THE GREA

THE
GREAT
GAMBLE

THE SOVIET WAR
IN AFGHANISTAN

GREGORY FEIFER

HARPER ● PERENNIAL

NEW YORK • LONDON • TORONTO • SYDNEY • NEW DELHI • AUCKLAND

A hardcover edition of this book was published 2009 by
HarperCollins Publishers.

THE GREAT GAMBLE. Copyright © 2009 by Russ Intellectual Properties,
LLC. All rights reserved. Printed in the United States of America. No
part of this book may be used or reproduced in any manner whatso-
ever without written permission except in the case of brief quotations
embodied in critical articles and reviews. For information address
HarperCollins Publishers, 10 East 53rd Street, New York, NY 10022.

HarperCollins books may be purchased for educational, business, or
sales promotional use. For information please write: Special Markets
Department, HarperCollins Publishers, 10 East 53rd Street,
New York, NY 10022.

First Harper Perennial edition published 2010.

Designed by William Ruoto

The Library of Congress has catalogued the hardcover edition as follows:

Feifer, Gregory.
The great gamble : the Soviet war in Afghanistan / Gregory Feifer.—
1st ed.
p. cm.
Includes bibliographical references.
ISBN 978-0-06-114318-2
1. Afghanistan—History—Soviet occupation, 1979–1989. 2. Soviet
Union—History, Military. I. Title.
DS371.2.F45 2009
958.104'5—dc22   2008022594

ISBN 978-0-06-114319-9 (pbk.)

HB 06.06.2022

For my father, PB

CONTENTS

CONTENTS

THE GREAT GAMBLE

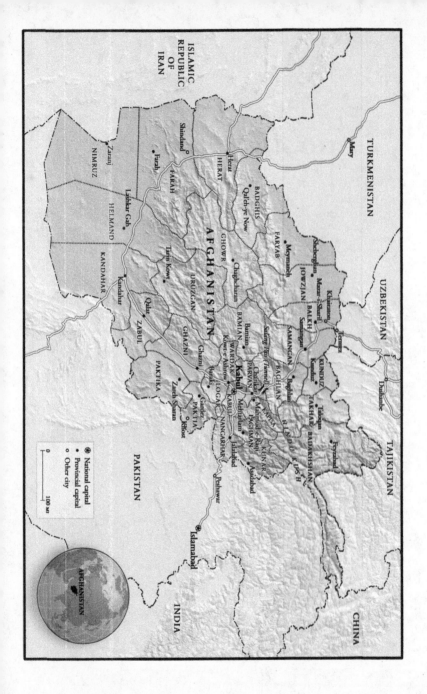

Map 1: Afghanistan

INTRODUCTION

I

Near the end of the overnight flight from Moscow to Kabul on Afghanistan's Ariana Airlines, the sun rises over that beautiful, battered country. As I peered down from a rattling jet during a recent trip in late fall, the dawn light of a cloudless morning revealed an endless succession of dusty, reddish brown mountain peaks and valleys. Reputed for its harshness, the small, deeply impoverished country—lodged between Iran and Pakistan, just below old Soviet Central Asia—is also physically stunning. I could understand how millennia of conquerors had been seduced. I was traveling there to learn how one of a long line of invading armies—in this case, belonging to a global superpower with virtually no limit to the amount it could spend on its military—became the latest to find defeat at the hands of local rebels.

Afghanistan's fate has been determined, more than anything, by its position on the globe. A persuasive current of scholarly theory about the nature of empires has it that geographic determinism—the lay of the land as well as its weather—helps define which territories become centers of empires and which remain battle-scarred frontier lands lodged between competing powers. Confluences of waterways and other transportation routes and natural defenses help form the centers of power. At the same time, mountains and other geographical features on the peripheries have long been intrinsic impediments to conquest. Deserts, river valleys, and narrow mountain passes, in which Afghanistan is rich, have greatly favored the resident peoples who know them.

Most Americans view the Soviet invasion of Afghanistan as a naked act of aggression by a ruthless, totalitarian state. The reality was far more complex. For more than a year, Soviet leaders rejected pleas from the Afghan communist government to send troops to help put down rebellion by the rural population protesting the regime's merciless modernization programs. After Moscow did invade, it found itself locked in conflict—essentially, a civil war—it could barely comprehend. While it cannot be said that Afghanistan triggered the Soviet collapse, it did project an image of a failing empire unable to deal with a handful of bedraggled partisans in a remote part of its southern frontier.

Of course, the war was also a tragic human story. Relating his part in it, Leonid Bogdanov, the KGB's chief representative in Kabul in 1979, described a meeting soon after the Soviet invasion. It was with the former head of Afghanistan's intelligence service, Asadullah Sarwari, who had fled the country in a KGB escape plot Bogdanov had planned.

"You know about everything you've taken part in here," the Afghan told Bogdanov. "You really should write a book about it."

"I don't know. . . . No one would believe it," the Russian replied. "It would read too much like a detective thriller."

During my interview with Bogdanov, we agreed that the war involved many levels of authority and many stages of psychological moods or emotional contortions. Some of the events and intrigues that led to the invasion strain the capacity to believe, so tight were the twists and uncanny the coincidences. Did the decision to go to war really turn on such random timing and seemingly insignificant personal matters?

Brezhnev's superficial but emotional tie to the country's first communist president, Mohammed Taraki, was a principal cause of the Soviet invasion. The president's ouster and murder offended the Soviet leader, especially because Hafizullah Amin, Taraki's rival, had promised the Kremlin he'd do no such thing. Nevertheless, Taraki's killing served more as a pretext for action than a motive. Since taking power the year before, Afghanistan's communist government had accelerated a reform program, including education for women and land redistribution, that had dragged on for most of the twentieth century. But now the government's violence rivaled some of Afghanistan's bloodiest chapters. And the red flags, orchestrated pro-government demonstrations, and other highly visible examples of communist pomp under Taraki particularly riled the rural population—and helped lead to a volatile situation and increasing attacks, mostly against government officials. The Kremlin blamed much of the trouble on Amin—who, compared to Taraki before him and the Soviet-installed Babrak Karmal after—was actually a relatively able if utterly ruthless leader.

The Cold War, the backdrop for Afghanistan's internal strife, was another key factor in Moscow's intervention. Although the Politburo would disingenuously accuse the Americans of planning to invade Afghanistan—mostly to justify its own meddling in a sovereign state's affairs—it was genuinely apprehensive that the fall of the Iranian shah in 1979 would prompt Washington to expand its influence in the region by boosting its presence in Afghanistan. Having spent decades and billions of dollars on the country's leadership in an attempt to establish hegemony, Moscow was determined not to let it fall under the influence of its superpower rival.

The Soviet leaders also perceived Afghanistan's proximity to Soviet Central Asia as a threat, fearing its largely Muslim population might become sympathetic to anticommunist activities across the border. Unaware of the real problems plaguing the country, the Politburo was swayed by its own rhetoric of "international duty" to Afghanistan's proletariat. In the end, the slightly senile Politburo all but jumped at the seemingly easy solution of a coup d'état.

Soviet critics of that course could hardly believe the Kremlin's refusal to remember the reasons for the American failure in Vietnam, a conflict Moscow itself had helped protract. But the Soviet leadership indeed ignored the lessons in its certainty that a quick invasion to prop up a friendly regime would not only increase its influence in Afghanistan but also send a message to all continents that Moscow remained a vital world power.

The actual result was virtually opposite. The Red Army found itself pushed by circumstances and events it had failed to foresee into a brutal struggle against a population that refused to tolerate invaders no matter how friendly they declared themselves to be. The Brezhnev regime's great gamble brought devastating consequences on an epic scale. While the official figure of Soviet war deaths is around 15,000, the real number is believed to be far higher, perhaps even as high as the 75,000 cited by many veterans. Conservative estimates put Afghan deaths at 1.25 million, or 9 percent of the population, with another three-quarters of a million wounded.

Needless to say of the Soviets, it was the soldiers on the ground who suffered the worst consequences of intervening in a complex conflict they didn't fully understand. The conclusions from their narratives throw strong light on how and why Cold War proxy-fighting in Afghanistan helped breed a new kind of global Islamic terrorism. They also suggest what the United States and other Western countries now must do in Afghanistan, Iraq, and other regions where ideology-driven guerrilla fighters face, and sometimes get the better of, conventional military forces.

II

The Soviet war in Afghanistan again confirmed that no power ever successfully conquered that land, which, for all its remoteness, lies at a strategically important crossroad of empires. The Persian ruler Cyrus the Great invaded it in the sixth century BC. Alexander the Great followed three hundred years later, as did the British in the nineteenth century. They vied for control over Afghanistan with the Russian tsarist empire for decades in what came to be called the Great Game. But while foreign forces have often moved into

Afghanistan with relative ease, they've never been able to maintain control. The country's long history of invasion helped spawn a culture of warfare among disparate local tribes and ethnic groups, which fought relentlessly among themselves until united by the common goal of repelling outside encroachers.

Modern Afghanistan, a country of roughly the size of Texas, was established just over a century ago. The British surveyors who drew its borders near the end of the nineteenth century sought to create a buffer state between British India and Russian-controlled Central Asia. In the north, the boundary follows the Amu Dar'ya River, and in the west, the Hari Rud River. In the south, Afghanistan borders the bleak desert territory of Pakistan's Baluchistan. In the east, the British cut through the middle of lands occupied by the Pashtun ethnic group. The scheme favored British interests in India (which abutted Afghanistan until the creation of Pakistan), and has weakened Afghanistan's ability to function as a viable state by physically splitting the Pashtuns—who haven't entirely given up the idea of creating a greater Pashtunistan, something the British were eager to prevent.

Afghanistan's central mountain range, the Hindu Kush, occupies much of the country and helps separate its various ethnic groups. There is no national ethnic group. Although "Afghan" was long equated with "Pashtun," it essentially denotes a resident of the country. The northern population consists chiefly of Turkic peoples—mostly Uzbeks, Tajiks, and Turkmen. Hazaras live in the mountains of central Afghanistan, an area called the Hazarajat. The Turks and Hazaras have traditionally opposed the rule of the Pashtuns to the south—Afghanistan's most powerful grouping, which comprises more than 40 percent of the population. Afghanistan's many smaller groups include the Nuristanis, who live in Hindu Kush valleys in northeast Afghanistan and sometimes have light hair and eyes.

Before the Soviet invasion, the population reached almost 17 million people, some 90 percent of whom were illiterate. Despite the strenuous efforts at modernization and secularization by its twentieth-century rulers, the persistently provincial and impoverished country is still largely governed by tribal sensibilities.

Local chiefs and mullahs often wield as much influence as heads of state, and much of the population has been quick to defend the rural way of life—often represented by Islamic codes—from threats of modernization. More than a century ago, a twenty-three-year-old reporter named Winston Churchill followed the British campaign in Afghanistan for the *Daily Telegraph*. Describing the Pashtun tribes, the future prime minister wrote that "Their system of ethics, which regards treachery and violence as virtues rather than vices, has produced a code of honour so strange and inconsistent that it is incomprehensible to a logical mind." Many Soviets would later agree.

III

Some British later liked to say the Soviets invaded Afghanistan only because they'd never read Rudyard Kipling's tales of betrayal and suffering in Afghanistan a century earlier. But even after its own debacle, Moscow never learned the lessons of its war in Afghanistan. Five years after it ended, the Kremlin launched another senseless conflict, this time in Chechnya, where Russian soldiers unable to fight rebels hiding in the Caucasus Mountains ravaged the civilian population instead. The soldiers employed strategy and tactics used in Afghanistan. The post-Soviet Kremlin was already looking backward for its models. When resurgent Russia, giddy from its massive oil wealth, invaded Georgia fifteen years later—Moscow's first attack against an independent country since the end of communism—it had already reverted to nineteenth-century notions about projecting power.

Western failure to understand the history of the Soviet war in Afghanistan has been even more damaging. Establishment of a viable central government in Afghanistan, an ambitious goal to begin with, has no chance of success without great attention and care from the United States and other Western countries. However, American forces are caught up in hostilities in Iraq, where the population is increasingly angry about the tens or hundreds of thousands of civilian deaths from terrorist bombings and U.S. military operations.

The United States enabled an insurgency in Afghanistan to best the mighty Red Army in 1989. Only a decade and a half later, the White House said it would be able to withdraw from Iraq mere months after invading, a belief that was paradoxical and bewildering. America attacked to seed democracy in a country with no tradition of representative government. The Soviet Union attempted to build communism in nearby, essentially tribal Afghanistan. Neither approach has worked, partly because the planners assumed that their own political systems would instantly take root in utterly alien territory—never mind that wars against indigenous insurgencies have almost never succeeded, in Afghanistan or anywhere else.

For all the USSR's destructive history—the tens of millions of Russians and other nationalities murdered and many more subjected to terror and dictatorship—a large number of the Afghanistan War's Soviet soldiers and officers genuinely believed they were helping the local population break free of oppression. On the day of the invasion, December 27, 1979, a Soviet military doctor resuscitated Afghan leader Amin after the KGB had poisoned him— the result of an astonishing lack of communication between Soviet intelligence, military, and diplomatic officials. Amin regained consciousness to find his luxurious palace enveloped in a hail of gunfire: Soviet troops were storming in to finally finish him off. The following day, the doctor heard a Radio Kabul report denouncing his patient Amin. The former fellow communist, as the Afghan president had once been praised—at least in official propaganda— was now a murderous enemy of the people. As he was describing the report years later, the doctor's irony was plain. "If it's announced on the radio," he said, "we felt it must be true."

While my account of the disaster includes testimony from the Afghan side, most comes from participating Soviets. Their perception of the war they experienced and endured may help dispel some American illusions about *our* wars, and also make us more sensitive to the volatility of the regions now determining the success or failure of our foreign policy.

CHAPTER 1

INVASION CONSIDERED

A Short, Victorious War

I

Dusk had already fallen in the late afternoon of December 12, 1979, when select members of the Soviet Union's top leadership gathered in a Kremlin conference room. They were there for a brief discussion of an issue that had given them much trouble during the better part of the outgoing year: political crisis in the USSR's southern neighbor Afghanistan. The informal assemblage of mostly white-haired gerontocrats wasn't an official meeting of the state's top governing body, the Politburo of the Communist Party's Central Committee. They formed a much smaller group of oligarchs who held the state's real political power, making decisions secretly among themselves. The elders ran the Soviet Union collegially, arriving at resolutions by the consensus that enabled them to share responsibility and absolve individual blame. What exactly happened during their secret midwinter meeting remains the subject of debate.

General Secretary Leonid Brezhnev presided. He had less than two years to live. Television appearances of the ailing leader had made him a public laughingstock. Propped between the shoulders of fellow Politburo members, the bloated, bushy-browed bear of a man made supreme efforts to mumble through euphemistic texts written by his advisers. (Slurring the frequently used bureaucratic word "systematically" was among his most mocked gaffes. It emerged from his lips sounding much like a juvenile term for women's breasts.) During important Politburo meetings, the master of tedium went through the motions of approving decisions already made by members of his immediate entourage, who even wrote his responses for him. One reason for his longevity in office was that the rest of the Soviet leadership—some of whose members were far from incompetent—worried that the West would interpret any changes in its makeup as a sign of the Party's instability.

Brezhnev had come to power in October 1964, promising to do away with Nikita Khrushchev's anti-Stalinist campaigns and boat-rocking reforms. Supported by vast cadres of Party functionaries, the new general secretary put an end to embarrassing and potentially ruinous questions about past activities. He provided stability for the Communist *nomenklatura*—the politically dependable men who occupied senior positions in the bureaucracy and lived much better than others on the patronage. Dissidents were once again put on public trial. After the Czechoslovakian reform movement known as "socialism with a human face" was crushed along with the Prague Spring in 1968, Brezhnev's tenure developed into what became known as *zastoi*—the stagnation. The economy, beset by massive inefficiencies from central planning and institutions such as Stalin's agricultural collectivization, declined more or less consistently, and was further dragged down by a ballooning military-industrial complex overseen by Defense Minister Dmitri Ustinov. Prevented from making significant improvements by the nature of his rule and no doubt his own nature too, Brezhnev presided over a system that managed to hobble ahead only because the fruit of corruption spread from the Party elite to the rest of society. The economy's raw materials and articles of production were largely—maybe even chiefly—distributed by thievery, bribery, and black marketeering.

Chief Party ideologue Mikhail Suslov, KGB Chairman Yuri Andropov, Foreign Minister Andrei Gromyko, and Defense Minister Ustinov also attended the December 12 meeting. Some claim—although people close to the Soviet leadership deny—that Prime Minister Alexei Kosygin was there as well. If he wasn't, it may have been because Kosygin, as is widely believed, opposed the idea of invading Afghanistan—or because he was ill.

Although the imposing, six-foot-tall Suslov was generally regarded as Brezhnev's likely successor, most Politburo decisions were made by a triumvirate composed of Andropov, Gromyko, and Ustinov. They simplified and prettified the issues in their reports to Brezhnev. Using good old ideological terms such as "the interests of the proletariat" and "the spread of the world socialist revolution," they also usually told the Soviet leader what they believed he wanted to hear. Possibly in the hope of succeeding him, Ustinov was particularly sycophantic, singing Brezhnev's praises in official pronouncements and refusing to say anything that would prompt his ire.

The defense minister had no monopoly on kowtowing or backslapping, however. Frequent awards ceremonies were venues for fierce jockeying to secure places closest to the general secretary so that the following day's newspaper photographs would display the "winners." When Brezhnev pinned on Kosygin the latest of the prime minister's countless medals—that one for the Order of the October Revolution—he commented that the award looked pretty, then turned to fellow Politburo member Konstantin Chernenko. "Kostya," the general secretary said, "I don't have one of those." Several days later—probably the time it took for the Politburo to find an excuse to make the award—a place was found on Brezhnev's bulging chestful of decorations for a new Order of the October Revolution.

Shortly before the December Kremlin meeting, Andropov had sent Brezhnev a personal memorandum that had heavily influenced the debate over how Moscow should respond to a series of worrying developments in Afghanistan. A new communist government in Kabul was asking Moscow to send Red Army troops to quell increasing social unrest. The Soviet leadership had been turning down the requests for almost a year. Public opposition had especially spiked after Afghanistan's president, Nur Mohammed Taraki, was ousted by his deputy, Prime Minister Hafizullah Amin, in September, a situation KGB chairman Andropov now characterized as "an undesirable turn for us." Andropov criticized Amin's mass repressions and the "alarming information" that Amin was conducting secret activities that might lead to a "possible political shift to the West."

Andropov too is believed to have earlier opposed the idea of invading Afghanistan, but Vladimir Kryuchkov, his hawkish and secretive deputy, prevailed upon him to change his mind. In his memorandum, Andropov went on to say that Afghans living outside the country were supporting Amin's rival Babrak Karmal—whom Taraki had exiled to Prague as Afghanistan's ambassador to Czechoslovakia—and they were developing a plan to oust the new leader. Andropov suggested moving Soviet military units close to the Afghanistan border to provide "assistance" for such an event. The Soviet ambassador to the United States, Anatoly Dobrynin—from whose notes Andropov's text survives—believed the memorandum was central to convincing Brezhnev of the need to invade Afghanistan.

Defense Minister Ustinov, another prime advocate of increased Soviet military involvement in Afghanistan, probably also pushed for invasion at the December 12 meeting. Ustinov was disliked by most of his subordinates, who regarded him as a technocrat with scant combat experience. Although the Red Army's top generals had warned of the dangers of invading Afghanistan, Marshal Ustinov was more concerned about countering possible American military plans in the region. The 1979 Iranian Revolution had much eroded Washington's authority in the Middle East. Ustinov wanted to prevent any restoration of that influence.

Deputy Foreign Minister Georgy Kornienko believed Andropov may have played the key role on December 12. He would later write that his boss, Foreign Minister Gromyko, spoke against invasion until October, when he apparently bent to growing pressure from Ustinov and Andropov following Taraki's assassination.

But Leonid Shebarshin, who was then the KGB's Tehran station chief, told me the pressure came from another Politburo member, Mikhail Suslov. Shebarshin was one of the service's top Afghanistan experts, who would rise to KGB chairmanship—for a day—after the attempted putsch in 1991. Sitting in the Moscow offices of his private security company, he said Suslov, not Andropov, played the main role on December 12. The Party's stalwart ideologue, Suslov was said to have insisted that Moscow protect Afghanistan's socialist regime by removing the threat posed by Amin, who was thought to have ties to the CIA.

However, what Suslov and the others actually said during their meeting—or exactly how the group reached its consensus that day—will almost certainly never be known. The conduct and substance of that fateful conference remains one of the Cold War's greatest mysteries. None of the participants, now all dead, recorded their versions of what took place, or even related them to others. Debate continues to this day—even among the most knowledgeable people, who personally knew the Politburo members—about who influenced whom and with what arguments. What *is* clear, however, is that when the de facto Soviet leadership emerged from its discussion, it had made the decision to invade.

The only document recording at least a summary of the critical meeting is a cryptic note handwritten by Chernenko, who later became Soviet leader. Kept in a special Central Committee safe, the paper that remained "super top secret" for many years was signed by Brezhnev and later seconded with the signatures of most members of the full Politburo: Andropov, Ustinov, Gromyko, Suslov, Chernenko, Arvid Pelshe, Victor Grishin, Nikolai Tikhonov, Andrei Kirilenko, and Vladimir Shcherbitsky.

Written in the Soviet bureaucratese that hid evidence of the decision-making process, the note speaks of the secrecy in which the plan to invade was approved. For extra protection against any charge of illegal maneuvering or unauthorized activity, the signers took the additional precaution of having the entire Politburo also approve it. The note titled "Concerning the Situation in 'A,'" as

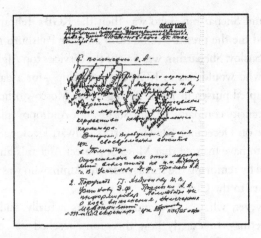

"On the Situation in 'A'," the Politburo note that resulted
from the December 12, 1979, meeting authorizing Amin's
overthrow. (*Alexander Liakhovskii archive*)

Afghanistan was referred to, made no mention of military action,
saying only that "measures" were to be executed by "Andropov Y.
V., Ustinov D. F., and Gromyko A. A."

Fifteen days later, on December 27, the so-called Limited Contingent of Armed Forces of the Soviet Union—including special
forces, motorized rifle, paratroop, and other divisions—launched
their invasion. Some of the Soviet leaders would soon be dead of
old age or illness. It's unlikely that they realized the gravity or full
ramifications of their decision. It would start a war that would last
nine years and cost tens of thousands of Soviet lives.

II

Eleven months before the December 12 meeting, in January 1979,
Valery Kurilov was serving as a KGB counterintelligence officer. The

English-speaking twenty-nine-year-old was drafted into a training program for a group of elite special forces, *spetsnaz* (short for "special purpose"), under the KGB's foreign intelligence wing, the flagship First Chief Directorate. Members of the Zenit, or Zenith, unit were used as so-called diversionary brigades outside Soviet borders. Only officers of superior mental and physical soundness were selected. Graduates were enlisted in reserve units for later formation into *spetsnaz* groups that would be inserted behind enemy lines or used for other covert activities.

Kurilov received the recruitment call on one of the blurry days following the prolonged celebration of the New Year, the atheist Soviet Union's main holiday, analogous to Western Christmas. Work all but ceased for up to two weeks while most citizens gave themselves to private or collective drinking. Kurilov left his wife and daughter for Balashikha, a suburban town northeast of Moscow, where a "saboteurs" course was conducted, with lessons in how to parachute, lay mines, fire sniper rifles, use radio communications, draw maps, and cope with hard physical tasks.

Conditions were spartan in the old log barracks at the *spetsnaz* group's headquarters in a dense stretch of woods. The snow was deep and temperatures low. In the cold, the recruits were taught to stage attacks, conduct ambushes, and free hostages. They learned to fight with newly distributed Finnish combat knives. They were also taught to throw scissors and nails, and to strangle with shoelaces. They became skilled in using plastic explosives and digging ditches with their hands for laying bombs that would go unnoticed by guards patrolling train tracks. They practiced building secret shelters for hiding during the day. Fierce competition among the men accelerated their transformation into expert warriors. They shed weight, their faces became craggy, and they were told they were the best of the best.

The commander of Kurilov's group was KGB Colonel Grigory Boyarinov, head of the First Directorate's Department Eight, for special operations. The highly decorated officer had cut his teeth in the deadly Soviet-Finnish War that preceded World War II. Boyarinov was a demanding commander, but his clear concern for his subordinates helped earn him their respect and devotion.

Spring brought a measure of relief and the course abruptly ended in May, just as the officers were preparing to travel to the south of Russia for mountain training. They were informed they'd be going to Afghanistan instead, where, they were told, enemies of that country's 1978 communist revolution were still active. The Soviet embassy and its advisers needed protection from possible threat.

Along with new summer and winter-white uniforms, the officers were given false documents describing them as engineers, meteorologists, and other specialists. The group was driven to the Chkalov military airport near Moscow, where fifty-odd men boarded a military plane with Aeroflot markings bound for the Uzbek capital, Tashkent. The following day, the men flew on to Kabul, accompanied by a plane loaded with supplies.

Zenit's transport was part of a large transfer of Soviet equipment and troops to Afghanistan that swelled with Moscow's increasing concern about the country's growing instability. The officers were to help evacuate Soviet embassy staff and advisers in the event of a crisis. Two months earlier, in March, eight Mi-8 transport helicopters, a squadron of An-12 turboprop cargo planes, a signal center, and a paratroop battalion had been sent to the Bagram air base on the sun-baked, dusty flats forty-five miles north of Kabul. The aircraft crews wore Afghan uniforms, the paratroops were disguised as advisers, the helicopters and planes bore Afghan markings. A month later, in April, General Alexei Yepishev, head of the General Staff's Main Political Directorate (called GLAVPUR), led a delegation of top military officials to assess the situation in Afghanistan. In August, General Ivan Pavlovskii, the well-respected chief of Soviet ground forces, followed with a group of sixty officers on a training and reconnaissance tour that lasted several weeks.

A new battalion of paratroops and *spetsnaz* troops from Central Asian republics was also formed in May. Based in neighboring Uzbekistan and organized to serve as guard troops for the beleaguered Afghan president Taraki, the men were never dispatched for that purpose. Instead, they would form a so-called Muslim battalion, part of a scheme to soften the impact of the Soviet presence in Afghanistan by including Tajiks, Uzbeks, Turkmen, and members of other ethnic groups that also lived in Afghanistan.

Also in the spring of 1979, Yuri Andropov ordered Oleg Kalugin—the KGB general who headed counterintelligence for the First Chief Directorate—to draft a report for the Politburo detailing recommendations for Soviet activity in Afghanistan. Kalugin stressed the need to win the propaganda war. He suggested publicly accusing Pakistan of aggressively threatening the Afghan revolution. He also proposed calling Afghan rebels American and Zionist agents. The young KGB general also suggested creating local committees to support the revolution, forming several strike units of loyal troops outfitted with the most advanced technology, and readying Soviet military forces on the border with Afghanistan to parachute into the country to protect or evacuate Soviet citizens under threat—and then guard important Afghan government installations. The last recommendation was a step toward advising a full invasion.

The Kremlin assembled four representatives to inform the Politburo about the situation in Afghanistan and implement decisions on the ground. The group included KGB chief liaison Boris Ivanov, who was a respected intelligence veteran; Soviet Ambassador Alexander Puzanov, a bland Party apparatchik; top military envoy and World War II hero General Ivan Pavlovskii; and bull-necked former paratrooper Leonid Gorelov, chief Soviet military adviser to the Afghan government. Each of the four had his own line of communication to Moscow, which began receiving conflicting reports about the deepening political crisis.

From Moscow, Kryuchkov ordered the four men to combine the channels of information by jointly drafting one report, chiefly to avoid upsetting Brezhnev with bad news. Pressure to muzzle the representatives came from Andropov and Ustinov, who were especially eager to please the ailing leader. The decision helped create the effect of a vicious circle. The top Soviet apparatchiks were too concerned with their own careers to want to be caught on the wrong side of the general secretary's decisions: most opinions in the Politburo swayed with Brezhnev's. Now the growing information vacuum meant the Kremlin would essentially stop receiving any objective evaluations about Afghanistan's fast-worsening developments. The rosy reports would serve to diminish opposition by Prime Minister Kosygin to the opinions of Politburo hawks like Suslov and his associate, Central Committee member Boris Ponomaryov, that Afghanistan was staging breakthroughs in the world revolutionary process and needed help shoring them up.

In May, the KGB's Zenit group—sent to protect Soviet embassy staff—set up in the embassy's school, which had just let out for summer. The complex stood in a northwestern suburb of Kabul; a number of Soviets lived in the surrounding houses. The first task was to examine the compound's security and locate possible places where attacks against it could be mounted. The officers installed an alarm system and worked out defensive positions on the embassy's flat roofs, which they protected with sandbags. Then they scouted

Valery Kurilov, of the KGB's Zenit *spetsnaz* group, took part in the storming of President Amin's Taj-Bek palace on December 27, 1979, the first day of the Soviet invasion. (*Alexander Liakhovskii archive*)

the neighborhood, learning, with the help of Afghan counterintelligence, about its residents and their sympathies.

Despite Afghanistan's proximity to Soviet Central Asia, Kurilov had seen nothing like it before. The Soviet republics were sedate by comparison. Noisy, dusty Kabul was a jumble of cars, carts pulled by men and donkeys, and crowds of pedestrians. Countless small shops and stalls lined the roads. Dramatic brown mountains surrounding the warren of downtown streets helped lend an air of beauty. But eclecticism ruled: houses built terrace-like into the hills appeared medieval, while concrete government buildings and rows of prefabricated, Soviet-constructed residential buildings provided signs of rushed modernization in the outskirts.

Kurilov found the security situation disheartening. Zenit would be the embassy's sole protection if violence were to break out. He saw no evidence of the Afghan government soldiers he'd been told were exercising authority on Kabul's streets. Shootings took place constantly. Houses were torched. Members of the ruling People's Democratic Party of Afghanistan, or PDPA, whose more extremist Khalq wing held power, were staging ambushes of relatively moderate rival Parcham members, many of whom were in hiding. Kurilov came to believe the PDPA had come to power as if by chance and had no real understanding of how to run the country. The government was simply imitating its powerful neighbor, the Soviet Union. Proclaiming they were building socialism, officials were doing little more than confiscating land for redistribution as the PDPA's members descended into an orgy of infighting. The revolution, as many were beginning to say in despair, was eating its young.

Zenit's KGB officers had arrived pumped up by their training. Back at the Balashikha camp outside Moscow, some of the men most eager for action had even started a barroom brawl, beaten a police officer, and been arrested. But now the group's mandate extended only to defending the embassy, and they sat bored behind machine guns and sandbags on the complex's roof.

One afternoon, three civilians set upon a government soldier walking past the compound's walls. Kurilov could only look on from his position on a balcony of the embassy's hospital clinic—where, dressed in a doctor's white coat and hat, he manned a machine gun. In August, a unit of government troops rebelled by seizing the towering fifth-century Bala Hissar fortress on a hill in the city's southern outskirts. The soldiers beat their commanders and political officers. Afghan Army soldiers accompanied by several Soviet-built T-34 tanks dug in across the street from the embassy to protect the compound. Again, with a mandate only to protect Soviet staff, the Zenit men could do nothing but listen to the shelling and a helicopter attack before the rebellion was put down.

Although Kurilov found much of the political reasoning in Afghanistan positively Neanderthal, it seemed a pleasant society. Most of the Afghans he met were friendly and eager to please. He found local kebab and rice pilaf dishes delicious, and despite its violence, dusty Kabul could sometimes feel relaxing. Still, reminders of the vast difference between his sensibilities and most Afghans' were jarring. During the summer, a Zenit squad began coaching government army officers in counterintelligence skills; Kurilov was in charge of physical training. One of his first trainees boasted of using his new skills to drown a fellow communist party member who belonged to a rival faction.

"But he's one of your party," Kurilov said, taken aback.

"They're enemies," the Afghan officer replied with a straight face. "They want to sell us to the Americans."

The communist believers Kurilov encountered didn't see any contradiction between the concept of international brotherhood and an apparently ancient proclivity for savage retribution. Seeking out an Afghan Army captain for debriefing, Kurilov found him listed as a patient in a hospital after his car had been hit by machine-gun fire outside Kabul. A guard at the hospital who went to find him reappeared minutes later, roughly dragging the wounded officer behind him. Again Kurilov couldn't understand the treatment to which Afghans subjected one another; this time, the men were on the same side, with no apparent split. The guard had simply assumed the officer was to be punished for something he'd done wrong. Rather than protest, the wounded man, who had lost half his tongue in the attack, mumbled to Kurilov that "protecting" the revolution was the only way to save Afghanistan. It was his duty to fight the rebels who were appearing everywhere, he said.

III

If Afghan politics had ever been simple, they weren't now. The PDPA had come to power in April 1978, after the overthrow of President Mohammed Daoud: what was spoken of as The Revolution. Despite the KGB's many highly placed sources in the Afghan government—including even some ministers—the revolt took Moscow by surprise. The Soviet leadership learned the news from a Reuters report. Paradoxically, Brezhnev wasn't pleased. But paradox would become a hallmark of the coming saga.

The Soviet Union had long enjoyed a mostly cooperative relationship with Afghanistan, the first country to recognize the Bolshevik government after the 1917 Revolution. (Soviet Russia, in turn, was the first to recognize the modern nation-state of Afghanistan two years later.) King Zahir Shah was crowned in 1933 at the age of nineteen, after the assassination of his father, Nadir Shah. Under young King Zahir, Afghanistan was largely ruled by members of the royal family, chiefly his cousin Prince Mohammed Daoud Khan, the future president, who later also became the king's brother-in-law.

As part of the government's ongoing drive to modernize the country, many Afghans were sent to the Soviet Union for education. After their political indoctrination there, it was probably inevitable that a communist party would form in Afghanistan. Communist in all but name, the PDPA was founded on January 1, 1965, at the Kabul house of Nur Mohammed Taraki, a journalist and writer who would remain active in politics until his murder helped provoke the Soviet invasion fourteen years later.

The party received funding from the KGB and maintained close ties to the Kremlin. It soon split into two wings. Taraki retained control of the Khalq, or the People, group. The more radical of the two, it was chiefly composed of poor, rural Pashtuns. A well-spoken lawyer named Babrak Karmal headed the Parcham, or Banner, wing, which included many better-educated urban supporters, among them a large number of Tajiks and Uzbeks. Seen as more intellectual, Parcham adopted a more gradualist approach to reform, advocating change from within the system.

In 1973, the wily Daoud seized power when King Zahir was on a trip to Italy, and declared a republic. The army—of which Daoud was chief patron—supported his action. Much of the military's officer corps had also trained in the Soviet Union, where it too was influenced by revolutionary rhetoric. Many high-ranking officers were members of the fundamentally communist PDPA. Nevertheless, Daoud, who worried that Afghanistan had drifted too close to Moscow, risked losing the army's support by purging his government of PDPA members and ejecting some of the growing number of Soviet military advisers in the country.

Daoud's heavy-handed rule, including press censorship and other autocratic measures, prompted criticism from students and leftists in urban centers, especially Kabul. His efforts to modernize the tribal rules and sensibilities of the mostly rural country also drew the ire of committed Islamists. Daoud responded by jailing opponents. In 1977, he oversaw the passing of a new constitution, and was soon elected to the powerful new post of president.

Since the end of World War II, Afghanistan had received financial and political support from the United States as well as the Soviet Union. Although both Cold War rivals sent engineers and advisers to build roads, airports, factories, and other infrastructure, Kabul retained a closer relationship with its northern neighbor. But Daoud's announced policy of independent nonalignment increasingly upset the Kremlin. He liked to "light Soviet cigarettes with American matches," a KGB officer said of his tactic of playing the superpowers against each other.

When Brezhnev summoned the new president to Moscow to complain about his overtures to Egypt, Saudi Arabia, and other countries with ties to the United States, Daoud retorted by saying his country was a sovereign state that made its own policy. Whether or not he banged his fist on a table, as reported, Brezhnev was furious. And Daoud's popularity continued sinking back home, especially after Moscow successfully encouraged the PDPA's Khalq and Parcham wings to reunify, a reconciliation that posed the president a serious threat.

When a top communist activist named Mir Akbar Khyber was assassinated in April 1978, most Afghans blamed the secret police. His funeral turned into an antigovernment demonstration by fifteen thousand protesters. Daoud reacted by arresting a number of communist leaders, prompting an even stronger backlash. On April 27, several armored units surrounded the presidential palace in the center of Kabul. Army troops seized the airport while air force MiG-21 fighters took to the air to shoot at the palace, where Daoud was in residence.

The army's Seventh Division, which remained loyal to Daoud, attempted to retake the city but was stopped by more air attacks from rebelling military units. Daoud's eighteen-hundred-strong guard fought through the night to try to break the palace siege until rebels broke in, killing Daoud and his family. The communist coup d'état—dubbed the Saur, or April, Revolution—caused some two thousand deaths. Marxist military officers immediately gave power to the PDPA, which proclaimed itself the head of the Democratic Republic of Afghanistan, the DRA.

In Washington, two days after the regime change, a secret memorandum from an assistant informed U.S. Secretary of State Cyrus Vance that American allies in the region, notably Pakistan, Iran, and Saudi Arabia, saw the development as a clear pro-Soviet coup. The Americans did not know the KGB, which had seen no looming problems in Afghanistan, was actually caught completely off-guard. But although few in the Kremlin had heard of the journalist-activist Nur Mohammed Taraki or other top Afghan politicians, Suslov, Ponomaryov, and the other Soviet ideologues jumped at the chance to applaud the April Revolution for fostering the spread of the communist agenda.

Taraki, who still headed the Khalq wing, was named the new president. Babrak Karmal of the Parcham group was appointed deputy premier, but the two factions immediately split again and Taraki soon purged the government of Parcham members. He exiled Karmal by appointing him ambassador to Czechoslovakia. By the end of the year, the Khalq wing controlled all levers of power.

The new government brought the country solidly under Moscow's influence, partly by inviting a new wave of Soviet political, military, and other advisers. The Soviet general staff ordered them to establish a political directorate—the kind that exercises control— within the Afghan Army. In August, KGB foreign intelligence chief Kryuchkov flew to Kabul, where he oversaw the drafting of a cooperation agreement between the KGB and Afghanistan's new intelligence service.

Taraki's government set out to transform the country into a modern, and now socialist, state. His campaign was every bit as— if not more than—ruthless as Daoud's. But Taraki faced relatively little resistance at first, except in the north, where tribes in eastern Nuristan, the Hazarajat—home to the Hazaras in central Afghanistan—and northern Tajik areas chafed at the new regime's largely Pashtun composition. Aware of the rural resistance to modernization, the PDPA tried to mask its radical reform program by saying it would undertake to defend "the principles of Islam, democracy, freedom and the inviolability of the person." Foreign policy would be based on neutrality.

Afghanistan's biggest social division lay between urban and rural populations. That became starkly clear in October, when the government unveiled a new flag, red replacing traditional Islamic green. Even worse for the defenders of tradition was an announcement that the administration would push for women's education, equal rights, land reform, and national status for a number of ethnic groups, including Uzbek, Turkmen, Baluchi, and Nuristani.

The government said it intended to bring stability, provide education, and generally improve the lot of the people. But despite such promises, land reform, the most important of the changes, often consisted of rounding up landowners and farmers, shooting them, and burying their bodies with bulldozers. The direct attack on the rural mode of life, as it was seen, prompted unrest all over the country.

The government enforced its authority by executing thousands, some after mass arrests and torture. Even more died in brutal repression of revolts. Religious and tribal leaders were especially targeted, as well as political activists, scholars, and members of intellectual and other elite social groups deemed a threat to the regime. Tens of thousands suffered, many in the Pul-i-Charkhi prison outside Kabul, designed by the French and long since crammed and filthy. The ultimate goal—besides consolidating political control—was to brutally punish society into modernizing.

IV

KGB officer Leonid Bogdanov knew something about Afghanistan and its penchant for violence. When the savvy Middle East expert first visited the country in 1971, a boy peddling Coca-Cola at a rural kiosk offered to sell him an American Thompson machine gun. Seven years later, when the April Revolution took place, the balding intelligence officer with a growing waistline had recently returned to Moscow from a tour in Iran. Although his wife was ill and his daughter was about to enter the university—so they couldn't leave Moscow—Bogdanov was sent to assess the situation on the ground in Afghanistan.

Bogdanov was appointed head of a project to establish formal relations between the KGB and the Afghan intelligence service. The new organization, responsible directly to Taraki, would be called AGSA, after the Pashto acronym for Organization for the Defense of Afghan Interests. Bogdanov would remain in Kabul to serve as the KGB's chief representative in Afghanistan—he'd work alongside the station chief, or *rezident*, and the KGB's main adviser to the Afghan government.

It didn't take long for Bogdanov to grow concerned about the regional significance of Afghanistan's recent turmoil. In Tehran, where he'd gotten on well with the Iranian shah, he'd nevertheless been acutely aware of Iran's alliance with the United States. Now he was worried the situation in Afghanistan would prompt new agreements between Tehran and Washington that would increase American influence in what he saw as the soft Soviet underbelly south of Central Asia.

Afghanistan's relations with Pakistan also troubled him. Many Pakistanis had never accepted the British-drawn Durand line of 1893, which delineated the border with Afghanistan. That boundary divided the area of Baluchistan and its largely Pashtun population in half, and Islamabad had long sought to undermine Afghanistan's stability in the hope of annexing territory north of the Pakistani border.

Thus Bogdanov saw the United States, Iran, and Pakistan possibly working together to foment unrest in Afghanistan's part of Baluchistan. At the same time, he was concerned Afghanistan's PDPA party hadn't given up the old hope of expanding south. The deputy prime minister, Columbia University–educated Hafizullah Amin, even jokingly promised him a swim in the Indian Ocean.

Bogdanov arrived in Kabul in early August 1978 in the company of foreign intelligence chief Kryuchkov and foreign counterespionage chief Oleg Kalugin, who came to draw up Moscow's intelligence collaboration agreement with Afghan Security Services Chief Asadullah Sarwari. During an early tête-à-tête with Deputy Prime Minister Amin, the KGB's new representative noticed a split between Amin and Taraki. Since Afghanistan had no officially designated intelligence service, Bogdanov asked Amin whether he'd receive credentials from Amin or Taraki himself. Amin replied that a newly formed group was already conducting intelligence. Although it was formally subordinate to Taraki, "I, as his deputy, supervise the security services." Bogdanov realized that if Amin didn't already have effective control over the levers of power, he wanted them.

When Bogdanov was introduced to Taraki, the Afghan leader appeared more interested in ideology than countering threats to his power. The shah of Iran wouldn't be pleased if he knew the KGB officer was now serving in Afghanistan, the president boasted when informed that Bogdanov had recently served there. "We've done better than you did in Iran. We carried out *our* revolution while you were trying to talk us out of it." Taraki complained about women wearing the veil, and promised Afghanistan's mosques would be emptied within the year. He also indicated his approval of the KGB. "We know about your kind of diplomacy. We're happy you're here."

Amin apparently agreed because he soon asked for help overhauling the intelligence service to resemble the KGB in structure. Bogdanov submitted a plan for providing technology, training, and Soviet funding. It included forming a counterintelligence agency

In front row, left to right: Afghan Deputy Prime Minister Hafizullah Amin *(far left)*, Soviet Foreign Minister Andrei Gromyko *(third)*, Afghan President Nur Mohammed Taraki *(fourth)*, Soviet Secretary General Leonid Brezhnev *(fifth)*, and Soviet Prime Minister Alexei Kosygin *(sixth)* in Moscow at the signing of the friendship and cooperation agreement between Afghanistan and the Soviet Union on December 5, 1978. *(Alexander Liakhovskii archive)*

subordinate to the Defense Ministry, and a border troop service under the Interior Ministry. Amin duly approved the scheme.

Despite the government's eagerness for help and advice, Bogdanov was shocked by its approach to modernization. He later came to believe that only government weakness was responsible for the country's relative calm at the time. Little contact with the regional leaders left top officials in Kabul with scant knowledge of what was happening in the provinces. Amin told Bogdanov the regional governors were largely free to run their fiefs as they wanted, provided they paid levies to the treasury. Most of the local resistance to the central authorities was instigated or supplied by criminal bands.

The Soviets urged the central government to strengthen its hand by beefing up the PDPA's regional grassroots structure, but it proved too weak even for that. Instead, the government created Soviet-style political departments to enforce ideology, much like the Red Army's system of commissars who exercised the Communist Party's authority within the ranks. PDPA representatives were sent to strategically important industrial and agricultural areas, but for now, most of the country was left largely alone, while the government's reforms served only to further undermine its authority.

The KGB's chief Kabul representative, Leonid Bogdanov (left), with General Andrei Vlasov, the chief Soviet border guards adviser, in Kabul, October 1979. (*Alexander Liakhovskii archive*)

Clumsy in their attempts to modernize and secularize, PDPA members committed cardinal social sins, such as intervening in marriage ceremonies—a grave offense in Pashtun culture. Party officials stormed into houses and scolded the local elite in front of their families—violating the Islamic code that prevents guests from glimpsing the household's women. Economic intrusion was no less insulting. By law, dispossessed landowners were allowed to keep thirty hectares of their land, around seventy-five acres, but the parcels allocated were often too far from their houses to make farming practical. As for the confiscated land, some was distributed to peasants too poor to acquire tools to cultivate their new plots, let alone provide proper irrigation. Raising the issue with Interior Minister Aslam Mohammed Watanjar, Bogdanov said he was seeing evidence of growing resistance funded by dispossessed landlords. He said he believed the country was sliding toward a dangerous civil conflict that would be unavoidable if the PDPA didn't soften its approach. Bogdanov would soon take his argument to his superiors in Moscow. But he would find his audience less than receptive.

V

The PDPA's problems deepened. A year after the April Revolution, Pashtun tribesmen formed antigovernment strongholds in the eastern Hindu Kush, the Kunar Valley, and northeastern Badakshan. As general resistance to the murderous government grew, army soldiers deserted by the thousands, taking their weapons with them.

In February 1979, Islamic radicals kidnapped U.S. Ambassador Adolph Dubs. When, against American wishes, Afghan troops advised by the KGB burst into the Hotel Kabul, where he was being held, they accidentally killed the diplomat along with his captors. Washington could do little beyond speeding its own decision to cut off the small amount of aid it still provided Afghanistan.

In March, protests against the inclusion of women in a government literacy campaign helped prompt a major uprising in the western city of Herat. The revolt would produce a serious watershed for the opposition. Rather than follow government orders to stop the rebellion, the Afghan Army's Seventeenth Division mutinied and joined the riots. Kabul lost control of the city for three days. Rebels raided weapons stockpiles, then hunted down officials, Soviet advisers, and their families. Bodies of the publicly tortured and murdered were paraded on pikes.

Bogdanov learned about the uprising on March 14 from Soviet Ambassador Puzanov. The elderly diplomat had once been an influential Party official, a former prime minister of the Russian Republic, the largest of the Soviet Union's fifteen republics. He had been sent to Afghanistan for semiretirement seven years earlier, when the ambassadorship there had been a cushy posting in a friendly country. Now events were pulling Puzanov in over his head. The latest news worried him greatly: a Soviet trade representative in Herat had telephoned him to report that crowds were marching in the streets and directing residents to beat all non-Muslims in the city. Then the line went dead. A mob killed the representative, although neighbors saved his badly beaten wife. Top Soviet military adviser Gorelov later described rebel supporters streaming into Herat from the surrounding countryside. In an attempt to stop the crowds, the army opened fire, killing hundreds of civilians, before mutinous officers turned their tank cannons on their own men.

Three Soviet advisers who managed to flee in their cars headed north for the town of Kushka, located in a gorge on the Soviet border. When the drivers of the first two cars noticed the third had disappeared, they turned back. They found their colleague's vehicle next to a mud-walled village, surrounded by crowds that dispersed when the Soviets drove up. The driver was inside his car, sliced open, disemboweled, and stuffed with straw. His mouth was filled with sand. Other Soviets fared better. A tank battalion still loyal to the government escorted a group of them to the airport, along with their wives and children.

On hearing the news, Bogdanov rushed to the Afghan intelligence service's new headquarters, which he found inoperative. But the chief of Afghan counterintelligence was there, and was able to describe the Seventeenth Division's mutiny. Secret police chief Sarwari, arriving from a meeting with Taraki, said military units loyal to the PDPA's Khalq wing were preparing to attack Herat from the surrounding hills. Taraki ordered units from Kandahar to surround the city while two armored brigades moved in from Kabul. Soviet-made Il-28 bombers from nearby Shindand struck parts of the city as ground forces retook the streets.

Bogdanov would later see the Herat uprising, which took the lives of some five thousand people, as the start of civil war. The mutiny sparked the PDPA's first major appeal to Moscow for help. Taraki asked how long it might take Soviet forces to enter Afghanistan to assist the government. Speaking to Soviet Premier Kosygin by telephone in mid-March, the Afgan president told him the situation was "bad and getting worse."

"Do you have support among the workers, city dwellers, the petty bourgeoisie, and the white-collar workers in Herat?" Kosygin asked. "Is there still anyone on your side?"

"There's no active support on the part of the population," Taraki replied. "It's almost wholly under the influence of Shiite slogans—follow not the heathens, but follow us. That's what underpins the propaganda."

"Are there many workers there?"

"Very few. Between a thousand and two thousand people in all."

"What are the prospects?"

"We're convinced the enemy will form new units and develop an offensive."

"Don't you have the forces to rout them?" Kosygin asked.

"I wish that were the case," the president lamented, then switched to an appeal. "We ask that you extend practical and technical assistance involving people and arms."

"It's a very complex matter," Kosygin replied.

"If you launch a decisive attack on Herat now, it will be possible to save the revolution," Taraki said.

Of all Politburo members, Kosygin was probably the least inclined to support an invasion. "The whole world would immediately learn of that," he replied. "The rebels have portable radio transmitters and will report it directly."

"I ask you to extend assistance," Taraki implored. "I suggest you place Afghan markings on your tanks and aircraft and no one will know the difference. Your troops could advance from the direction of Kushka and Kabul. In our view, no one would catch on. They'd think they were government troops."

"I don't want to disappoint you, but it wouldn't be possible to conceal that," Kosygin answered. "Two hours later the whole world would know about it. Everyone would begin shouting that the Soviet Union's intervention in Afghanistan had begun. If we quickly airlift tanks, the necessary ammunition, and make mortars available to you, will you find specialists who can use these weapons?"

"I'm unable to answer that question. The Soviet advisers can answer it."

"Hundreds of Afghan officers were trained in the Soviet Union. Where are they all now?"

"Most of them are Muslim reactionaries. We're unable to rely on them, we have no confidence in them. . . . Why can't the Soviet Union send Uzbeks, Tajiks, and Turkmen in civilian clothing? No one would recognize them. We want you to send them. They could drive the tanks, because we have all those nationalities in Afghanistan. Put them in Afghan costume and give them Afghan badges and no one will recognize them. It's very easy work, in our view."

"You're of course oversimplifying the issue. It's a complex political and international issue, but irrespective of that, we'll hold consultations again and get back to you. . . . We're comrades waging a common struggle and that's why we shouldn't stand on ceremony with each other. Everything must be subordinate to that," Kosygin replied, ending the conversation.

On March 20, Taraki secretly flew to Moscow, where Kosygin

formally delivered the news that the Kremlin had decided against sending Soviet troops into Afghanistan. The move would worsen the situation for both the USSR and Taraki himself, Kosygin explained. Brezhnev repeated the negative answer later that day, reading from a prepared text on behalf of the Soviet leadership.

Meanwhile, desertions and mutinies continued in the eastern city of Jalalabad, south of Kabul in Ghazni, and elsewhere in Afghanistan. In May, a mechanized brigade from the Afghan Army's Seventh Division defected to the resistance. In June, government troops fired into a demonstration in Kabul, killing many civilians. In August, the Fifth Brigade of the Ninth Infantry Division joined a revolt in the broad, fertile Kunar Valley in the northeast of the country.

After Moscow sent more aid to Kabul—including two hundred T-55 and a hundred T-62 tanks and twelve Mi-24 gunship helicopters—Taraki ordered some of the aircraft into the strategically important valley. They destroyed villages, killing many residents, including more than a thousand in the town of Kerala. A historian noted that "this atrocity" became "one of the best known in a war replete with atrocities." Also in August, government troops retook Kabul's Bala Hissar fortress after the mutiny Zenit officer Valery Kurilov heard from the Soviet embassy.

Some Soviet military authorities in Moscow began thinking that aid to Kabul would be a good excuse to strike a quick blow against the Afghan rebels and provide Red Army paratroops with useful combat experience. The idea wasn't lost on Defense Minister Ustinov.

VI

Growing rebelliousness in the provinces helped feed the power struggle between Taraki and Amin. For his part, Taraki fostered a budding cult of personality, partly through mass rallies in which marching supporters carried his portraits. But most Afghans perceived the aging former journalist and KGB agent since 1951 as a relatively ineffectual leader of a generation whose time was passing. In contrast, the younger, energetic Amin clearly burned with ambition. After receiving his Columbia University master's degree in educational science—he failed to earn a doctorate—Amin returned to Afghanistan in 1965 to join the PDPA's militant Khalq wing. Fourteen years later, in the spring of 1979, he held the post of foreign minister and was soon to become prime minister as well. The driving force behind the government's reform effort, Amin was also responsible for much of the violence carried out in its name: disappearances, torture, and summary executions, together with bombings and mass killings of civilians during suppressions of rural rebellions.

Plotting to capture the presidency, Amin quietly installed loyal subordinates in government positions. Communications Minister Said Mohammed Guliabzoi was one of four top cabinet members who stood in his way. The others included Interior Minister Aslam Mohammed Watanjar, Border Affairs Minister Sherjan Mazduriar, and the feared security services chief Asadullah Sarwari. While Taraki failed to register Amin's maneuvers—or simply ignored them—his top supporters did their best to stop Amin. Short, neatly mustachioed Guliabzoi believed his patron Taraki bore responsibility for some of the government's violence, but he blamed Amin's overzealous ruthlessness for withering whatever support the April Revolution had had among the people.

Visiting a wealthy friend, Guliabzoi overheard another visitor, also a party official, jeer to the host, "Your time has come!"—meaning his land was scheduled for redistribution and he'd soon be left with nothing. That kind of crudeness made Guliabzoi regret that the PDPA, which was a little more than a decade old, lacked the experience to carry out its ambitious program competently. Guliabzoi—who had helped overthrow King Zahir Shah in 1973 and was himself no stranger to the use of violence—nevertheless increasingly worried about the motives and methods of Amin, who ordered rivals jailed without informing the head of police—Interior Minister Watanjar—or security chief Sarwari. Guliabzoi, Watanjar, Mazduriar, and Sarwari knew the prime minister was also behind the deaths of a number of top officials, and that he increasingly acted alone, keeping Taraki in the dark.

The friction between the two leaders was clear during a meeting after the president returned from a trip abroad. Amin was pleased. "Our supporters have recently staged another revolution," he crowed. To Taraki's inquisitive look, Amin announced that several family members of moderate religious leader Sibgatullah Mojaddedi had been killed.

"Why?" Taraki asked. "You know Mojaddedi has many followers. He's a popular figure."

Amin took other actions without informing Taraki even afterward. When the president's aides informed him Amin had ordered the houses of villagers in the Kunar Valley burned and the inhabitants buried alive, Taraki was visibly upset. "We carried out the revolution for the people, not to kill them," he said. But Taraki's lack of resolution to do more than chastise Amin—even if it was really over who was in charge of the killing and not the killing itself—seemed only to provoke more aggression from his rival. When the president and his top four ministers at last moved to stop Amin, he went on the attack.

The KGB's Bogdanov saw signs of Amin's plotting over the summer, and evidence of ever more murderous antagonisms between Khalq and Parcham. Soon after arriving in Kabul, Bogdanov attended a going-away party for a Soviet adviser at a small, well-guarded Kabul restaurant. When secret police chief Sarwari joined them, he informed Bogdanov that the head of the army's general staff, General Shakhur, was plotting a military coup with American help. Sarwari, a tough former air force pilot, went on to accuse an unnamed superior of Shakhur's of masterminding the alleged plot. As he described the alleged plot's details, Bogdanov mulled over whom Sarwari was really accusing of treason. It could only be Defense Minister Abdul Qadir, a rival Parcham group member, he decided—but since the coup story sounded far-fetched, the real explanation was almost certainly that Sarwari was preparing the way for the defense minister's removal.

Before leaving the restaurant, Bogdanov spoke again to Sarwari. "I don't quite understand," he said, "but I believe your government has a split and that's very dangerous. You should be united."

Then Bogdanov drove to see Ambassador Puzanov at the Soviet embassy. "They're going to arrest Qadir," he said.

"That can't be true!" Puzanov replied. "The Party made him a full member"—from the candidate member he'd been—"only three days ago. He was drinking champagne with [chief Soviet military adviser] Gorelov today."

Still new to Kabul, Bogdanov decided not to argue. He limited himself to saying, "Alexander Mikhailovich, maybe they're only trying to lull him into dropping his guard." Puzanov was unconvinced.

The following day, Bogdanov drove to the airport to see off the Soviet adviser. Ambassador Puzanov and Sarwari were also there. Approaching Bogdanov, Sarwari took his hand. "You remember what I told you yesterday? It was Qadir. We arrested him in the presidential palace this morning."

"Why don't you tell Alexander Mikhailovich about it?" Bogdanov replied offhandedly, referring to Ambassador Puzanov.

Worried by the news, Puzanov asked Bogdanov to accompany him to the embassy, where they called a meeting of the top Soviet military advisers. Gorelov described his meeting with Qadir the previous morning. Gorelov was not known for his intelligence, but he was a decorated paratroop general whose division had led the Soviet attack against Czechoslovakia to put down the Prague Spring in 1968, ably seizing government buildings and airports. Gorelov had been sent to Afghanistan in 1975, when it was ruled by Daoud. Suspecting Gorelov because of his ties to the executed former leader, Amin had asked Moscow to replace him, along with Ambassador Puzanov—requests the Kremlin ignored for now.

Gorelov said he'd left Qadir anxious. The two were drinking

champagne around eight o'clock in his office when the telephone rang. It was Taraki, requesting the defense minister's presence. The presidential palace was a ten-minute walk away. Qadir had asked Gorelov to wait for him and left unarmed. It would be the last time Gorelov saw him.

At around nine thirty a.m., Interior Minister Watanjar—whom KGB chief Andropov liked to call "the Yeti," for his stocky frame—walked into Qadir's office. "Qadir's under arrest," he announced. "I've been appointed acting defense minister."

As the Soviet military advisers debated the text of a report to Moscow, Sarwari accused several politicians of plotting against the general staff. Bogdanov again warned his embassy to expect purges that were sure to follow. A number of arrests three days later earned him the ambassador's complete trust.

Qadir's removal was far from the only sign of turmoil at the top. Earlier, Bogdanov—together with visiting KGB foreign intelligence chief Kryuchkov and foreign counterintelligence head Kalugin—had met Amin for dinner. After a relaxed meal with good food and conversation, the Soviets asked Amin what purpose the vicious sparring between his Khalq wing and the moderate Parchamists could serve.

"There's no struggle," Amin replied. "We cooperate well."

Bogdanov repeated his question as the Russians prepared to leave. "Is it differences over tactics . . . or something else?"

"Everything's fine," Amin reassured him. "There are two Parcham members sitting in the cabinet. What better sign of cooperation can there be?"

Back at the Soviet embassy, Kryuchkov scolded Bogdanov for harping on the question. Bogdanov defended himself. "You and Kalugin will be leaving soon," he said, "but I have to establish an intelligence service for these people. You watch, they're going to rid the government of every Parcham member." Convinced the key to stabilizing Afghanistan was stopping the intra-party rivalry, Bogdanov believed only Soviet pressure would make Amin's Khalq group relent.

"The next time something flares up, I'm going to tell Amin, 'You assured me there aren't any problems between the two sides. This is none of my business, but you solve your issues within your party.' He'll get the point."

Shortly after, during the summer, when Soviet Central Committee member Boris Ponomaryov—another leading advocate of intervening in Afghanistan—traveled to Afghanistan, Bogdanov urged him to lean on Amin and to take up the issue of Afghan infighting in the Kremlin. Ponomaryov returned to Afghanistan a year later, in July 1979. When he was leaving, Bogdanov—who was heading to Latvia for vacation at the time and happened to be on the same flight from Kabul to Bukhara—again pressed his point. "There's no military solution to the Afghanistan issue," he assured the top Politburo hawk. But he believed ever fewer Soviet officials shared his view.

VII

Taraki appointed Amin prime minister in March. Bogdanov was in Moscow at the time. On his return, Sarwari praised the president for his political smarts: he was holding his most dangerous rival close. The conversation took place in Sarwari's office. When his translator left the room, the security chief whispered into Bogdanov's ear: "Amin is a very dangerous person. He'll do anything to get what he wants." The exchange prompted another cable to Moscow warning of a serious threat within the party. Soon Amin began pressuring Puzanov to lean on Taraki to appoint Amin defense minister as well.

Taraki finally appeared to worry about his split with Amin. During a Politburo meeting in July, Amin blamed Taraki for the government's failures. Taraki returned the fire in August, accusing Amin of nepotism. Taraki's four closest advisers succeeded in transferring some of Amin's powers to the presidency. Still, the four

Taraki and Amin at the presidential palace in Kabul, 1978. *(Alexander Liakhovskii archive)*

ministers worried the rumors they were conveying to Taraki about Amin plotting to seize power weren't taken with the necessary seriousness. Entreaties to rein in his independent activities left Amin unmoved.

Amin saw an opportunity in September 1979, when Cuba was due to host a summit conference of nonaligned countries. On the urging of the four ministers, Taraki ordered Amin to represent Afghanistan. But the prime minister outmaneuvered them by arguing that only the leader of the "revolutionary East"—Taraki—could properly represent its interests. At a party conference he initiated, Amin announced the president's decision to go, adding that the country appreciated his efforts. The flattery worked on Taraki, and to seal the decision, Amin informed Moscow in a cable requesting a plane for the trip.

Several of the officials accompanying Taraki on his flight to Havana on August 30 were there because Amin had contrived for them to go. After an uneventful conference, the president's return flight on September 10 stopped in Moscow, where Bogdanov was at home, having just returned from vacation.

A KGB duty officer called him there to say the Afghan president would be staying in a mansion in the city's leafy Lenin Hills, near Moscow State University. There was more: a security official in Taraki's entourage had urgently requested to speak to the KGB's Kabul representative. Suspecting that conditions had further changed during his monthlong absence from Afghanistan, Bogdanov tried to postpone, saying he was out of the loop. The meeting could easily be held the following week, when he'd be back in Kabul. Nevertheless, he agreed to the requests, informed his superiors, then drove to his office at the KGB's new suburban headquarters. Reading the latest reports from Afghanistan there, he worried the situation had worsened even more than he'd expected. There were now rumors that Amin was plotting to kill Taraki and evidence that he'd overridden the Taraki supporters who'd urged the president not to go to Cuba.

Bogdanov called Kryuchkov and offered to warn Taraki of Amin's possible intentions. The foreign intelligence chief declined, partly on the grounds that Taraki was scheduled to meet with Brezhnev. But several Central Committee members with whom Bogdanov pressed his case eventually persuaded Kryuchkov to arrange a meeting.

Bogdanov joined a group of Soviets, including other KGB officers and Foreign Ministry diplomats, who had met their Afghan guests at Sheremetyevo Airport and accompanied them to Lenin Hills. As Taraki dined in his guesthouse prior to being driven to the Kremlin to meet Brezhnev, one of the Afghans approached Bogdanov to say Amin had ordered him to relay important information to Kabul's KGB representative—strictly in private. The man said Amin had absolutely insisted the translator be Sayed Tarun, Taraki's chief of staff, who was also traveling with the president. Bogdanov was an experienced intelligence officer, but his interlocutor's next words startled him: "Everything I tell you will be untrue. We must meet alone later."

Bogdanov had met Tarun in Kabul many times, and he knew him as a tough man who often enthusiastically backed the arrests of top government figures. The KGB colonel got along with Taraki's chief of staff well enough, but he didn't know the mustachioed officer was actually a top Amin loyalist who secretly used his position to spy on the president. Amin had engineered Tarun's installation as Taraki's chief aide, and would soon lobby for him to replace Sarwari as security chief.

Now standing nearby, Tarun seemed surprised to hear the request to translate. But not too surprised; the graduate of Leningrad's Meteorological Institute spoke fluent Russian. He joined the two men in one of the mansion's bedrooms. There, the mysterious Afghan, through Tarun, accused Taraki of plotting to kill Amin, adding that the four ministers were engaged in a conspiracy against the prime minister. When the Afghan left, Bogdanov asked Tarun whether he agreed with the accusations. Tarun agreed and said he also believed the plot included his own murder.

"But why would they want to kill you?"

"Whoever lives well today wants to live better tomorrow," Tarun replied.

Bogdanov was a little shaken. "Do you realize what you're saying?" he asked. "It's a very serious accusation. Will you confront the ministers?"

"Of course. Because I support Amin. We'll fight our enemies."

Bogdanov could scarcely believe Taraki's closest personal assistant could be Amin's agent. Suppressing his surprise, he asked Tarun what he thought of the Afghan president.

"An old fool! He has no idea what he's doing."

Bogdanov struggled to conceal his astonishment until Tarun excused himself, saying he needed to have his suit pressed for the Kremlin meeting. When Bogdanov left the bedroom, the Afghan official who'd initially approached him came forward again. This time, Bogdanov called over a Soviet Foreign Ministry translator.

"Everything Tarun told you was a lie," the Afghan now insisted.

"There's no conspiracy against Amin. He's trying to fool you. It's Amin who wants to get rid of Taraki. And the four ministers are in his way. He wants them *out* before taking on Taraki himself." The official added that the coup Amin was planning would take place within days. It was chilling if not entirely shocking news. The claims appeared to confirm the KGB's reports from Afghanistan that Bogdanov had read earlier in the day.

Taraki soon left to meet Brezhnev in the Kremlin, where the Soviet leader greeted him with a sloppy kiss. Then the general secretary read a Central Committee memorandum that warned of Soviet concerns about Amin's plan to seize power, which would pose a threat to the Afghan revolution. Brezhnev gave authorization—coded in bureaucratese—for Taraki to fire his prime minister.

When the Afghan president returned to the Lenin Hills guesthouse, a KGB officer again warned him about Amin's plot, now in no uncertain terms. It turned out that Brezhnev's blessing to fire Amin had been too cryptic. "Comrade Brezhnev hinted about it but I didn't quite understand what he was getting at," Taraki confided.

Now it was his turn to spin disbelief. "But not to worry," the president assured the KGB officer. "Thanks for the information, but please tell my Soviet comrades there's no reason to be concerned. I'm completely in control of the situation in Afghanistan. Nothing can happen without my knowledge."

Thus calming the Soviet leadership, Taraki left for Kabul, followed by Bogdanov two days later, on September 12. Brezhnev's timely warning to the Afghan president had indicated to the KGB representative that the Soviet leadership had other channels to Kabul that bypassed him. When Taraki confronted Amin days later, the prime minister denied all the accusations against him and humbly offered to resign his post if requested by the Soviets. His only condition was that the resignation be approved by a plenum of the PDPA's Central Committee. Amin's nephew later told Bogdanov that during Taraki's absence, Amin had called all thirty-odd Central Committee members individually into his office. All were asked whom they supported, Amin or Taraki—while the nephew held a pistol to their temples.

Some Soviet advisers were already urging Moscow to take matters into its own hands. They'd come up with a solution to Afghanistan's problems: assassinate Amin. By September, the KGB's Zenit group developed a plan to kidnap the prime minister and bring him to the Soviet Union, where he would probably be killed. But no order to execute the operation was issued.

VIII

During Taraki's absence, Amin had continued staffing government offices with relatives and supporters. He purged Taraki loyalists partly by accusing them of leading dissolute lifestyles. The four ministers—Interior Minister Watanjar, Communications Minister Guliabzoi, Border Affairs Minister Mazduriar, and Security Services Chief Sarwari—were among those to whom special pressure was applied. Hoping to save their jobs, and concerned about the threat of Taraki's ouster, they appealed to the president for help. He refused, after which "the gang of four," as Amin now dubbed them—in what couldn't be missed as a reference to recently ousted Communist Party leaders in China—began speaking out against the prime minister.

The officials Amin had sent to spy on the president in Cuba hadn't been present when he met with the Soviet leadership in the Kremlin. Fearing what Taraki may have been told in the Kremlin, the prime minister ordered an antiaircraft battery on a hill near Kabul to shoot down the president's plane as it approached the airport. However, Sarwari's intelligence service learned of the plan and disarmed the artillery unit.

As the plane's scheduled arrival neared, Amin sat listening in his office. Hearing no explosions, he knew his plan had failed. He urgently called the airport to order the plane to circle for another approach. The maneuver gave him enough time to drive there and greet Taraki with an embrace.

Taraki was unaware of how much had changed during his brief absence. When he convened a cabinet meeting the following day to discuss his trip to Cuba, the president made a consequential misstep. Where, he asked, were Guliabzoi and another minister who were late to the meeting? "Have they been arrested?" Sarwari, Mazduriar, and Watanjar believed the question showed he was aware of Amin's plotting. Then the president made a tactical mistake: "There's a cancer in the party and it needs to be cut out!" he announced. For Amin and his supporters, the writing appeared to be on the wall.

Two days later, Amin and Taraki spent the entire day closeted in Taraki's office, where Amin accused the gang of four of staging an attempt to assassinate him and demanded their resignations.

When Bogdanov arrived in Kabul from Moscow, Sarwari was waiting in his office. The Afghan security chief—whose reputation for cruelty was reinforced by rumors he personally took part in torture and executions—said Amin had ordered his arrest and execution, along with the rest of the gang of four. Bogdanov asked Sarwari to call a meeting with Taraki, then left for the embassy to report. Ambassador Puzanov relayed Bogdanov's information to the Kremlin, which again ordered that peace be made between Amin and Taraki.

The four ministers appeared at the Soviet embassy to seek protection. While they were there, Amin telephoned and asked to speak to Interior Minister Watanjar. "So, you honorable guardians of the revolution got scared!" he taunted. "You're hiding from me like rats!" Amin handed the receiver to Taraki, who assured the ministers they were safe and asked them to return home.

That night, when Sarwari was again told that Amin had ordered the assassinations of the four ministers, his informant added that it would happen the following day, September 13. Early the next morning, the Soviet representatives learned that one of Sarwari's deputies had burst into his boss's office with several other armed men who announced that Sarwari had been replaced with counterintelligence chief Aziz Akbari. The men tried to break into Sarwari's desk. One of Sarwari's loyal adjutants, Mohammed Qulassem, ordered the deputy, who actually served Amin, to leave. When he refused, the adjutant shot and killed him. Amin's men returned fire and killed Qulassem.

Nevertheless, Taraki still refused to take steps that would prevent Amin from carrying out a coup. When the four ministers urged him to announce Amin's intentions to the Politburo and on radio and television, Taraki again balked. "I don't want to swat any flies for my own sake," he said. "Amin is the party's problem and the Politburo's. They should solve it on their own."

After Taraki's rejection, the ministers returned to the Soviet embassy while Ambassador Puzanov left under military escort for the presidential palace. There Taraki said Amin had told him he intended to fire the gang of four for failure to carry out their duties. Taraki refused to approve the move and invited the four top Soviet representatives to discuss the matter the following day.

Later that day, Bogdanov and KGB chief liaison Boris Ivanov met Amin in his Defense Ministry office. Ivanov—distinctive for his thick, horn-rimmed glasses ahd generally bookish appearance— was a talented speaker of several foreign languages, respected by his subordinates for his ability to think beyond the narrow confines of Party dogma. Although surprised by the visit, the prime minister appeared ready to discuss a truce. Still, he continued insisting the gang of four be dismissed, and now added a demand that the president's chief of staff, Tarun, be appointed head of the intelligence service. Amin gave Taraki three days to reply. Hearing the offer soon after, Taraki tentatively agreed to replace Sarwari, but insisted the other three ministers remain in office. Despite the evidence about Amin's intentions, Taraki even now continued to trust him, or so he professed to Gorelov.

During Bogdanov and Ivanov's meeting with Amin, Afghan military chief of staff Mohammed Yaqub interrupted to say something in Pashto to the prime minister that the Soviet interpreter didn't catch. Shortly after Yaqub left, Tarun entered the room and addressed Amin. "I've come with an invitation to dinner with the president," he said. "But I advise you not to attend . . . he's given orders to kill you. He has a Kalashnikov and two pistols already prepared." Tarun then excused himself, and Amin turned to Bogdanov. "Well, what do you think?" he asked sarcastically. "Should I go to the palace tomorrow? Yaqub just told me the same thing, you know." Despite the warnings, Ivanov and Bogdanov pressed him to go.

That evening, Guliabzoi received a telephone call at home. During a meeting of a number of cabinet and party members, the caller informed him, Amin accused the gang of four of plotting a coup—and again threatened to fire them. The four ministers lived on different floors of a Soviet-built, concrete-slab building in Microrayon, a Kabul suburb. Three convened in Guliabzoi's apartment, from where they telephoned Taraki to inform him.

"You're all so young," the president responded. "Don't do anything rash. I'll solve this."

They drove to the Soviet embassy to press Soviet chief military adviser Gorelov to intervene on their behalf. After Mazduriar arrived from a visit to the dreaded Pul-i-Charkhi prison to join them, the ministers left for the presidential palace, where Taraki informed them that he'd finally decided to sack Sarwari in an effort to appease Amin. Again Taraki told the ministers not to worry.

Soon counterintelligence chief Akbari—an Amin supporter— informed the ministers he'd removed the security around their building and was sending a tank battalion to take them away. Still, Taraki repeated his assurance that he'd solve the problem.

"How?" Guliabzoi asked. When Taraki produced no convincing answer, Guliabzoi urged him to ask for Soviet military intervention. "Son," the president said, "I'm a Pashtun. And no other Pashtun will accept that I've used a Russian battalion to rescue you."

Finally, however, Taraki advised the ministers to hide. Their refuge was a safe house in a poor neighborhood on one of the hills overlooking the city. Taraki and his supporters had converted the house when they'd been threatened with assassination under Daoud's rule. That night, Amin announced the gang of four had been fired on Taraki's order.

When the four top Soviet representatives appeared for dinner at Taraki's residence the following day, the president told them Amin had refused to attend. Taraki telephoned the prime minister to insist on his presence. Amin replied that he'd learned Taraki was trying to assassinate him. The president handed the receiver to Puzanov, who, pressing Amin to come, guaranteed his safety. After consulting with his top advisers, Amin finally consented.

He arrived at Taraki's palace with four armed bodyguards in two Mercedes cars. Tarun met him at the entrance and led the way to the dining room on the second floor. Passing an outdoor pool, the visitors approached a set of stairs leading to the meeting room. The guards at the top refused to let the armed men pass. Tarun— whom some describe as acting as if he'd already been appointed Afghanistan's security chief—was carrying an automatic rifle slung around his neck. He ordered Taraki's guards to stand aside. Instead, one of the soldiers opened fire, killing Tarun instantly. Amin's men shot back. In the exchange of fire that followed, Amin's bodyguard Waziz Zirrak was injured. A ricocheting bullet grazed the prime minister, who'd been hiding behind a corner. Covered by his three remaining guards, Amin ran back to his car and sped to the nearby general-staff building. When he telephoned Taraki to demand an explanation, the president said the shooting was the result of a misunderstanding on the part of his guards. Taraki pressed him to return for discussions, but Amin accused the president's guards of purposely killing Tarun and refused. Sarwari later told the four Soviet representatives that Taraki's guards had orders to let no one armed inside.

The four Soviets left Taraki for Amin's office to try to explain the incident. Although outwardly calm, Amin pointed to blood splattered on his suit and steadfastly accused Taraki of planning to kill him. "If you ever want to meet Taraki again," he said, "you should do it only after informing me. I don't want any more 'misunderstandings.'" The ironic request would turn out to be unnecessary. None of the Soviets would again lay eyes on Taraki.

While the Soviets were meeting with Amin, the president ordered the air force to bomb the general-staff building. Told the four Soviet representatives were inside, he replied that it "doesn't matter." His order was refused. Already in de facto control of the government, Amin ordered the army to surround Taraki's residence, barricading him inside and cutting the telephone and electricity lines. The following day, Amin convened a plenum of the PDPA Central Committee, during which the president was deposed and arrested. The committee named Amin general secretary of the party.

Ambassador Puzanov and his fellow Soviet representatives later met with Amin to press him not to harm Taraki. He told them the deposed leader and his family would not be jailed but placed under house arrest for their own safety. When, almost a month later, on October 9, KGB officers in Kabul asked Amin to spare Taraki's life, he told them the former president was ill, but still alive. In fact, one of his own guards had, on Amin's orders, smothered him to death with a pillow in the Pul-i-Charkhi prison, after which he was quickly buried. His wife and children were arrested. The Bakhtar news agency later announced Taraki had died of a "serious illness."

Gromyko cabled the Soviet advisers to continue working "as normal," and not to take part in any actions directed against Amin. But Brezhnev was infuriated. News of the death of a man he'd so recently greeted warmly in Moscow, and to whom he'd also given his assurance of support, deeply rankled. "What a scum that Amin is to smother a person with whom I took part in revolution," the Soviet general secretary said. Brezhnev's emotional response and sense of personal insult gave strong impetus to the ongoing discussions about removing Amin, and other Politburo members took their cue. Old rumors that Amin was a CIA agent contributed to KGB chief Andropov's decision to order new plans for ousting him.

Meanwhile, unrest in the Afghan countryside continued to grow, and Amin, for all his cunning and ambition, had no better luck quelling it. He did, however, put down an uprising by the Afghan Army's Seventh Division. The Kremlin looked on as the crisis spun its new communist neighbor ever further from its influence.

IX

The Cold War had overshadowed every move made in Afghanistan by Moscow and Washington. If the United States gradually lost interest in the country following World War II, the Soviet Union had increased its attentions. Before 1979, the Kremlin had provided more than $1 billion in military aid and $1.25 billion in economic aid. (Some of that investment was returned through a Soviet-built natural gas pipeline that ran from northern Badakshan to the USSR.) The current risk of PDPA collapse threatened the Kremlin with the loss of decades' worth of influence-building in Kabul.

One of Moscow's main considerations was the possible American response, especially the effect intervention might have on Cold War dynamics. In late 1978, a top-secret cable from Cyrus Vance warned the U.S. embassy in Kabul that diminished American activity in Afghanistan would contribute to the major Soviet goal of reducing Western influence in the region. Such a present to Moscow would not be in American interests, the communiqué stressed.

With suspicions rising, the U.S. embassy kept a close eye on the Soviets. A cable to Washington on May 9, 1979, informed of a marked increase in the Soviet presence in Afghanistan over the preceding several weeks. As for the possibility of Soviet military units entering the country, the cable said the Soviets would surely not allow their investments to be lost.

Soviet distrust of Washington was also growing, especially after that year's worrying events in Iran. Afghanistan's western neighbor was swept up by the Islamist revolution of Ayatollah Khomeini, a fierce opponent of Washington, who forced the abdication of the shah, its key regional ally. On November 4, Iranian college students took the U.S. embassy staff in Tehran hostage, and American listening posts on the nearby Soviet Union were lost, together with bases and airfields. Afghanistan suddenly became much more interesting to Washington, and the possibility that it might send in American forces concerned Moscow.

Deluded by the relatively upbeat cables Andropov had arranged for Soviet personnel in Kabul to send, most of the Politburo saw Afghanistan's unrest as a spontaneous tribal uprising against the government rather than a deepening civil conflict. A new regime in Kabul might favor siding with Washington—which the Soviet leaders assumed was aiding the rebels—instead of Moscow. And an American ally on the USSR's southern border would pose a major threat.

Waiting could make matters worse. The Kremlin knew Washington recognized the Afghan government was part of the Soviet sphere of influence, but maybe only for now. That was an argument for invasion sooner rather than later. Surely American demoralization after Vietnam reduced the chances that it would do anything now to counter quick Soviet action.

Iran's revolution affected Soviet policy in other ways. Moscow now faced a potentially hostile Islamist state bordering the Muslim republics of Soviet Central Asia. Taking control of Afghanistan would push the perceived front line of Soviet influence south of the Hindu Kush mountain range—instead of waiting for religious radicalism to possibly move north. And with many thousands of Muslim subjects also living in the Russian republic—the largest of the fifteen Soviet republics—Islamic radicalism could not be ignored. Aiding the fellow communist regime seemed increasingly appealing. In other words, invasion.

X

In Kabul, Amin set about purging the government of its remaining Taraki supporters, killing some of them. The KGB's Zenit group had already enacted a plan to save the gang of four—Watanjar, Guliabzoi, Mazduriar, and Sarwari—who were most at risk. In the early afternoon of September 14, Taraki's last day as president, Guliabzoi, Watanjar, and Sarwari had driven to the house of a KGB operative near the Soviet embassy, from where they were secretly spirited to the embassy. The cars in which they were driven were later burned.

The ministers were brought to a Zenit safe house, where Leonid Bogdanov visited them, bearing vodka and red caviar. They refused to touch it. He assured them Taraki was safe and that the KGB had matters under control.

"Just give me a platoon of soldiers and we'll get those bastards," Sarwari appealed, half in jest. "Send us some Cubans, they'll do the job." Bogdanov replied that since the ministers had become Moscow's responsibility, he couldn't let them out of hiding. He also insisted they hand over their weapons: two Kalashnikovs, an Uzi, and Watanjar's Czechoslovakian pistol, a present from Soviet First Deputy Interior Minister Victor Paputin.

The ministers' mustaches were shaved and they were dressed in Zenit uniforms. From their hiding place in a second-floor room of the *spetsnaz* group's building, they ventured outside to stretch their legs only at night. Zenit officer Valery Kurilov, who sometimes escorted them on their walks, befriended Sarwari, and since the security chief's Russian was weak, they communicated in English. Sarwari promised that if he made it out of his predicament, he'd ensure Kurilov would live like a king.

The Afghan government's counterintelligence, now securely under Amin's control, was searching hard for the vanished ministers. Amin accused them of helping Taraki plot to kill him, adding that the four chief Soviet representatives—Ivanov, Puzanov, Gorelov, and Pavlovskii—were involved and, despite Ambassador Puzanov's denials, that the KGB was hiding three of the ministers. (Mazduriar was still living in his own house.) Worried the ministers would soon be found and killed, the KGB prepared to evacuate its Afghan charges. The operation, of Bogdanov's devising, was called

Raduga—"Rainbow." Kryuchkov authorized the plan over a secure line to Bogdanov on September 15. The ministers agreed to it the following day.

The plan was for Zenit to fly the Afghans out of the Bagram air base—more secure than Kabul Airport—under a cover story about routine rotation of personnel. But that meant a half-hour drive outside the capital. The ministers would travel in ammunition boxes equipped by a Moscow workshop with air holes and mattresses. With the ministers inside, the green boxes would be loaded onto buses, hidden under supplies, and driven to the airport. Kurilov's commanding officer directed him to draft written portraits of each minister so they'd be recognized on arrival. (Standard for surveillance operations, written portraits are rigorous descriptions of physical appearance, including head, face, and eye shape, hair color, scars, and other attributes.) Since Zenit officers would be accompanying the ministers to the Soviet Union, Kurilov wondered about the need for the extra precaution.

On September 18, a large Il-76 transport plane landed in Bagram airport with ten Zenit officers, several KGB makeup artists, document forgers, and other specialists, and two trucks, one loaded with the special green containers. The following day, the ministers were loaded into the boxes at the embassy, then onto a truck. Several Zenit officers uninformed of the nature of the cargo climbed onto the truck, others onto an accompanying bus. The small convoy pulled out of the embassy compound and headed north for Bagram, skirting the city's heavily guarded center.

The KGB's worry that Afghan counterintelligence suspected what the Soviets were up to appeared well founded when a Toyota pickup with what looked like several Afghan intelligence officers began trailing behind. At a checkpoint stop along the way, a lieutenant in the Toyota approached the driver of the Soviet truck. "What do you want?" asked the driver, a Zenit officer.

"To check what you're carrying," the lieutenant replied.

"Nothing. We're going home. We have people in the bus, our clothes, that's it."

"You must be transferring weapons."

"No weapons."

"I want to have a look." At the back of the truck, the Afghan saw KGB officers sitting on several trunks inside. He reached out to one of the boxes containing the ministers. A Zenit officer swiftly stepped on his hand. Trying to free it, the Afghan used his other hand to reach for his pistol. Before he could find it, the *spetsnaz* officer stuck the muzzle of his Kalashnikov rifle into the man's face. The Afghan froze. The Zenit officer lifted his foot; the lieutenant pulled back. Turning around, he saw two more Zenit officers, who'd debarked from their bus, one brandishing a combat knife. The Afghan quickly walked back to his Toyota to confer with his colleagues, then waved the convoy on its way.

Arriving at Bagram, the truck carrying the ministers drove straight onto a waiting plane. Mechanics lashed down its wheels and the plane took off. As it gained altitude, Kurilov's next worry was that the Afghan Air Force would send pursuit fighters. He asked an engineer where the plane was headed. "Secret," the man replied. Kurilov now realized, to his dismay, that the written portraits of the ministers he'd drafted might indeed be needed. In case they wouldn't make it out alive—a strong case, it seemed to him at the moment—the men would have to be identified.

Putting the thought out of his head, he began opening the ministers' boxes. The men inside, drenched in sweat and clutching pistols, hadn't been told where they'd be taken. When Kurilov informed them at least where they were going *from*, Sarwari shouted "Why?!" and again demanded to know where they were being taken. "We're Afghans! I'll muster my people! We'll overthrow Amin's bloody regime!"

A bottle of vodka produced by another officer helped Kurilov calm the former minister enough so that his questions focused on where they were going.

"I don't know," Kurilov replied. "Probably the Soviet Union."

The men laid a tarpaulin on the aircraft's metal floor and opened some rations. In less than two hours, the plane landed in

Tashkent, the capital of the Uzbek Socialist Republic—the city through which Kurilov's unit had flown into Kabul, some 450 miles almost due south, in May. The ministers were escorted off and hurried into waiting Volga cars. Just under a month later, on October 14, they would be flown to wait out Amin's regime in the Bulgarian capital of Sofia. Meanwhile, the Zenit officers flew on to Moscow in the airplane that had carried them from Bagram. Landing at the Chkalov military airfield, they drove the same truck, still identified by its Afghan license plates, to Zenit's headquarters at Balashikha, the suburban town where the "saboteurs" course was conducted.

Kurilov was ready to return to Afghanistan immediately, but his group was granted two months' leave. Back at his old KGB counterintelligence job, he was forbidden to speak about his Zenit activities. But his summons to sign for a salary bonus sparked rumors, and he was bombarded with questions about his absence. He answered none. Two months later, he'd be back in Afghanistan in time to take part in a far more serious operation.

CHAPTER 2

STORM-333

The Invasion

I

Despite the Kremlin's worries, Amin essentially remained loyal to Moscow. Soviet military support was his best bet for shoring up the Afghan government against growing unrest. Nevertheless, Moscow increasingly blamed the country's problems on him. When Soviet Ambassador Puzanov refused to grant the new leader's request for a meeting, Amin began to suspect the KGB officers and Soviet political advisers in Kabul no longer trusted him. But he continued requesting Soviet military intervention, now mainly through chief military adviser Gorelov, to whom he increasingly grew closer. Moscow did not budge.

In October, Puzanov called a meeting with Gorelov and KGB head representative Bogdanov to discuss a new uprising by the Afghan Army's Seventh Division.

"A tank battalion is moving toward Kabul," he informed them. "It's already shelled a telephone exchange building. If it gets here it's going to destroy the city."

Bogdanov addressed Gorelov. "Lev Nikolaevich, don't you have advisers with the Seventh?"

"We've lost contact," Gorelov replied.

"Do we know *anything* about the rebels' intentions?"

"They're saying, 'Long live Taraki! Long live the Afghan-Soviet friendship!'" Gorelov said. "I've already ordered a regiment of commandos from the Bala Hissar fortress to surround the division. Helicopters are ready to strike."

Bogdanov was flabbergasted. "Lev, what are you doing!" he said. "They're *against* Amin. That means they're on *our* side! How can you destroy people who are *for* friendship with the Soviet Union? We shouldn't get involved in this one. It's not our business."

Gorelov protested. "Leonid," he told Bogdanov. "Tell me honestly, *who's* on our side? Are you really sure?" Nevertheless, Gorelov called off his attack. The Soviets later learned that only a handful of officers in command of three tanks—and not an entire battalion—had rebelled.

But soon real military uprisings against Amin *were* taking place, including in Jalalabad.

||

Said Mohammed Guliabzoi's account of his fate following Taraki's arrest differs from that of Bogdanov, who devised the plan to spirit him and Taraki's other allies out of the country, and from that of the Zenit officers who carried it out. The then-communications minister insists that he, unlike the other members of the gang of four, spent sixteen days hiding in a mountain safe house outside Kabul. He later fled the capital, but remained in Afghanistan to help plot a coup against Amin, scheduled for October 12. His version had the army's Seventh and Eighth divisions set to participate, together with the Fifteenth Air Force Division—almost three hundred military officers in all, including forty-seven in Amin's guard. One of the division's jet fighters was to give the signal on October 12 by firing a rocket over Kabul.

Only the Seventh Division began to act, however. Learning of the plans, Amin arrested most of the complicit officers, including the pilot meant to give the starting signal, and had some of them executed. Nevertheless, according to Guliabzoi, other plots to kill the president were devised, including a plan for a sword-bearing guard to cut off his head. What's not in doubt is that Amin, no longer able to fully trust many of those around him, requested a Soviet guard and increasingly relied on Soviet protection. Moscow advised him to move to the Taj-Bek palace on the city's outskirts, where the Soviet soldiers would be less visible to Kabul residents.

In late November 1979, Soviet First Deputy Interior Minister Victor Paputin flew to Kabul to review his ministry's units in Afghanistan. He used his time there to prepare a report for Moscow on the general situation in the country. Desertions and eroding discipline had made the problems in the Afghan Army critical, he observed, and the opposition was on the verge of taking power. He called for the immediate dispatch of Red Army forces to the shaky country. Paputin's cable wasn't signed, as required, by three of the top Soviet representatives in Afghanistan. They'd recently been recalled, and their replacements were unavailable or deemed too green. Paputin's blunt report was not received well by the Soviet leadership. After returning to Moscow in December, he committed suicide under mysterious circumstances. Paputin's motives remain a mystery, but they're believed to have been linked to pressure over having contributed to the Soviet invasion. On December 10, Defense Minister Ustinov summoned Victor Zaplatin, the chief Soviet political adviser to the Afghan Army, to Moscow for an urgent explanation of the worrying news. Zaplatin's testimony was less alarming than Paputin's, but still failed to concur with the doctored reports the Politburo had been relaying to Brezhnev, who by that time was spending most of his time at his dacha.

Ustinov was angry. "You in Kabul can't even agree among yourselves about what's going on," he hissed. "But we in Moscow have to make the decisions. How are we supposed to do that?"

Concern was now growing in Moscow that if nothing was

done to help stop Afghanistan's growing rebellion, Amin might ask Washington to send its military into the country. In early December, KGB chief Yuri Andropov sent his memorandum to Brezhnev arguing the need to take resolute action. Most accounts attribute the decisive push that convinced the Soviet leader of the need to invade to that memorandum. In case the decision would be taken, preparations were begun. The 520 officers and men of the Soviet 154th Separate *Spetsnaz* Detachment—the "Muslim battalion"—landed in Bagram on December 9 and 10.

Two days later, the Politburo's ruling minority resolved to remove Amin. The secrecy surrounding the meeting and the vagueness of the resulting directive have kept the Politburo's exact role in Amin's assassination and the beginning of the war a subject of debate, despite their pivotal significance. The conflict's preeminent historian, General Alexander Liakhovskii, who later took part in the war, is convinced that contrary to common belief, the Soviet leadership gave no straightforward order to send Soviet troops into Afghanistan. According to Liakhovskii, the December 12 decision directly concerned only Amin's removal. The inclusion of ground forces—to play a supporting role—was almost an afterthought. No one who advocated action envisioned that seizing the government would spark an ongoing war.

Nevertheless, on December 13, the KGB put in motion a plan to poison the three men it now deemed to hold real power in Afghanistan: Amin; Amin's nephew Asadullah Amin, whose many posts included counterintelligence chief; and Mohammed Yaqub, head of the general staff. Babrak Karmal was back in Afghanistan from Prague, where Taraki had sent him as ambassador to Czechoslovakia. He and three of the "gang of four" ministers who'd been spirited out of Afghanistan were waiting for the Soviets to strike and install them in power.

The Muslim battalion and a unit of Soviet paratroopers would help take over the Communications Ministry and other key objects in Kabul. The Soviet Union's Turkestan military district had been ordered to mobilize its forces and prepare for full combat readiness.

It had no knowledge of the intention to eliminate Amin, for the Politburo had not called for an invasion plan when its members made the December 12 decision to assassinate the Afghan president.

According to at least one general staff officer, no one *ever* actually ordered the invasion of Afghanistan. Instead, between December 10 and 30, various units were given some thirty various directives to prepare for action. Defense Minister Ustinov's lack of combat experience helps explain the absence of centralized implementation. A career spent building the military-industrial complex gave him scant knowledge of how to command the invasion of a sovereign state. Since it was beneath the marshal to ask subordinates for advice, staff activity remained largely uncoordinated.

On December 13, one of Amin's Soviet cooks slipped KGB-provided poison into a lunch prepared for the new president and his nephew. The chemicals were estimated to start working after six hours. The Soviets hunkered down to wait for signs of panic at the presidential palace, after which a signal would be given to take over Kabul's key military and communications installations. When nothing happened after the allotted time had passed, the KGB station called Moscow to request further orders. It was decided to cable Amin from Moscow, providing a way to ascertain the president's health by delivering the message to the palace. After a personal communiqué was sent around eleven p.m., a military intelligence officer and an interpreter set out to deliver it to Amin. The Soviets had extra trouble passing the palace guard because of a nighttime curfew. But when they were finally admitted, Amin and his nephew Asadullah were there. Amin looked pale but showed no other signs of sickness. He listened while the interpreter read the telegram, thanked his visitors, and asked them to send his compliments to Brezhnev, Andropov, and the rest of the Soviet leadership.

Amin's poison had been dissolved in a glass of his favorite drink, Coca-Cola. Its bubbles rendered the concoction almost harmless. Amin's nephew Asadullah was less lucky. He became seriously ill by the following day, but survived after his evacuation to Moscow for treatment.

When the vexing news was relayed to Moscow, an order was given to proceed with the ground-force operation anyway. Another paratroop battalion flew to Bagram to take part in storming the palace. The units obeyed a command to prepare until a second order came to stand down. There would be no coup d'état attempt that day.

The leading Soviet representatives later cabled Moscow that a successful operation would require more troops. According to General Liakhovskii, that document was the main genesis of outright military invasion. After the failed assassination attempts, the operation grew into a full-scale assault as if on its own—thanks first to postponement, then inertia. Incredible as it may seem, no further Politburo meetings took place after December 12. Either the final decision was given orally or the directive was destroyed (together with many other single-copy documents) on Andropov's later orders. In any case, December 27 was picked as the day for "Storm–333": a new operation to kill Amin.

III

Zenit officer Valery Kurilov had been recalled to duty in November. Unable to tell even his wife where he was going, he could say only that he'd be gone six months. She nevertheless guessed the truth from sand she found in his uniform's seams. Back at the Balashikha base outside Moscow, Kurilov and many colleagues from his previous tour engaged in traditional conjecture about their new destination. Poland, then beset by a stagnant economy and growing labor unrest, was a possibility. But given their recent mission in Afghanistan and their knowledge of its growing instability, the men concluded they could only be returning there, this time to help oust Amin.

Officers of the KGB's Zenit *spetsnaz* next to an Il-76 cargo plane at Bagram air base in November 1979. *(Alexander Liakhovskii archive)*

Disguised as a sappers unit, a thirty-two-man group flew to Tashkent, where the officers spent a week killing time in a hotel. Then they traveled to the Bagram air base north of Kabul in early December, landing at night in the middle of a sandstorm. They set up tents inside the base and waited for orders. With freezing temperatures outside, no place to wash, and rations largely limited to canned meat, the men quickly became restless. They grew beards and played cards to pass the days.

Walking the perimeter of the air base one evening, Kurilov noticed a familiar figure dressed in a long brown overcoat: Sarwari, one of the gang of four. Stifling his surprise, he approached the former Afghan security chief, who embraced him. Sarwari had been talking to ex-Communications Minister Guliabzoi and a third Afghan, whom Kurilov didn't recognize. All were wearing the same overcoats, part of a uniform he hadn't seen before. The third man was Babrak Karmal, whom the Soviets were planning to install as the new president. They had been flown into Bagram that day.

Kurilov briefly spoke to Sarwari, who asked whether his Zenit comrades were with him. "I hope you'll help us," he said.

"We'll do everything necessary," Kurilov promised.

"We'll be victorious!" the Afghan replied.

After they parted and Kurilov began walking away, a guard with no markings on his uniform approached and demanded to know why he'd spoken to Sarwari. When the Zenit officer failed to answer directly, the two almost came to blows. Kurilov would later find out his challenger was another *spetsnaz* officer assigned to guard the Afghan VIPs. It was his first meeting with a member of "Group A," later called Alpha, an elite unit formed by KGB chief Andropov. Kurilov and the other officer, Alyosha Baev, would become friends after the onset of fighting drew them together.

Group A and Zenit would participate in the new operation to assassinate Amin, together with another thirty-two-man group, called Grom—"Thunder." Sarwari and Guliabzoi were also to take part by identifying Amin for the Soviet *spetsnaz* groups during their attack.

On December 13—the day set for the first, failed attempt on Amin's life—Kurilov's unit convened to receive orders for an assault on the presidential palace. But the men lacked a proper map of the city. Reliance on a Zenit officer's tourist map made Kurilov uneasy. "Who's planning this thing?" he wondered. Group commander Yakov Semyonov read the men's orders. They would join soldiers from the Muslim battalion outfitted with ancient BTRs, short for armored personnel carriers, eight-wheeled vehicles that the soldiers would drive to the presidential palace, ram through the gates, and burst inside. The BTRs' high-caliber 14.5-mm guns would cover the *spetsnaz* officers by firing into the upper floors. Once inside, Kurilov would help secure the first floor. An Afghan interpreter using a megaphone would attempt to induce palace guards to surrender by announcing the arrival of a "new stage" of the April Revolution. There were no orders about what to do once the building had been taken.

The plan sounded suicidal to Kurilov. The BTR heavy machine guns' fire could reach only the second floor. The third and fourth floors would remain uncovered.

There were other problems with the BTRs. Slamming through the palace gates would require the vehicles to pick up considerable speed. But their approach to the palace would have to be by a road running in front of the complex, then a sharp turn that would afford too little distance, Kurilov believed, to gain the needed momentum. But no alteration was permitted in the plan, whose drafter, whoever it was, Kurilov cursed. "Probably someone sitting in Moscow," he told himself.

Semyonov was as embarrassed as his subordinates were wary. As Zenit braced itself for the worst, Kurilov and a fellow officer agreed to finish off one another if either was seriously wounded. The unit prepared for the assault, but the attack was called off as the hour approached because, Kurilov would later learn, Coca-Cola bubbles had foiled an attempt to poison Amin.

President-in-waiting Karmal was summoned to Moscow the following day, and Zenit transferred from its bivouac in Bagram to Kabul, where Amin had been informed he'd receive extra protection from the *spetsnaz* officers. Following Soviet advice, the Afghan president had moved from the main presidential residence to the Taj-Bek palace on a barren hill in Duralaman, the southwestern outskirts, where he believed he was more secure. Several of the Muslim battalion's BTRs broke down while transferring the *spetsnaz* officers to their new billet in a cluster of half-constructed

The Soviets advised Amin to take up residence at the Taj-Bek palace for his security. (*Alexander Liakhovskii archive*)

barracks seven hundred yards from the palace. The officers covered the missing windows and doors of their new quarters with material cut from tents, and scrounged for at least enough fuel for the stoves to take the edge off the cold. Wood was so scarce that supplies for more important phases of the coming assault had to be sent from the Soviet Union, so inefficient was operational planning. The soldiers' rations on which the officers survived set Kurilov's teeth on edge. To get away from the miserable conditions, he volunteered to escort convoys between Kabul and Bagram, despite the danger of that duty.

It was only on December 24, two weeks after the Politburo's decision to remove Amin, that Defense Minister Ustinov informed his top generals about it. That day, he signed a directive ordering troops to be sent to provide "international help" to the Democratic Republic of Afghanistan and "avert possible threats to the Soviet Union."

Advance divisions of the invading force, under the Fortieth Army, first entered Afghanistan on December 25. Engineers began constructing a pontoon bridge from Termez in Uzbekistan, on the other side of the Amu Dar'ya River. Waves of aircraft from the 105th Airborne Division based in Fergana, Uzbekistan, and the 103rd Airborne Division headquartered in Vitebsk, in Belorussia, began landing on the Soviet side of the Afghan border, and in Bagram and Kabul. Evidently on the assumption that the invasion would succeed with minimal losses—the mere presence of Soviet soldiers would supposedly subdue any opposition—few concrete orders were issued for what they should do once they entered Afghanistan.

Aircraft carrying Soviet troops began landing in Kabul airport in earnest on December 27, surprising many residents of the capital. The 108th Motorized Rifle Division, or MRD, would invade from Termez over the new pontoon bridge and move toward Bagram and Kabul along the main route south through the Hindu Kush, including a three-kilometer, Soviet-built tunnel along the Salang Pass. The 5th MRD would enter farther west, from Kushka in Turkmenistan, then head to Herat and Kandahar. In Kabul, advance units of the 345th Separate Paratroop Regiment and Soviet military advisers already serving in Afghanistan would help the *spetsnaz* forces and Muslim battalion storm Amin's palace and take twelve other key objectives in the city. The 860th Separate Motorized Rifle Regiment, 56th Separate Air Assault Brigade, 2nd Air Defense Brigade, and 34th Composite Aviation Corps would also participate. Amin's continuing requests for Soviet troops greatly aided the planning process. Now Moscow was happy to comply, landing troops without causing alarm—except that they wouldn't be helping Amin. The stage was set for what would essentially be the seizure of the country, even if the Kremlin didn't see it that way.

IV

KGB General Yuri Drozdov was a chief architect of the Soviet attack. On December 25, he met with the heads of the special forces units that would take part in the operation. Even then, the scheme was vague; Drozdov didn't even have a floor plan of Amin's palace, which the KGB would put together later.

Kurilov's unit was given its orders on the morning of December 27. He himself remained part of the group that would secure the luxurious Taj-Bek palace's first floor. His personal main objective was a room containing a safe with the building's most sensitive documents, which several Pashto-speaking soldiers would quickly sort. The *spetsnaz* officers were instructed to allow no one to leave the palace and to shoot-to-kill anyone who tried. Flak jackets were distributed, but they did little to help calm nerves. Kurilov's was too short, leaving part of his chest and stomach exposed. He put it on anyway, beneath a winter Afghan military uniform also distributed to the Zenit group.

Zenit officers in view of the Taj-Bek palace on December 26, the day before they helped storm the building on the first day of the Soviet invasion. *(Alexander Liakhovskii archive)*

The officers worried their Afghan uniforms—meant to confuse the enemy—would make them indistinguishable from their foes, especially during a night operation. To avoid casualties from "friendly fire," they decided to wear gauze bandages around their arms for identification, then settled on more visible white cotton strips torn from bedsheets. As evening approached, the special forces troops readied themselves. The storming was scheduled for ten p.m., then advanced to seven thirty.

Zenit's top commander, Boyarinov, arrived to rally his men. Each received two shots of vodka, and Boyarinov checked that his officers hadn't eaten lunch, so that stomach wounds would be less likely to become infected. "Don't stay in one place," the veteran officer told his subordinates needlessly. "Move around so you won't be easily targeted. Everything will turn out all right. I'll be with you." The mood was tense, but the men appeared jovial, if only to help steady their nerves.

Tripod-mounted antiaircraft guns had been fixed to some of the BTRs that would transport the Zenit officers to the palace. They would be driven by Muslim battalion soldiers, who would break into small units to provide cover outside the building but not take part in the storming itself. When the men approached the armored vehicles as seven thirty drew near, a loud explosion sounded in the city center: the signal to launch the attack. The blast blew open an underground shaft holding international telephone and military communications cables next to the central telephone exchange. (The operation didn't take place entirely smoothly. Soviet soldiers disguised as technicians placed the explosives successfully, but were forced to return because they'd forgotten to start the timer.)

As they heard fire erupt at the palace, the Zenit men relieved themselves on the wheels of their BTRs for good luck. Tracer fire, grenades, and automatic rifle rounds all around the building brought to life the Afghan military units guarding it. Rockets soared over Kurilov's head toward the palace. A military intelligence colonel approached the group and announced that there would be no opposition at the palace. Then Kurilov's unit was ordered to begin its operation, and the men clambered down the hatches of their BTRs.

The column of four personnel carriers rumbled off. The Uzbek driver of Kurilov's BTR drove with his head sticking out of his open hatch.

"Close that thing!" Kurilov yelled over the belching diesel's din. "We'll all be killed!"

"I can't see with it closed!" the man replied, but then complied.

The Zenit men were jammed together and laden with knives, shovels, and other equipment in addition to their body armor and automatic rifles. Kurilov sat pressed up against the man in front of him, an officer from the small northern city of Petrozavodsk, near Finland. "Stop pushing me," the man complained.

"Okay, Volodya," Kurilov soothed.

Then Volodya voiced a more important complaint. "I won't fit through that damned hatch," he said.

"Don't you worry, you will," Kurilov assured him.

"No I won't. What'll I do?"

After some time, the BTR halted, then jolted forward again. Machine-gun fire had disabled the column's first vehicle as it approached the palace. Again the personnel carrier shuddered to a halt, and Kurilov heard what sounded like hail hitting its steel shell. He thought that strange until he realized bullets were making the noise. The officer from Petrozavodsk opened the hatch, began climbing, and got stuck halfway out. Kurilov grabbed his legs and pushed as hard as he could. The officer shot out of the hatch and tumbled down. Kurilov followed, landing hard on the cold ground.

As he lay at the base of the palace hill, projectiles from firing that seemed to come from everywhere landed all around him. Floodlights that the palace guards had miraculously failed to turn off illuminated the building. The black sky was partially red from tracer bullets. Kurilov paused to gather his concentration before the rush toward the palace.

V

The plan to take Kabul on December 27 was largely the same as the abandoned one of December 13, except that many more troops were taking part and the Taj-Bek palace was a significantly easier target than the main Ark presidential complex in the city center.

In the days leading up to the invasion, Soviet advisers and troops had used several ploys to disable Afghan government forces loyal to Amin. An Afghan tank unit surrounding the Kabul radio station was instructed to drain its vehicles of fuel because it was supposedly about to receive newer models. Some of the Afghan Army's Seventh and Eighth divisions were told to make an inventory of faulty ammunition—which would require them to unload shells from their tanks. Soviet instructions to other Afghan units to remove their batteries for winterization immobilized two hundred vehicles.

Suspecting none of that—on the contrary, gratified by the landing of Soviet planes full of troops and equipment over the preceding days—Amin was in a jubilant mood on the morning of December 27. Having finally convinced Moscow to send him Soviet forces, the president arranged a celebratory lunch at the Taj-Bek palace to mark the occasion with some ministers and top Politburo members. He'd then address the army's chief political directorate in the general staff building.

Among those who attended the lunch at the palace was education minister and Afghan Politburo member Abdul Rakhman Jalili, one of Amin's leading supporters in the government. The rector of Kabul University before the April Revolution, Jalili had been educated in the West—he attended college and graduate school in Wyoming—and spoke English flawlessly. Now he believed the PDPA's reforms, however ruthlessly implemented, had set his country on the right course, specifically that the revolution would help pull the Afghan people out of illiteracy and poverty. He also believed most of them supported the government's efforts. The pivotal Herat uprising in April 1979, he thought, was orchestrated by military officers with ties to Iran, and far fewer civilians died in the violence than the rebels claimed.

Afghanistan's Politburo usually held meetings on Sunday mornings. The meeting on December 27 was unusual for taking place on a Thursday—on which celebrations for the PDPA's fourteenth anniversary were due to be held. After Jalili delivered a speech condemning Babrak Karmal, his aide told him an urgent call from Amin's office ordered him to the Taj-Bek palace. Amin wanted the Politburo to approve some new party slogans. He also wanted to discuss the text of his speech that afternoon announcing Moscow's next arms shipments. Afghanistan's leadership had to have noticed that an extraordinary number of Soviet troops had accompanied the weapons and matériel. So Amin's speech would also promise the Soviet forces would be leaving on December 28, via Khairaton, a railhead in the north of the country.

After approving the new slogans, the officials were called to lunch, prepared by the president's Soviet cooks, at around one p.m.

This time, the KGB agents delivered the poison in a creamy vegetable soup Jalili found especially tasty. Emerging into a corridor outside the dining room after the meal, the Politburo members felt sleepy. Jalili instantly suspected a plot, but he couldn't imagine who stood behind it, and it was already too late to act. He and most of the other officials were driven to the hospital.

When Amin failed to appear at the general staff building at two p.m. as scheduled, Afghan political directorate chief Ekbar Waziri drove to the Taj-Bek palace and found Amin unconscious. Waziri immediately departed for the Soviet embassy to ask for doctors to be sent to the president. The new Soviet ambassador, Fikriat Tabeev, knew no more than anyone in the Foreign Ministry in Moscow about the KGB's plan to poison Amin and launch an invasion. Responding to Waziri's request, the embassy sent Anatoly Alexeev, chief Soviet surgeon at the Kabul military hospital, and another Soviet doctor, named Victor Kuznichenko, to aid the president.

When the doctors entered the palace's vestibule, they saw several high-ranking PDPA and government officials lying on sofas and the floor in agony, limbs splayed. The doctors immediately understood they'd been poisoned. Amin was in a bedroom on the verge of death. In a deep coma, he breathed with difficulty.

Attempting to revive him, Alexeev administered liquids to help flush out the poison by forcing diuresis, gave numerous injections, and attached intravenous drips to both arms. Three hours later, at roughly seven p.m., Amin opened his eyes, and the doctors removed his oxygen mask. The president immediately reached for a telephone on a stool beside his bed. The line was dead. Although Amin was less than fully coherent, he realized something was wrong.

Waziri told Amin that Tabeev, the new Soviet ambassador, had telephoned around two p.m. and asked to talk to him about his official announcement concerning the transfer of Soviet troops to Afghanistan. Waziri now suspected that the real purpose of the call was to learn whether the president had been successfully poisoned during lunch. Although the KGB had expected the chemicals to take effect only after six hours, they actually began working almost immediately.

KGB General Drozdov, responsible for overseeing the assault on Kabul, was to determine the operation's launch time. But despite centralized overall planning of the attack on the palace, its execution was completely decentralized, the commander of each operation in Kabul conducting his own reconnaissance before developing his plan of attack. No group knew much about the activities or even existence of the others.

At the Taj-Bek palace, Soviet Army battalions had been directed to neutralize the guards posted outside; the rest was up to the KGB's *spetsnaz* groups. Amin's guards manned positions within the palace, machine-gun posts outside on the palace hill, traffic-control posts on the approach road, and an over-watch position on a nearby hill, while the security brigade also maintained a cordon around the building. Three Afghan Army tanks stood on high ground from where they could fire on anyone crossing the open territory surrounding the palace, also protected from air attack by an army antiaircraft regiment positioned nearby. The regiment's twelve 100-mm antiaircraft guns and sixteen dual-barreled DShK heavy machine-guns could also fire on ground targets while approaching the palace. The guard totaled some 2,500 personnel. Another two tank brigades could rapidly reinforce them from garrisons near Kabul.

Inside the palace, Alexeev was told that Amin's eldest daughter was also dying. Before leaving to treat her, Alexeev ordered the president to a hospital, but he refused to go. Waziri left for the Defense Ministry and when almost there, heard an explosion near the Communications Ministry: the signal to launch the attack. Inside the general staff chief's office, he encountered Soviet soldiers and a general giving orders.

Groups of KGB and GRU (military intelligence) *spetsnaz*, paratroopers, advisers, and several pro-Soviet Afghan Army units fanned out to take the twelve key Kabul objectives in addition to the Taj-Bek palace. They seized the PDPA's central committee building; the Defense, Interior, Foreign Affairs, and Communications ministries; the general staff building; the central army corps headquarters; the military counterintelligence building; the radio and television center; a prison for political prisoners; and the central post and telegraph offices. With the speed of their attack, the Soviets successfully prevented forces loyal to Amin from deploying.

VI

A tall, handsome, twenty-seven-year-old lieutenant named Valery Vostrotin led an elite company in the 345th Separate Paratroop Regiment. Company 9, which would become one of the most famed units of the Soviet-Afghan War, had been sent to Bagram on December 9. For much of the previous year, Vostrotin and his men had been trained for possible operations in Iran, including careful instruction about dealing with local Muslim populations. Now the company's initial task was to guard a squadron of Antonov-12 cargo planes that had been based in Afghanistan since July. On December 15, however, the unit was ordered to join four other Soviet companies guarding the Taj-Bek palace. Vostrotin's troops were given Afghan Army uniforms—to minimize hostility from the native population, they were told—and directed to march the forty-five miles south along the flat plain to Kabul.

Once there, Company 9 joined the Muslim battalion. The men were ordered to let no one within a radius of one kilometer of the palace in the event of any disturbance. Using night-vision goggles, they trained to drive their light armored personnel carriers on the capital's streets after dark.

At around three p.m. on December 27, KGB General Drozdov briefed Vostrotin and the assault's other battalion and company commanders. Amin was a CIA agent, he said, ordering the

Company 9's commander, Senior Lieutenant Valery Vostrotin. He would become the conflict's biggest hero in the eyes of many of its veterans. *(Alexander Liakhovskii archive)*

men to stop any of his supporters from crossing the palace grounds during the upcoming storming, which would begin that evening. Company 9 would advance toward the palace behind a formation of Group A BTRs, then help secure the perimeter. The mission would be Vostrotin's first combat.

When the operation began, he found it had been poorly planned in many respects and that his men weren't battle-ready. Worse still was the general chaos that reigned. Despite intense KGB observation of the palace for some time, the young lieutenant hadn't been told whether the road Company 9 was supposed to take was well maintained or riddled with the usual potholes.

Disobeying strict procedure that forbade officers from taking part in fighting when commanding their men, Vostrotin felt he had to take the controls of a BMD, an amphibious, tanklike infantry fighting vehicle used by paratroops. .

Under heavy fire, the men reached the palace perimeter they were to secure. Finding themselves at a concrete military drill ground, they fired at a set of barracks standing to one side. They didn't know that an Afghan Army battalion headquarters was positioned behind them. The Afghans managed to shoot a Company 9 man in the head, killing him.

Vostrotin ordered four of his soldiers to creep toward the buildings and capture the Afghan battalion commander. Interrogating the Afghan within an hour, he was surprised to learn he'd graduated from the Soviet air academy in Ryazan—Vostrotin's own alma mater.

"What do you want with us?" the commander asked in genuine shock. Vostrotin had ignored as much as he could of the ubiquitous propaganda proclaiming the friendship of the Afghan and Soviet people. He carried out orders—whether to protect Amin's government, as he'd believed he'd been sent to Afghanistan to do, or to help kill the president, as he'd been ordered to do hours earlier. His actions were the same; only the politics changed. But the Afghan's question made him realize that some took the propaganda about Afghan-Soviet friendship to heart.

"What do you want from us?" the commander repeated. "Stop the firing. I'll bring out all my men."

If that was the case, why fight? Letting the commander go to assemble his soldiers peacefully, Vostrotin radioed his own battalion commander and received a screaming earful in reply for trusting the Afghans. "I'll hand you over to a tribunal for a court martial!" bellowed the lieutenant's commanding officer. Thereupon the chastised lieutenant ordered his men to bring the Afghan commander back. After catching him, they delivered a beating before Vostrotin took him prisoner and his men secured their part of the palace perimeter as ordered.

VII

Zenit officer Valery Kurilov lay where he'd landed after tumbling from his BTR at the base of the Taj-Bek palace. Opening his eyes, which closed involuntarily when bullets landed nearby, Kurilov found himself at the base of a small, carefully laid parapet that formed one of the terraces surrounding the palace above him. He tried to ascertain who was shooting at what in the barrage of fire around him, and succeeded in making out the main palace entrance at the end of a winding approach road. A neoclassical front vestibule protruded from the rectangular building with rounded colonnaded sides. Although the battle had been raging for what seemed to have been hours, an oddly untouched black Soviet Volga sedan parked in front gleamed from a fresh wash. It was soon riddled with bullets and blazing with fire.

Through the palace's large windows, Kurilov saw lights inside. As he crawled forward in the dark, he felt stones underneath him. Examining one, he realized it was an unexploded grenade, with its ring still attached. Palace guards were lobbing them out of the windows. Soon Kurilov pulled himself over something wet and slippery: a dead body. Moving closer, he glimpsed a heavy machine gun firing in his direction from a palace window. Raising his Kalashnikov, he fired at the window, hoping a bullet would ricochet to hit the soldier inside, whom he couldn't see.

Closer to the palace, a Muslim battalion soldier sprawled motionless nearby, a tripod-mounted machine gun lying in front of him. Puzzled that a man so close to the palace was so inactive, Kurilov nudged him. "What are you doing?" he asked. His machine gun had jammed, the soldier replied. Kurilov picked it up and squeezed the trigger. It let off a round. He handed it back, instructing the soldier to shoot into the window from where the unseen enemy was firing at them. Then the firing stopped; the absence of its noise caused Kurilov's heart to skip. When the volleys started again, he instructed the soldier to throw a grenade and prepared to toss one of his own. On the count of three, both men hurled their explosives at the window; Kurilov's missed; the soldier forgot to pull his ring. They threw two more. This time, Kurilov's flew into the window and exploded.

Trying to continue forward but realizing he was pinned down and couldn't move in any direction, Kurilov noticed someone kneeling near him in the mayhem. Taking careful aim with his automatic rifle and shooting almost nonchalantly, as if at a firing range, the man was picking off palace guards one by one. The sharpshooter wore a strange cloth-covered helmet with a visor and a built-in radio receiver. Kurilov had never seen one before, and found himself thinking: "If I live through this, I'm going to get one just like it." He later learned that the well-outfitted fighter was an officer of the KGB's mysterious Group A, the second one he'd seen. The helmet was Swiss-made.

Suddenly there was another pause in the firing. Zenit chief Boyarinov, who had overall command of the palace assault and had been inside, emerged to urge his men on. Like the other Zenit officers, he was dressed in an Afghan Army uniform. Kurilov heard him shouting, "C'mon, men! Move forward!" Then Boyarinov was hit, by Soviet machine-gun fire, as Kurilov would later find out. A bullet ricocheted from the top of his flak jacket and pierced his neck.

Kurilov stood up to charge toward the palace. As he fired off rounds, something knocked his automatic rifle out of his hands. He picked it up, but it wouldn't function. Fighting an ache in his hand, he tried moving the breechblock to replace its cartridge, but it had jammed. Then he noticed that the bullet that had evidently hit his gun also left a hole in his palm, maybe after a ricochet. He would later calculate from the way he'd been holding his weapon that the bullet missed his face by centimeters.

He found another Kalashnikov on the ground. His wounded hand made it difficult to carry, but to his relief, it still had a strap, which he slung over his shoulder before another bullet pierced his left arm. The hit, which felt like a massive blow from a red-hot iron, left him unable to move his arm. He would have to operate his rifle with a single hand. Continuing toward the palace, he entered through the main door, turned right as he'd been instructed, and made his way down a hallway. *Spetsnaz* officers were blowing open locked doors on both sides with grenades and entering the rooms.

A third bullet pierced Kurilov's body armor and lodged under a rib, the force knocking him flat. Lying on the floor, he saw the Afghan guard who'd shot him and managed to find the trigger of his machine gun with his good hand. He fired in the man's direction. Then a grenade exploded nearby, sending shrapnel into Kurilov's face, arms, and legs. Blood oozed out in many places and he felt his tongue swelling. Barely able to move his powerfully aching body, let alone to continue fighting, Kurilov decided to leave the building. Then he realized his white armband was missing. In his Afghan uniform, he could easily be mistaken for an enemy soldier.

VIII

After treating Amin's daughter, the Soviet doctors heard automatic rifle fire echoing inside the high-ceilinged Taj-Bek palace. With no idea of what was happening, chief surgeon Alexeev assumed the attackers were Afghan rebels. The hills surrounding Kabul often echoed with their fire at night; the doctor believed now they'd come for Amin.

Cries, explosions, and rattling windows joined the noise of fire. Amin emerged from the room in which he'd been treated into a hallway. The president, in a T-shirt and underwear, was holding his IV bottles in his hands. Realizing he no longer needed the drips, Alexeev removed the needles, and held Amin's arms to stop the bleeding. Then the doctors walked the president to a bar in the hallway, where his five-year-old son appeared, threw his arms around his father's legs, and began crying. While Amin calmed his son, Kuznichenko whispered to his colleague, "Let's go, Anatoly Petrovich. It's dangerous here. He doesn't need us anymore."

The doctors had turned away and started down a hallway when automatic rifle fire rang out at the other end. A shockwave propelled them into a conference room where windows shattered from more rounds. The men pressed themselves against the far wall, where Alexeev, hearing loud Russian swearing outside, realized Soviet soldiers were storming the palace—to save Amin from the rebel attack, he assumed. A Soviet soldier burst in, shooting his automatic rifle from his hip, spraying the room with bullets. Alexeev heard a groan from the direction of Kuznichenko, who began bleeding heavily from his chest.

Back at the hallway bar, an officer of Group A shot Amin. For good measure, the Soviet assassins rolled a grenade toward him. It exploded near his head, achieving the Soviet Politburo's main objective, and also killing his son.

A handful of *spetsnaz* officers had been killed. Many more were wounded. Kurilov, dripping blood as he crawled toward the palace entrance, heard someone calling out the name of a Zenit commander: "Misha Yasin! Misha Yasin!" Outside, he saw the operation was winding down. Soldiers were leading prisoners and wounded from the palace. He felt extremely sick. Someone gave him water to drink and helped bandage some of his wounds.

Alexeev and a soldier carried the dying doctor down some stairs and outside, where they tried loading him onto a BTR. An officer looked him over and ordered them to leave the dead behind.

Deposited into a personnel carrier, Kurilov noticed he was sitting next to Alyosha Baev, the Group A officer who had challenged him at Bagram. A grenade had injured Baev's back and lodged shrapnel in his neck. Other Group A officers were having difficulty lowering a wounded comrade into the BTR. The man's head dropped onto Kurilov's legs; his feet stuck out of the vehicle and had to be forced in for the hatch to close. Finally, the BTR rumbled to life and started off. Kurilov offered his comrade water from a canteen before realizing he had died.

Back at their half-constructed barracks, white-coated medics bandaged the many wounded Zenit men and gave them morphine injections. No guard had been left behind and everything inside the buildings had been looted, probably by Afghan soldiers. Kurilov was placed on a table, where a medic cut off his uniform and removed his damaged body armor. He ached everywhere and couldn't move his left arm, but the morphine began working. Feeling better, he began considering his circumstances for the first time. "We won," he found himself thinking. "We'll be heroes!" He looked over at a fellow Zenit officer, who smiled weakly back at him. The two men agreed to find some vodka to celebrate. Instead they were evacuated to the Soviet embassy hospital together with the other wounded.

From the back of another BTR, Kurilov saw one of his commanders, Alexander Golubev, who headed KGB counterintelligence in Afghanistan. "Titych!" he yelled, using a nickname derived from Golubev's patronymic, Titovich. Kurilov was still numbed from the morphine. "Get me out of here!"

"Valera!" Golubev replied, using Kurilov's informal name. He'd been searching for his men. "I thought you were dead!"

At the hospital, Kurilov realized he was covered in shrapnel. His face was swollen almost beyond recognition. A harried nurse removed some of the metal slivers, then gave him a needle to finish the job himself in front of a mirror. The bullet lodged under his ribs would be removed later, at an army hospital in Uzbekistan.

IX

Elsewhere in the city, the Soviet assault group assigned to take the general staff building was having trouble after the unit commander was shot early in the operation. Some fifteen paratroops were also killed at the Bagram air base after Afghan Army soldiers managed to organize some resistance there, and a Soviet soldier was killed taking the Interior Ministry building. The Afghans fighting for Amin suffered large casualties, probably several hundred.

There was no trouble at the television and radio building: ex-Interior Minister Watanjar, who was with the Soviet forces and dressed in combat fatigues and helmet, negotiated with the Afghan tank division guarding it not to fight. Then he went on the airwaves to order the government to work the following morning.

For Lieutenant Vostrotin, most of the fighting at the Taj-Bek palace was over by midnight. When three Afghan tanks approached about two hours later, Company 9 fired at them and they surrendered. At four a.m., Vostrotin ordered his men to deposit Afghan corpses into a large ditch that had been dug for the foundation of a new building. He sent his prisoners under escort to the Soviet command post at the palace. The lieutenant then accompanied the bodies of two of his men to the same station, where his company was ordered to help guard the palace.

The sun was rising when, some time after seven a.m., an explosion sounded outside the building. Vostrotin looked out to see soldiers from another Soviet paratroop division attacking. Evidently not knowing the palace was in Soviet hands, they had been ordered to take it, unaware the white armbands on his own men's Afghan uniforms signaled they were friendly forces. Vostrotin quickily alerted his superiors, but six to ten men died during the two hours it took for the KGB and military hierarchies to stop the attacks.

Despite the confusion and remarkable lack of communication between units, the operation to assume control of Kabul was a great success. Elite troops took control of government buildings, major utilities, and other critical spots in a matter of hours. The officially dubbed Limited Contingent of Armed Forces of the Soviet Union streamed into the heart of Afghanistan on December 27 and 28. Motorized divisions secured bases for supplies and second-wave divisions, and the country's other major cities were quickly subdued. Within a week, at least 750 tanks and 2,100 other military vehicles were spread out across the country. By the end of the month, there were eighty thousand Soviet troops stationed in Afghanistan.

Babrak Karmal, the future president with a beak-shaped nose and slicked-back hair, traveled by convoy to Kabul, where he arrived at dawn on December 28. That morning, Radio Kabul announced in Russian that Amin had been tried and shot as an enemy of the people.

X

Former Education Minister Abdul Rakhman Jalili learned of Karmal's appointment from the radio report, which was broadcast not in Kabul, but over the border in Tashkent. From his hospital bed, to which he'd been taken after his poisoning the night before, he'd heard firing from the Kabul airport and the radio and television offices.

Jalili was arrested in the hospital later on December 28, together with the rest of Amin's cabinet and a number of Central Committee members. Those with connections to Watanjar and other high-ranking Taraki supporters were soon freed, while those less lucky, Jalili among them, were taken to the massive Pul-i-Charkhi prison. Kept in a small, dark room with a waterlogged floor, the former minister was beaten and refused visits to the toilet. Intelligence officers later transferred him to a security service prison for interrogation.

Jalili survived several failed plots to have him and other former members of the cabinet executed. Then he was condemned to death. But under pressure from friends who emerged from the change of regime unharmed, a court commuted his sentence to life in prison. He would serve the next decade there, including six years in solitary confinement.

Like most Afghans, the invasion caught Jalili by surprise. He, in particular, had believed no real differences, let alone enmity, divided Amin's government from the Kremlin. He later came to believe the Soviets had feigned friendship until the final minute, after collaborating with the gang of four and other Taraki supporters to drive a wedge between the two leaders. Jalili believed the gang of four had plotted to kill Amin all along, including on the night Sayed Tarun—Taraki's chief of staff—had been shot, and that Soviet Ambassador Puzanov had approved.

But that was in hindsight. At the hospital, listening to the radio announcement of Karmal's appointment, Jalili couldn't fathom why the Kremlin, which he'd always considered to be wise, would take the huge risk of backing the ineffectual Karmal as its best hope for restoring stability to Afghanistan. He later decided Karmal and the gang of four had talked the Kremlin into believing Afghans would welcome Soviet forces.

Whatever hopes the Kremlin had for Karmal, there was no doubt about its final judgment of Amin and whether or not working with the late president might have been better than killing him. Soviet radio and television reports following the invasion painted him as a murderous despot who'd been removed just in time to save the Afghan people from crisis.

Several days after the invasion, on January 2, the KGB's foreign counterintelligence chief Oleg Kalugin met Yuri Andropov in his Moscow office. A telephone call interrupted their discussion. The caller was Boris Ivanov, the KGB's liaison in Kabul, whose report about the post-invasion situation agitated Andropov. "Look, Boris, tell Karmal he should immediately appear on television," Andropov said. "It's been three days since the coup and there's been no appearance. He must understand the people need an explanation. Do everything to make it happen as soon as possible!" Karmal began making impromptu appearances throughout the country the following month.

Andropov himself visited fog-shrouded, snow-blanketed Kabul on January 28. The KGB chairman was in a good mood and began lunch on his first day discussing Soviet hockey teams with Marshal Sergei Sokolov, the new head of Soviet forces in Afghanistan. Back in Moscow, Brezhnev considered the Afghanistan matter closed and ordered the troops out. Still, the triumvirate of

Andropov, Foreign Minister Gromyko, and Defense Minister Ustinov argued withdrawing would be a serious mistake. Amin may have been removed, but it would take time for Karmal to exert his authority and stabilize Afghanistan. Soviet forces should remain until the Afghan government was strengthened, they explained in a report to Brezhnev. Pulling out would prompt Afghans to claim Moscow was an unreliable partner. They needed to stay and help.

The gap between reasoning at the top and in the field widened. In June 1980, a plenum of the Central Committee unanimously approved the decision to invade, without actually calling it that. No discussion preceded the approval, nor did any participant ask a single question. Increasing attacks on Soviet convoys and garrisons by rebels holding out in the Hindu Kush and elsewhere raised little concern. But Soviet personnel on the ground held a different view. In January, KGB Kabul representative Bogdanov met with Marshal Sokolov, who outlined the military's general view. "You know what I'm afraid of?" Sokolov asked. "That the Afghan Army is going to melt away and leave us face-to-face with the guerrillas."

Former Communications Minister Guliabzoi was also worried. Before the invasion, he'd met with Babrak Karmal to discuss forming a Soviet-backed unity party, and was named interior minister when the new government was formed. Guliabzoi would remain chief of police for most of the next decade despite quitting three times. After one resignation, he stewed at home for two weeks before being asked back to help restore order: supporters of his Khalq wing had killed three hundred rival Parchamists in their ongoing feud.

Guliabzoi soon told Marshal Sokolov that however much he'd relied on Soviet support, Afghanistan would never be at peace as long as Soviet troops remained in the country. Beyond removing all Russians from the Interior Ministry's staff, he was in no position to exert pressure. But he advised that Soviet troops stay off Kabul's streets during the day and that Soviet advisers and diplomats also maintain a low profile.

Even if such advice had been heeded, it was becoming too late to win public approval of the intervention. Many rural Afghans who had chafed under Amin's reforms were now on the verge of joining spontaneous resistance. They called themselves mujahideen, derived from "jihad" to mean "holy warriors." Suspicious of Soviet forces that claimed they were there only to help them, and armed with nineteenth-century muskets, World War II–era British Lee Enfield rifles, and AK-47s—many of them plundered from government stockpiles—the mujahideen prepared to fight against what they saw as the latest in a series of foreign invasions of Afghanistan.

The KGB's Leonid Bogdanov was among those who feared for the future, but not for long. He left Kabul for good in April.

CHAPTER 3

THE SOVIETS
DIG IN

I

The Soviet invasion of Afghanistan caused the immediate expiration of Cold War détente. Washington was outraged. The spirit of wary accommodation that had followed the Cuban Missile Crisis of 1962—years that had brought surprisingly positive results during summit meetings between Brezhnev and President Richard Nixon—was replaced by renewed hostility.

President Jimmy Carter called Moscow's aggression in Afghanistan "the greatest threat to peace since the Second World War." He could do little to back up his words, however, because his attention was fixed on the Iran hostage crisis. In early November 1979, seven weeks before the Soviet invasion, Iranian students had seized sixty-six diplomats in the American embassy in Tehran, forcing the hand of the new radical Islamist regime of Ayatollah Khomeini to keep them hostage. The shock event was aimed at shoring up the Islamic Revolution by preventing Washington from intervening.

As for Afghanistan, even if the White House had been inclined to take serious countermeasures to the Soviet action, the memory of America's debacle in Vietnam all but eliminated the possibility. Washington engaged in a reheated propaganda war, but wasn't willing to do much more than issue bitter denunciations of Moscow.

The State Department and other agencies began feeding stories to the media that Soviet forces were using chemical weapons in Afghanistan. Carter also canceled grain sales to Moscow, restricted Soviet fishing rights in U.S. waters, and postponed submission of the SALT II nuclear arms limitations treaty to Congress. Washington's most severe reaction was the announcement that America would boycott the forthcoming 1980 Olympic Games, to be hosted by Moscow. The United States also worked to rally world opinion against the invasion. On January 14, the United Nations General Assembly approved, by 104 to 18 votes, a resolution calling for an "immediate, unconditional and total withdrawal" of Soviet troops from Afghanistan.

Many in the West saw the invasion as an extension of Soviet imperialist expansion. That view was supported by the belief the Soviet presence in Afghanistan brought it closer toward acquiring a warm-weather port on the Indian Ocean—one of the ambitions that had driven the British to engage in the Great Game against Russia for control of Afghanistan and other parts of Central Asia in the nineteenth century. But the USSR was far from securing such a strategic port. Weeks after Kremlin hawks hailed the invasion as a great success, attacks by local Afghans—the kind that had bedeviled all previous invaders, from Darius I and Alexander the Great—began dogging Soviet units.

The support Babrak Karmal's new regime had expected from Amin's removal failed to materialize. Moscow's blame of the assassinated leader for many of the country's problems—and refusal to realize that whatever slim popular support the PDPA had was fast evaporating—did it no good. The Red Army soon would make the situation worse. Instead of helping the Afghan government establish control over the country, it precipitated the creation of a deadly opposition that quickly spread in the open and mountainous countryside.

In the days after his company had seized the Taj-Bek palace, Lieutenant Valery Vostrotin remained there to help secure its grounds. Making it through his first combat operation buoyed his spirits, and helping guard one of the symbols of Afghan power sustained them. He was recommended for promotion to captain and to receive the prestigious Hero of the Soviet Union award.

Vostrotin's ideas about how an officer in his position should act came partly from the cinema screen. The Soviet Union was awash in films about the remarkable victories of World War II, some of which showed soldiers taking cigarettes and schnapps flasks from Germans as trophies. Adding to that, neither he nor Company 9's political officer knew that military regulations forbade looting, in which their men now engaged in a massive spree. Vostrotin himself took pistols, hats, and carpets to line the inside of his tent back at Bagram. A sewing machine would help mend uniforms. But consumer goods unobtainable in the Soviet Union—Panasonic television sets, Sharp boom boxes—were the most valuable prizes.

The fun lasted two days. On New Year's Eve, Company 9 was ordered to rejoin other units of the 345th Regiment, which had arrived at Bagram after the storming of the palace. Vostrotin commandeered a ZiL flatbed truck to load the goods he'd looted for distribution to each of the platoons at his base. The truck followed the paratroops' BMD personnel carriers from Kabul back north to the air base. A military band was playing when Vostrotin arrived in the evening. His men were greeted as heroes by the troops who'd only just arrived.

Vostrotin's soldiers pitched tents, took showers, and began to prepare for serious New Year's celebrations. The air was thick with euphoria when the battle alarm sounded. Company 9's men were ordered to dress for combat and scramble to line up in front of the regimental staff headquarters. They had five minutes. Vostrotin could only guess the reason. He'd decided his battle-hardened company must have been picked to take part in quelling a fresh rebel attack when the 345th Regiment's commander arrived. Grim-faced Colonel Nikolai Serdyukov sternly eyed the line of men before speaking.

"We thought you men were heroes!" he barked. "But you've turned out to be nothing more than marauders and simple criminals!"

Turning to one of his aides, Serdyukov ordered for Vostrotin and his men to be frisked. Their BMDs were also searched. Following that humiliation, the ZiL and all its cherished trophies were confiscated. Vostrotin lost his promotion and his award, and was lucky not to have suffered more serious punishment.

Company 9 was disgraced, but not for long. The unit would go on to become one of the war's best known. Its soldiers' legend was already growing, and their battle experience meant Company 9 would be picked before other units to take part in especially important operations. Later, that experience helped Fortieth Army commanders plan future operations. Already by May 1980, Company 9 would be the most decorated unit in Afghanistan.

Vostrotin would continue to be lucky in other ways. Twice wounded, he would rise to the rank of general and eventually win a Hero of the Soviet Union decoration, the highest honor bestowed on Soviets. After four years in Afghanistan, he'd leave for studies in a military academy, but return as a regimental commander in 1986, worshipped by his men as a gifted, just leader, and respected as a defender of conscripts' interests by almost everyone else who took part in what he'd come to believe to be an increasingly senseless conflict.

II

Twenty-five-year-old army lieutenant Vladimir Polyakov was stationed in Potsdam, near Berlin, where he headed a reconnaissance platoon of an artillery battalion of the Soviet Army Group in East

Germany. When the tall, dark-haired officer received orders to depart for Afghanistan along with other forces massing in December 1979, his high-ranking KGB officer father offered to help get him reassigned to safer duty. "But you sent me to a military academy," Polyakov protested. "I've been trained for war—and now, when my country needs me, you want me to stay away?" Rumors were circulating that Washington was also planning to invade Afghanistan, and Soviet forces were racing to beat them there. Brimming with patriotism, Polyakov prepared to protect his motherland by helping the Afghan peasant population defend itself.

From Termez in southern Uzbekistan, his regiment, part of the 108th Motorized Rifle Division, crossed into Afghanistan on a frigid night in early February, and joined a stream of men and machines moving south toward Kabul. Polyakov rode in a modified BTR armored personnel carrier. In place of the usual heavy cannon, it was outfitted for scouting duties with night-vision equipment, long-range sights, and a 14.5-mm high-caliber machine gun.

The procession traveled under light snow along the mountainous Salang Pass and through its remarkable three-kilometer tunnel recently completed by Soviet metro engineers who bored through the barren, white-capped Hindu Kush to complete the country's only full-length north-south road. Masses of heavy machinery, including antiaircraft battalions, reflected Soviet military planners' misconception of the kind of engagements the invasion force would face. Each motorized rifle battalion consisted of three motorized rifle companies, MRCs, each with about a hundred personnel. MRCs also included a mortar battery, five platoons (including antitank, grenade launcher, air defense, signal, and support platoons), and a battalion aid station. (Later, MRDs were reinforced with tank companies, artillery batteries, and other units.)

Crossing the shallow Amu Dar'ya River on the new pontoon bridge to the Afghan town of Khairaton, Polyakov marveled at the barrenness and beauty of the land. Flat desert plains in the northern regions of Balkh and Samangan one day and the next, winding mountain passages of Baghlan Province—where the climb took him past windswept jagged peaks—made him feel as if he were on another planet. Some of the hills were further decorated by dramatic piles of sand and stone from rockslides, their colors changing from reddish to gray. Many of the Afghans he saw wore turbans; those who weren't barefoot wore sandals or flimsy rubber shoes. They seemed untouched by the twentieth century, living in mud-walled villages that were difficult to make out because they merged with the landscape. It was utterly strange to a Russian. There was no shortage of deprivation in the Soviet Union, but there at least the state controlled all aspects of life. Afghanistan appeared wild.

The Fortieth Army's procession along the Salang Pass was a jumble of constant traffic jams and frequent accidents. Soldiers crossing the pristine landscape inescapably poisoned their lungs with dense diesel exhaust spewed by each engine forced to crawl along the narrow roads, or to idle there. The worst was in the Salang Tunnel, which Soviet vehicles helped blacken with toxic fumes. At one point, tanks stuck there, as they were stuck everywhere along the passage, kept their engines running. Company 9's Lieutenant Vostrotin later heard that when drivers refused to turn them off because that would violate standard procedure, a major fired his pistol to overrule the regulation. Rumor had it that more than twenty men were asphyxiated in the tunnel, although some of the deaths were also said to have been caused by suicide.

From the desolate, freezing Salang Pass, the road wound down past mountain forests and streams into the scrubby plains above Kabul. Once they'd reached their destinations, soldiers set up barracks, mostly around airports or at some distance from urban centers. Their positions around the country were chiefly along the main roads, forming a triangular loop from Khairaton just across the border from Termez, south to Kandahar and east to Shindand. Polyakov's brigade pitched tents on the outskirts of Kabul along the road to Bagram, in an area his soldiers dubbed Tioplyi Stan, after a southern Moscow outskirt similarly distant from the city center. Other units from the 108th Motorized Rifle Division and a medical battalion soon joined. Making the best of the ascetic, extremely

The northern entrance to the Salang tunnel, along the Soviet supply lifeline leading south to Kabul from the Soviet Union. *(Alexander Liakhovskii archive)*

dull tent life, they hunkered down to wait for orders. Although the men were issued boots and warm coats to help fight the damp cold, their insufficient rations consisted mainly of fatty canned beef called *tushonka*. Stewed pork and cheese would come later, but only as a rare treat.

Many of the first wave of soldiers saw Afghanistan as relatively peaceful. The people who called the Russians "Shuravi" were busy scratching out livings from the dusty earth. Even children toiled, pulling carts and donkeys to markets. Although most houses had no outside-facing windows and many were surrounded by walls, Soviet soldiers occasionally glimpsed tidy carpeted floors and pillows inside. Later, officers would visit locals' houses to trade stolen military supplies for food, alcohol, and clothes.

Officers and soldiers came to covet the kebabs and beer for sale in Afghan stalls outside their new bases, and because they had no Afghani currency, they took to selling tent cloth, soap, and anything else the impoverished locals would buy. (Later, Afghan vendors began accepting Russian rubles and military *cheki*, or checks, virtually worthless coupons distributed in lieu of cash.) One of the Soviets' most popular acquisitions was *sharo*, an alcoholic drink distilled from grapes.

Robbing quickly became a favored means of obtaining local goods. Fair-haired Sergeant Alexander Kalandarashvili's 120-man reconnaissance battalion, part of the 56th Paratroop Brigade, had slipped from Turkmenistan across the Amu Dar'ya into the northern Afghan Kunduz Province three days before the invasion on December 24. The operation was well prepared, so easy that Kalandarashvili felt as if he were on a tourist trip. Not only because of the exotic landscape; his men had never seen such bountifully laden shop stalls. They were closed at night with small padlocks. Within a couple of weeks, most had new heavy locks that still didn't protect against rampant looting. Soldiers took whatever they saw; chickens were often the easiest game. After the dust had settled from the initial invasion, the first shots fired in the Afghanistan War, Kalandarashvili believes, were prompted by stealing.

When early in his tour Kalandarashvili passed a nearby village, he saw no one there. He was miffed. The Soviets had come to help the locals. Why were they hiding?

Several months after arriving, brigades began building small wooden and concrete buildings to replace their tents. Proper housing with air-conditioning to alleviate the fierce summer heat would not be built for years; for now, many men spent their own money to furnish the grim accommodations. But the paucity of supplies was somewhat easier to take at this initial stage because the forces setting up weren't expected to engage in combat, nor did they anticipate enduring their discomfort for long.

III

Still elated after the successful invasion, the Soviet military leadership worked to seal its victory and enable a withdrawal of forces. The military's main task was to secure the country's transport routes and industrial assets; the second was to protect the new government's representatives in Kabul and the regions. Companies or battalions were directed to guard the main administrative buildings in each province.

In Moscow, the Soviet media called the Red Army's arrival in Afghanistan a new stage of the April Revolution. President Babrak Karmal announced a broad-based unity government on December 28, the day after Amin's assassination. Six days later, on January 3, he held a news conference to announce that "fascist" Amin, collaborating with the CIA, had tried to cede the country's Pashtun territory to Pakistan. A new constitution would guarantee freedom for Afghanistan's people, Karmal promised. To court the country's Islamic clergy, he said it would be based on the tenets of Islam. Karmal also came to the rescue of his fellow members of the PDPA's Parcham wing, releasing thousands from Pul-i-Charkhi prison. Marginalized under Amin and Taraki's Khalq group, the Parcham faction used its new position of power to purge the government of Khalq members.

Despite the paeans to Karmal appearing in the Afghan and Soviet press, the new leader was soon generally perceived as weak. His love of liquor and pressing of others to drink posed some of the main hazards for his personal guards during the first months of the occupation. The Soviets countered by doubling the presidential entourage's guard—and choosing abstainers for duty. Members of Valery Kurilov's Zenit group were doing most of the guarding when Vladimir Redkoborodyi arrived in Kabul in early 1980. An officer of the KGB's Ninth Directorate, which provided security to General Secretary Brezhnev, among many other top officials, Redkoborodyi had been ordered to take charge of Karmal's security.

Forty-two-year-old Redkoborodyi—a dapper, mustachioed officer with a penchant for wearing the disguises his sensitive job required—had no inkling of what lay in store for him. He'd traveled to Afghanistan reluctantly. Given an automatic rifle and two hand grenades at the Bagram airport, he was driven to an apartment in Kabul. Night came very soon after the sun set behind the surrounding mountains, virtually emptying the streets of people. He found the scene depressing. Intermittent gunfire kept him awake all night. (Although he would soon become used to the shooting that would begin almost like clockwork at around ten p.m., taking the absence of gunfire as a bad sign, since it often indicated a larger attack was coming.)

Awakened by a loud din his first morning, Redkoborodyi raised the shades in his apartment prepared to defend himself against attack by a crowd of people outside. It turned out they were gathering to make their way to a nearby stadium, where clothes donated in Soviet Central Asia were being distributed. Later that morning, the Ninth Directorate officer and eight colleagues were taken to the Soviet embassy. Receiving their orders, they drove to Karmal's presidential palace.

The spectacle of the Afghan soldiers guarding the sprawling palace perimeter startled Redkoborodyi. Soviet soldiers called Afghan troops "greens," for their dark olive-colored uniforms. These uniforms, if they deserved the name, were mismatched; automatic rifles were propped up randomly against walls. The word "lax" had never been clearer to him, and the most disturbing aspect was the soldiers' scant attention to who was coming and going around them. Indoors, Soviet paratroops were in charge of security. Their circumstances were dreadful. The complex's several buildings were cold because there was insufficient coal to heat them, so the soldiers had to scrounge for supplementary firewood, also in desperately short supply. The same with food: there wasn't nearly enough. If matters were so bad in the presidential palace, what could they be like in the garrisons being set up elsewhere in the country?

IV

The invasion prompted sporadic fighting in the cities as the Afghan Army continued to melt away. In Kandahar, the Fifteenth Division mutinied on New Year's Day, while violence was breaking out in Herat and Kabul. When Marshal Sergei Sokolov sent the

Soviet 201st Motor Rifle Division—recently arrived to reinforce the Fortieth Army—to take control in Jalalabad on January 5, three battalions of the Afghan Eleventh Division deserted. Still, instead of worrying their presence was beginning to further fan the unrest they had been sent to calm, the Soviets saw it as an inevitable reaction—just the kind of ultimately insignificant resistance the Fortieth Army had been sent to Afghanistan to put down.

Like so many other Afghans, Major Yar Mohammed Stanizi, a district commander in Ghazni Province south of Kabul, heard about the Soviet invasion from Babrak Karmal's radio announcement from Tashkent. Although Stanizi had backed Soviet involvement in Afghanistan in the past, this was different. The Khalq supporter believed Karmal's Parcham wing was an organization for the wealthy elite. He'd criticized the new president and other Parcham leaders for having taken refuge abroad during Afghanistan's deepening crisis. His immediate impulse on hearing Karmal's address was to order units under his command to defend the regional capital against the Soviets. But he thought better of it and instead decided to wait for orders.

Fights between Karmal supporters and critics soon broke out around Stanizi's base. They prompted an eight-hour visit by Marshal Sokolov, who helped negotiate an end to them. But from then on, the major's view of the Soviets continued to deteriorate, despite a reluctant acceptance of their presence in his country. Now the Soviets had arrived, the alternative—continuing deterioration of the government's control over the country—would be worse.

But events would fail to back Stanizi's view. Soon he saw increasing attacks against fuel and supply convoys traversing Ghazni Province on the main road between Kabul and Kandahar. Even the government's stronghold Kabul couldn't be calmed. In February, a protest against what was being called the Soviet occupation turned into a riot in which three hundred people died. In a display of sympathy for the protesters, shops in the capital remained closed for a week, until a show of force by Soviet jets and helicopters restored an uneasy peace.

However, the Red Army's major problem was growing violence in the countryside. Marxism-Leninism offered little guidance to rural Afghan society, with its ancient concepts and ways. Since Moscow's obligatory ideological treatment of war—most important, between socialist and capitalist forces—did not include explanations of a popular uprising against an (at least nominal) socialist state, the Kremlin failed to understand its new mujahideen enemy.

Valery Vostrotin's lesser devotion to ideology would have made the future Soviet hero of the war better able to interpret events clearly. But he could already see them for himself before their spinning by political people who reported to the Politburo. The lieutenant's Company 9 paratroops were among the 15 percent of Fortieth Army forces he later estimated would actually engage the enemy instead of guarding roads and installations. But aside from its part storming the Taj-Bek palace, Company 9 wasn't yet rising in the hierarchy that would develop between regiments fighting in the field and those that rarely did; Vostrotin's men saw almost no fighting through the end of March. While they spent their days training and building rudimentary barracks, the Afghans he met continued to seem respectful. The Soviet military's massive display of strength in December evidently impressed them.

The company's first substantial operation was intended to reinforce such local deference. In April, Vostrotin and his men were sent east to the central Bamian Province. The going was tough on the five hundred miles they traveled, many by climbing narrow passages into the snowy mountains. Along the way, the Soviets attacked a local jail and released its prisoners as part of the show of force. At the end of their trip, soldiers dug several trenches. The idea was to show the locals the Soviets could move and operate wherever they wanted, but Vostrotin believed the effort was closer to a waste of time because it made no sense as a military operation. He saw supporting evidence for that opinion in the reception his men received. In many of the towns they crossed, people appeared in the streets holding red flags, portraits of Brezhnev, and banners proclaiming friendship between the Afghan and Soviet people. The Afghans often offered food and drink to the troops.

At the same time, Vostrotin also realized just how isolated much of the countryside was. He was amazed to hear locals saying they'd never heard of their new president, Babrak Karmal. Some believed Mohammed Daoud, who had been overthrown two years earlier, was still in power.

After three weeks in the mountains with no losses, Company 9 returned to its base. Vostrotin learned that an Order of the Red Banner was waiting for him back home: a delayed award for his role in the taking of the Taj-Bek palace, despite his looting. But any satisfaction in the success of the invasion would soon wear off.

V

Aka Yasin, a plucky Tajik student from Afghanistan's northeastern Badakhshan Region's mountainous Sangcharak District, was among the new recruits who began striking against Soviet formations. Soon after being expelled from secondary school for refusing to participate in PDPA-organized activities, he witnessed police arrest some two hundred people. With their hands tied behind their backs, they were herded by trucks into a freshly dug pit, where bulldozers buried them alive.

Yasin ran away to join a group of fighters in the mountains. Equipped with few modern weapons, they resorted to lobbing diesel fuel–filled Molotov cocktails in their first encounters with Soviet tank battalions. They dug traps and covered them with logs in the hope of disabling tanks. They also used rifles for sniping from holes in the mud walls of village houses. Other fighters even staged suicide attacks, among them a friend of Yasin who wrapped himself in a cloth, set it alight, and ran toward an oncoming tank—which shot him before he reached it. Later, Yasin and his fellow fighters undertook the highly dangerous work of making bullets by hand from spent casings, even though the unreliable finished products sometimes exploded in rifles.

Regardless of Soviet optimism, events the Red Army did not expect quickly propelled it into a struggle against a population that refused to tolerate invaders no matter how friendly they claimed to be. Soviet attempts to control uprisings in Kabul, Herat, and other centers only prompted further Afghan animosity. Military columns traveling through the countryside began coming under attack— still sporadic—from spontaneously formed insurgent mujahideen groups. The invasion had begun overcoming ethnic, tribal, geographic, and economic divisions, and solidifying Islam's role as a unifying ideology.

Rural tribal and religious leaders, including many who hadn't previously protested against Amin, joined the proclaiming of jihad against the Soviet-backed government. In addition to arms plundered from government stockpiles, weapons began flowing across the country's porous borders. Some of the strongest resistance came from the eastern mountains, the domain of the powerful Ghilzai tribe, whose members had access to Pakistan. Governments and groups eager to inflict damage on Soviet forces were shipping arms through Pakistan—even if few believed the invasion could be seriously countered.

Mujahideen forces began receiving funds and supplies from the United States, Saudi Arabia, Egypt, China, and elsewhere, as better-trained Afghan Army soldiers continued deserting by the brigade and hundreds of officials and professionals quit their jobs, some to join the mujahideen. Kabul residents staged a general strike in February. In the central Hazarajat area, a resistance movement took most control over Bamian, Ghowr, and Uruzgan provinces.

As the people increasingly took sides against the government, six Sunni Muslim mujahideen resistance groups banded together. Meeting in the Pakistani city of Peshawar in late January, they announced the formation of a united Islamic Alliance for the Liberation of Afghanistan. The groups included Sayed Ahmed Gailani's relatively moderate National Islamic Front of Afghanistan; Tajik linguist Burhanuddin Rabbani's Society of Islam (whose members included Ismail Khan of Herat and Ahmed Shah Massoud, soon to be titled "Lion of Panjshir"); fundamentalist Yunis Khalis's Islamic Party; Mohammed Nabi Mahommedi's Islamic Revolutionary Movement; and Sibgatullah Mojaddedi's National Liberation Front for Afghanistan. Rasul Sayyaf, who headed the Islamic Unity for Afghan Liberation Party, emerged as the compromise leader. The strongest—and perhaps most fundamentalist—of the mujahideen leaders, Gulbuddin Hekmatyar, boycotted the meeting, not wanting the others to dispute his power.

As the mujahideen groups considered coordinating their efforts, Soviet forces began responding to the growing attacks against them. In mid-January, military chief Marshal Sokolov established the Fortieth Army's headquarters in Bagram and sent the Fifth Motorized Rifle Division to the eastern province of Farah and the Fifty-fourth MRD to Herat, just to the north. In March, Soviet forces, launching their first major counterinsurgency operation from Jalalabad, took control of the restive Kunar Valley after a major desertion of Afghan soldiers from the Ninth Division. Elsewhere in the country, hostilities began more slowly and less ominously, largely because mujahideen Lee Enfield rifles were ineffective against Soviet armor, and automatic-rifle fire couldn't reach aircraft flying above. One of the rebels' early mistakes was attempting to form large combat formations, which were quickly decimated by far superior Red Army weaponry. In addition to their fire of far longer range and better accuracy, Soviet planes and helicopters could destroy anything on the ground, provided it could be located and identified.

Realizing they couldn't win battles by directly engaging Red Army forces, the vastly outgunned mujahideen soon began forming highly mobile units composed of ten to thirty men. With tactics changed to match, they began posing a serious challenge for the much more ponderous Soviet forces, which were unprepared for the new kind of combat. The ambush became the main form of attack. Many of the country's roads were surrounded on both sides by heights that served snipers well. Soviet vehicles were even more restricted on the narrow passes, whereas the mujahideen moved much more freely deep in the countryside and on well-known mountain paths used to stage many of their attacks. Damaging bridges to bring long armored columns to a screeching halt, well-planned mujahideen attacks filled Soviet soldiers with fear and opened a way to steal the arms being transported.

Afghans also attacked with acts of sabotage against government buildings, utilities, and fuel lines. Mujahideen fighters were highly courageous, as a rule. Mohammed Yousef, who headed the Pakistani intelligence agency's Afghan bureau, would later help train rebel commanders, but he faced difficulties convincing them to stage operations stealthily. He wrote that they preferred "noise and excitement" with plenty of opportunity for personal glory.

Tajik mujahideen fighter Aka Yasin joined Rabbani's Society of Islam. One of his first combat experiences came during a Soviet attack on the northern village of Sangcharak, when a bomb blew apart the roof of the house in which he'd taken refuge. Before he could hide elsewhere, a soldier jumped over the wall, but didn't see Yasin—who, having no ammunition for his Kalashnikov, removed its cartridge clip and tossed it at the Russian's face. Then he threw himself at the invader and the men fought. Yasin eventually prevailed and took the soldier prisoner.

VI

As the sun was setting over Afghanistan's snow-capped Hindu Kush Mountains on a cold evening in April 1980, four months after the Soviet invasion, an armored column approached a narrow passage wedged between a steep, barren mountain and a long precipice in the forbidding Panjshir Valley north of Kabul. Its progress was blocked by an attack on the front unit, seemingly from nowhere. Vladimir Polyakov, the patriotic young lieutenant who had been

A column moves along a narrow section of the Panjshir
Valley. *(Alexander Liakhovskii archive)*

sent to Afghanistan from Potsdam, scrambled after his soldiers,
who were jumping from their exposed personnel carrier to take
cover behind several large boulders.

A week earlier, his motorized rifle battalion had joined a crack
paratroop battalion in Charikar, near the foot of Panjshir, to rum-
ble up the narrow valley floor in their armored BTR vehicles. It
was his unit's first major operation after months of waiting and
boredom. Bulbous Mi-8 transport and fearsome Mi-24 gunship
helicopters—with their double canopies and stub wings loaded
with rockets—thundered overhead. Forward units swept for mines
while others searched villages for *dushmany*, or bandits, as the Soviets had come to call the mujahideen fighters.

The offensive had been ordered to take the Panjshir Valley,
above which a skilled resistance commander named Ahmed Shah
Massoud had stationed himself in the precipitous hills. From that
strategically valuable position, Massoud had been staging attacks
against the Bagram air base and the Salang highway, the crucial
supply line from the Soviet Union. Now Polyakov found himself
calculating how to stay alive. After several minutes under fire, he
and several of his men realized the mujahideen would eventually

pick them off from above. Their only hope would be to clamber up the rocky mountainside to attack the rebels targeting them. They slowly scrambled up—and found nothing: the Afghans had avoided them by the simple means of leaving for higher ground. At dawn, the group made its way back down. The sun rose to expose those who'd remained in the valley: some twenty-five men, now all dead.

The fighting took place near the village of Ruha, halfway up the valley. Later, after rebels fired at Polyakov's battalion from the general direction of the village, the Soviets responded by destroying many of its houses. Unable to pinpoint the enemy's exact location, the tanks fired randomly, often blowing up buildings more for target practice than anything else. The column then pushed on to another village, where children and elderly inhabitants emerged to observe the approaching machinery. While several soldiers distributed some of their rations to the obviously impoverished among them, other soldiers searched the group. They found a handful of bullets in the possession of a man apparently in his thirties. Seizing him, the Soviets ordered him to carry a heavy armful of ammunition up an incline that lay ahead. When the column reached the top, they shot him.

To flush out hidden mujahideen, Polyakov's battalion left its BTRs to climb a mountain path on one side of the valley. While a forward team moved ahead to scout, the rest split into two companies. Polyakov led the second. Suddenly more exhausted than the other men by the extremely difficult ascent, he fell behind together with two soldiers who helped carry his automatic rifle. They stopped to rest every fifteen minutes, the soldiers waking Polyakov when he fell asleep. He grew too weary even to worry that he was becoming too weak to fight. Luckily, his group found no enemy to engage, and the battalion stumbled back to the valley floor the following day.

The lieutenant's initial optimism about the invasion turned to bitterness. Had the Soviets been sent to the countryside as cannon fodder? The heroic fighting he'd expected was turning out to be slaughter. A handful of enemy snipers could tie up an entire column. As for defeating the mujahideen, his battalion had done no more than march from one end of the Panjshir Valley to the other and back again.

With scant strategy of any significance and negligible coordination between units, the fighting was mostly defensive, and on the enemy's initiative. Even the smallest tactical decisions had to be made at headquarters and took hours to receive. The main Soviet advantage of overwhelming air power provided little recognizable help to soldiers aware only of their immediate surroundings, from which the deadly bullets and projectiles were aimed at them. Polyakov couldn't understand why a joint effort of air and ground forces wasn't organized. As it was, he and his soldiers hardly knew what their immediate objectives were. Their training for engaging forces similar to their own, units equipped with tanks and airplanes in European fields and forests, was little help in countering partisan fighters in desert and mountain territory.

Simply locating the enemy was almost impossible. Hiding in caves and behind boulders high in the mountains, the rebels fought only when conditions favored them. Often using stolen or captured Soviet rocket grenades, they picked off Soviet personnel and vehicles from afar. Sharpshooters aimed lethally for the head—or the feet, making wounded soldiers burdens for their units. As the initial weeks of the conflict turned into months, fear became a normal part of Soviet soldiers' lives. Sometimes the raw, crippling dread of being killed or injured was overwhelming. The often enraged Soviet response of heavy barrages of grenade and artillery fire into the mountains had little effect because the troops rarely knew where the Afghans were.

Even worse, however, was that the soldiers hardly knew *whom* they were fighting, and not only because distinguishing resistance fighters from the native civilians was next to impossible. When Polyakov's battalion commander spoke with a provincial governor about the lay of his territory, it emerged that the Afghan received tributes from two of "his" villages. That shocked Polyakov, who had thought he was in the country to help peasants and workers, not corrupt capitalistic politicians, as he saw them, who took money from the rural poor. Simplistic as it may seem, that kind of ideological confusion would deepen the disillusionment of earnest officers like Polyakov, who quickly lost his idealism.

Unable to neutralize the mujahideen, the troops unleashed their firepower against civilians. Polyakov's men and other wary Soviet soldiers were now beginning their searches of mud-walled *kishlak*s, or villages, by throwing grenades. One paratroop's testimony about fighting in the Kunar Valley described a platoon's reaction to shots fired from the direction of a village building in which civilians were hiding. The Soviets blew up the structure's door with grenades, after which the Afghans began fleeing in different directions. The crowd included elderly, women, and children, as well as rebel fighters. The soldiers began slaughtering the Afghans. "Among those running out the door was an old man who tried to escape," the soldier recalled. "My friend shot at his feet. The old man jumped in fear and sat behind a bush to hide. My friend aimed directly at the bush and fired a round, after which just the legs slid into view under the bush. He was supposed to be hiding, my friend told me, laughing." Another time, the soldiers captured a small boy who had shot at them with an old musket, then brought the prisoner to a company commander. "He split the boy's skull with his rifle butt, killed the boy with one blow, without even getting up from his place."

Any sense of compassion Polyakov had for Afghan civilians was dulled the first time he'd seen the bodies of his dead Soviet comrades. He felt unable to fully control his actions, let alone his fate: he'd been given orders and he had to fulfill them. His overriding task was to stay alive. That meant taking as few risks as possible: any Afghan was a potential enemy. When Polyakov first saw a civilian shot—the villager in Ruha who had been found with a small number of bullets—he felt almost nothing, neither sympathy nor anger. Regret would come much later, away from the conflict. At the time, he felt zombified. He winced when he heard the first stories of women and children having been killed, but most

troops were even less interested in or capable of discriminating between mujahideen and the Afghan people. The desire to avenge the
deaths of their comrades—often by looting—was fast erasing that
difference.

VII

The Soviet decision to pack the invasion force with reserve troops
from largely Muslim Central Asian republics turned out to be a
grave miscalculation. Instead of generating trust and reducing resistance among Afghans, it actually stoked millennia-old animosities
between the country's dominant Pashtuns and its Tajiks, Uzbeks,
and other Central Asian ethnic groups. Hostility to the Soviets was
further deepened by the personal histories of many Tajiks, Uzbeks,
and Turkmen who lived in northern Afghanistan. Those who had
fled Communist repression in Soviet Central Asia disliked the Red
Army as much as, if not more than, the Pashtuns did. Antagonisms
also caused serious friction within the Soviet military. Ethnic Slavs
suspected their fellow soldiers from Central Asia of sympathizing
with the Afghan people. Russians and Central Asians wearing the
same uniforms—even Muslims of different backgrounds and per-
suasions—engaged in internecine fights and beatings.

Fortieth Army commanders aware of the problem withdrew
the Central Asian reserve by March, leaving chiefly interpreters
and those who'd proven their allegiance. But easing that trouble
did little to improve the general situation. It was hard to disguise
that the Afghan Army the Soviets had come to shore up was doing
as much to oppose them as help stabilize the country. The native
army would shrink from ninety thousand to about thirty thousand
men by mid-1980, and many of those who remained in uniform
were waiting for an opportunity to desert. Even Soviet officers and
soldiers who hadn't yet engaged the mujahideen knew how disheartening the general situation was becoming.

Some of the first heavy fighting of the Afghan War took place in the mountainous tribal regions of the east. In March 1980, the Soviet 201st Motor Rifle Division sent armored columns up the Kunar Valley north of Jalalabad to relieve what remained of the Afghan 9th Division in Asadabad. The 201st MRD's tactics typified the Soviet reliance on tanks and artillery. Using their heavy fire to take key towns, the Soviets pushed north, fighting off ambushes from above on either side and destroying villages as they advanced.

In May, the 201st again left Jalalabad to head north. When the column was stopped by fire from Afghans, Soviet troops began climbing the heights, but were hit hard by the mujahideen firing from behind rocks. The Soviet response was to call in artillery fire. The enemy took cover or melted away and settled in new positions farther up the valley.

According to a mujahideen commander named Mohammed Asef, the Soviet forces left behind two dead soldiers. When a detachment returned to collect the bodies, the Afghans opened fire from higher ground, killing seven more. The Russians retaliated by massacring livestock and villagers; mujahideen estimates put the number at eighteen hundred civilians in twelve days. "It was the first Soviet operation in the area," Asef would charge. "They came looking for U.S. and Chinese mercenaries and instead found frustration and an opportunity to murder and loot."

The mujahideen struck back the following month, when a battalion of the 201st MRD made its way southeast into the province of Paktia, along the road leading from the towns of Gardez to Khost toward the Pakistani border. After mujahideen attacks killed its officers and radiomen, the disorganized unit couldn't signal for help. Staying in their armored personnel carriers, the men fired until their ammunition ran out. Then the guerrillas overwhelmed them, destroying the battalion and leaving only a few survivors.

Sergeant Alexander Kalandarashvili's reconnaissance unit was assigned to escort convoys and search Afghan camel and truck cara-

A BMP personnel carrier. *(Alexander Liakhovskii archive)*

vans for contraband in the mountainous territory east of Kunduz. The soldiers rode on BMP infantry fighting vehicles, which were replacing the smaller, more lightly armored paratroop version, the BMD, in which they had arrived in Afghanistan.

Seeing civilians killed for the first time, Kalandarashvili appealed to his commanding lieutenant.

"Don't you worry about it," the officer replied. "Your main task is to get yourself home."

In February, a well-planned ambush above a narrow mountain pass near Kunduz wiped out nearly an entire battalion of two hundred men. Kalandarashvili came under fire soon after, when his company searched a *kishlak* in nearby hills. His reconnaissance unit stole a mule from the village. As the men were returning to their BMPs, leading the animal, shots rang out from a mountain pass above them. The frightened mule took off, clambering up a path. The lieutenant who had wanted the animal as his prize sent a quaking private after it. Left no choice, he climbed up and unexpectedly found himself behind several Afghans aiming rifles at the Soviets below. He shot and killed them.

But it was a rare success. Despite the Soviet crimes against the local population, Kalandarashvili had initially felt good about his internationalist duty helping Afghanistan. His mood, like those of most around him, soon blackened.

The Soviets had some successes in July. Red Army units destroyed a mujahideen base camp moving north of Jalalabad. But guerrillas operating from the Panjshir Valley north of Kabul put the highway through the Salang Pass under serious threat later in the summer. Two major assaults were unable to get at the rebels because they moved too quickly for their attackers.

Throughout the summer, the Soviets focused their efforts on maintaining control over main roads and airfields. They set up fortified outposts along their lines of communication, leaving Afghan troops to guard them. The Soviets also cracked down in urban areas, where demonstrations, strikes, and assassinations of officials were common. But Babrak Karmal was unable to do much to expand his control, especially in the provinces, where the rebels were using their influence to deny the government legitimacy among the population.

If Lieutenant Kalandarashvili's disappointment grew over months, helicopter pilot Vladimir Pyshkov's was almost instant. Flying into Afghanistan weeks before the invasion, the tough young lieutenant traveled widely in his Mi-8, ferrying officers of various ranks. From what he saw and heard, he soon perceived that Moscow was involving itself in a struggle between a brutal, reform-minded government and an overwhelmingly rural people clinging to their ancient traditions. With that divide, and a laughable mandate to "help the Afghan people" instead of engaging in all-out war, Soviet forces could do little to control the situation.

Already in January 1980, Pyshkov was participating in attacks on countless rebel caravans of camels and horses crossing the border with Pakistan over the Hindu Kush Mountains. One group of more than a thousand mujahideen—whom the Soviets also called *dukhi*, or spirits, both as denigration and acknowledgment of their superior hiding skills—was caught with brand-new AK-47 automatic rifles smuggled from China. The lieutenant's own weapon, he complained to anyone who would listen, had been assembled in 1972.

Pyshkov began seeing in his three-man helicopter crew what

seemed to him animal reactions to the killing around them. Instead of escorting captured mujahideen to military bases for interrogation and imprisonment, they often threw terrified captives out of the aircraft to their deaths. When he was flying a peasant loyal to the government to a mujahideen base in his northern village that he'd agreed to identify, the man admiringly pointed at his own house as the helicopter approached. Before the interpreter had a chance to translate, the chopper's gunner destroyed the little structure with rocket fire. The Russian soldiers were amused as the Afghan clutched his head, then saved themselves the trouble of an explanation back at their base by shoving him out.

The mujahideen were no less cruel to their captives. One of their favorite tortures was skinning Soviet soldiers alive by slitting them around the waist, pulling their skin above their heads, and tying it there, leaving the doomed to suffer excruciating deaths.

Soviet forces were also increasingly troubled by mismanagement and misbehavior by their own. Supplies of heating fuel, wood, and food remained scarce on some bases. Hepatitis and typhus would soon infect a third of the army. And free distribution of hashish and heroin by locals would encourage widespread drug use, which often turned the routine hazing of fresh conscripts more malicious.

Pyshkov's duties included ferrying Marshal Sokolov, the deputy defense minister who headed military operations in Afghanistan and would later become Soviet defense minister. During the early months of the war, the pilot jokingly asked his world-weary, chain-smoking passenger how long it would be until he could expect a vacation. "Son," replied the former tank officer somberly, "this is only the beginning."

VIII

By the time Valery Vostrotin was awarded a second medal for an operation in May, he'd noticed significant changes in the burgeoning

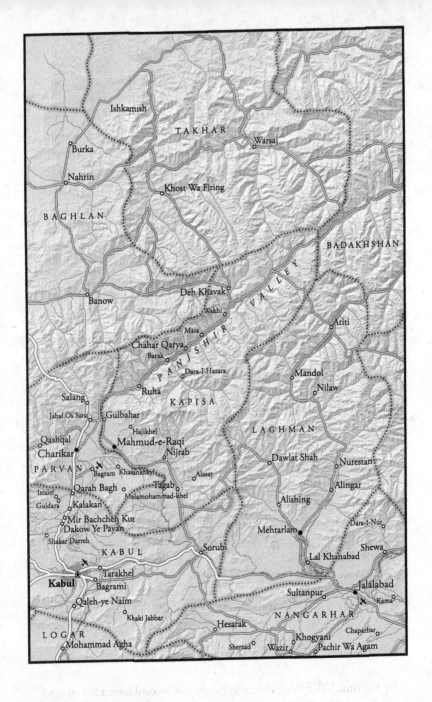

Map 2: Panjshir Valley

mujahideen movement. Many of the first groups were made up of criminals who were less interested in fighting than robbing travelers on mountain passes and in other remote areas. Resistance to the Soviets, let alone ideology of any kind, figured little in their actions.

That phase was brief, and even then—almost immediately—it became clear that the Panjshir Valley would be the country's key strategic ground. It didn't take long for it to become the central psychological battlefield too. Geography had much to do with it. The bottom of the ninety-mile valley opens onto passable ground a day's march above Bagram air base, about forty-five miles north of Kabul. The basin then cuts northeast through the Hindu Kush, its dirt road running along the Panjshir River. Although the valley's gray, rocky entrance is incredibly narrow, the passage widens farther north—where a series of villages occupy the valley floor—before it again narrows toward the north. The layout ensured the territory could be attacked only with large numbers from the south.

For centuries, the Panjshir Valley had functioned as a primary transport route between northern and southern Afghanistan. The Soviet construction of the Salang highway replaced it as such, but the valley's proximity to the main Soviet supply route made it an ideal place for staging attacks. Panjshir was also a serious threat to nearby Kabul. Many steep, gravelly "tributary" valleys offered further protection to the mujahideen and also provided escape and supply routes.

Twenty-seven-year-old Ahmed Shah Massoud, the talented mujahideen commander, stationed himself in Panjshir, helping to make it Afghanistan's central battlefield. An ethnic Tajik from the Panjshir Valley town of Jangalak, Massoud had attended a military academy, graduating in 1973. He then studied engineering at Kabul Polytechnic Institute before joining the rebellion against the government as a member of Rabbani's Islamic Society.

Massoud had led an attack in Panjshir on Daoud's troops as early as 1975. Now the Soviets were learning that he used modern tactics to split his men between highly mobile strike forces, defense units, and reserves. One of the few mujahideen commanders committed to unit discipline as well as training his men in specialized weapons, he even attempted to run a civil administration in the areas under his control. Western journalists who covered the war would find him particularly appealing, partly because of his fairly fluent French, which enabled him to publicize the mujahideen's struggle to the world. Eventually, even the Soviets who negotiated with him in the coming years openly respected him. His exploits became even more impressive because his predominantly Tajik resistance fighters were not attractive to weapons suppliers in Saudi Arabia and Pakistan, despite the importance of his position and the Panjshir Valley.

Massoud's attacks made the Soviet military leadership deeply determined to take the Panjshir Valley, far more than the country's other strategic areas, under its control. The resolve was further reinforced by the publicity Massoud won as he weathered attack after Soviet attack.

In the first major operation to take the valley, Vostrotin's Company 9 was sent to block a mountain passage in Sayat, at the foot of the valley east of Bagram. After it took the pass with little trouble, a Soviet mortar battalion of forty-odd men was assigned to guard its entrance from some two kilometers away on the valley floor. Mines

Ahmed Shah Massoud with supporters in the Panjshir Valley in 1980. (*Alexander Liakhovskii archive*)

had killed many of the first Soviet casualties in the area. But the mujahideen soon began staging direct attacks. After Vostrotin's unit had returned to Bagram, Massoud's men stormed the garrison, prompting Company 9 to return. Fighting them off, Vostrotin saw his first hand-to-hand combat with Afghan rebels. The far better equipped Company 9 won easily—if temporarily—and helped reinforce a key mujahideen tactic: avoiding direct combat with Soviet troops.

The battle experience helped Vostrotin conclude that the Afghan government troops who hadn't deserted couldn't be counted on for much. Officially, the Red Army was there to merely aid in establishing control of the countryside, but that was nonsense. Afghan soldiers were badly trained and ill-equipped. Their shoelaces came untied. Soldiers stumbled, tripped, and often gave up fighting after less than half an hour. Although the Afghans were supposed to engage the mujahideen in places where Vostrotin's men had gathered them by blocking passages, it was the Soviets who usually took over the fighting. The Fortieth Army was being dragged into serious warfare from the supporting role it had expected to assume.

The larger Soviet role escalated the country's already soaring tensions. The more villages destroyed and civilians killed by Russian soldiers, the more hatred they generated. In December 1979, when locals had greeted Vostrotin's soldiers waving red flags, he casually sent some of his men outside their base to gather firewood— not a real unit of any kind, just a couple of conscripts armed only with knives. The following June, that would have taken an entire battalion with air support. By then, Vostrotin had become impressed by the mujahideen he encountered around Bagram. They were committed to the war. They had begun fighting tenaciously despite a serious lack of equipment. They even manufactured their own mortar shells. But soon they acquired more damaging arms, including surface-to-air missiles. Deserting government troops brought rocket grenades with them, and Vostrotin suspected Soviet soldiers were selling the rebels their own weapons, too. Some mujahideen groups became so well armed that Soviet helicopters could no longer fly low enough to taunt them on foot and on horses.

In July, the Soviets changed their tactics by planning smaller operations against rebel bands and pursuing them more seriously. Company 9 and other units of the 345th Regiment were sent back toward Panjshir. Ordered to take an arduous route, the men hacked their way through vineyards to get there. Early on the morning of July 5, they set out for a routine search for rebels in a village called Khasankheyl, just east of Bagram in the green flats that stretched south of the valley's entrance.

Vostrotin had been temporarily promoted to acting battalion chief of staff, the unit's number-two commander. His lightly armored BMD personnel carrier followed ten others toward the settlement of squat mud houses set against a line of craggy mountains to the north. Commanders' vehicles weren't supposed to differ in any way from the others so they wouldn't be singled out for attack. But Vostrotin's noticeably did: the battalion's mechanics had failed to conceal its tall antennae or equip it with a standard gun turret and sights. Riskier still, Vostrotin rode alongside his battalion commander—a cardinal breaking of regulations: units' commanding officers were required to travel separately to minimize the chances they'd both be killed in an attack against any one vehicle.

As the column neared the settlement, a loud crack rang out. A BMD riding ahead blew apart before Vostrotin's eyes. It had hit an antitank mine, killing ten men. Then Vostrotin noticed a small Afghan jump out beside the column. He couldn't have been older than a teenager. Vostrotin saw him quickly load a rocket grenade and aim it at his BMD. The officer had no time to react before the missile launched toward him. Exploding against the vehicle's minimal armor, the grenade sent a shockwave at the commanding officers. Shrapnel hit both, gouging the left side of Vostrotin's face, including his eye, and his left arm.

The column had ground to a halt. Soldiers and then a medic performed first aid on the seriously wounded officers. They called in a Mi-8 helicopter, which evacuated them to Bagram. Doctors there operated on Vostrotin before sending him to Tashkent, then to the Soviet Union's top military hospital in Leningrad, where he spent the rest of the summer.

IX

Vladimir Redkoborodyi of the KGB's Ninth Directorate, who headed Babrak Karmal's security, had orders to spend most of his time inside the presidential palace. He had little choice, because his KGB unit had almost no vehicles at its disposal until it was allotted a number of four-wheel-drive Niva cars. The men dubbed them *chekavoz*, from Cheka, what the Soviets called one of the secret police's early incarnations. Although Nivas were simple to repair and could run on cheap, 76-octane fuel, the life expectancy of those few was short. As soon as the mujahideen learned the little jeep-like vehicles transported KGB personnel, they became especially prone to attack.

Trying to do the best with what he had, Redkoborodyi set up a hotline for Karmal's frequent conversations with the Kremlin. Although there was some fear the CIA would be able to eavesdrop, Redkoborodyi believed the talks—which Karmal conducted in a soundproof sealed booth—were secure. The unit chief also made his men and the Afghan soldiers assigned to the palace scrub clean the premises, even tidy the courtyard trees. He set up an Afghan palace guards corps and suggested to Karmal that the government provide them with uniforms, which boosted their morale and authority. The Russian classes he organized for them had the same effect, if less obviously.

Food supplies improved, but the palace remained cold in the winter, because coal—and wood as well—was virtually impossible to obtain while attacks on the country's roads diminished supplies. At the same time, frequent damage to power stations and cables made electricity sporadic. Still, Redkoborodyi believed the palace looked much more impressive than when he'd first arrived.

The KGB's Vladimir Redkoborodyi—head of security for Afghan President Babrak Karmal—dressed in Afghan attire, in front of Karmal, meeting crowds at a Kabul market, 1982. *(Vladimir Redkoborodyi archive)*

Soon Karmal took part in his first meeting with mujahideen leaders. Redkoborodyi and Soviet Ambassador Tabeev had already met with rebel commanders, including Massoud, to arrange for temporary cease-fires. With bribes perhaps even more a way of life in Afghanistan (where they were called *bakshish*) than in the Soviet Union, presents of fuel or other supplies were often enough to persuade rebel groups not to fire on this or that convoy.

Karmal also met ordinary Afghan civilians, but not without more urging from the Soviets. After Western media called him an apparent palace recluse who feared assassination, the four top Soviet advisers decided the president would do well to show more of himself to the people. A visit to various sites in Kabul was arranged, together with coverage by Soviet and Afghan television crews. With Redkoborodyi and his men wearing Afghan wool hats and baggy local costumes called *shalwar kameez*, the entourage visited a market and some shops, providing photo-ops that were deemed a big success the following day. But Karmal's protection wasn't airtight, and several subsequent assassination attempts almost succeeded. After the Afghan palace guards discovered explosives in a tin cup, security was beefed up. Although cooks were strip-searched, one managed to smuggle cyanide onto the grounds. He'd concealed the poison between his buttocks, and was discovered when he tried to administer the cyanide to a dish.

X

Vladimir Pyshkov flew his workhorse Mi-8 helicopter to deliver soldiers to guard bridges and tunnels. Traveling in a squadron of eight helicopters, he also dropped off conscripts to set up garrisons, then supplied them with food and ammunition. Arriving at outposts, he'd sometimes find the heads of men killed by mujahideen impaled on spikes.

To help reduce the arms and supplies from neighboring Pakistan and China, helicopters dropped mines on mountain passes. Afghanistan would soon become littered with mines, many of them plastic-encased "butterfly mines" that twirled to the ground, where they were difficult to spot. The weapons struck fear in participants of both sides of the conflict; they were a constant danger that could kill or remove a limb with one ill-fated step. Some of the most dreaded mines had to be planted by hand. "Jumping mines" shot up from underground when triggered by a tripwire, and were designed to maim victims by exploding at waist level.

Dropping mines from helicopters, pilots often crossed the border into Pakistan, sometimes because they had no way of telling the difference apart from the better construction of some of the houses. Pyshkov spent a week helping mine Pakistani territory before realizing his mistake. In time, so many areas would become mined that even Soviets disembarking from helicopters would step on them. Some Afghans took to clearing passages through minefields by sending herds of sheep through them.

Helicopter crews learned to operate with greater efficiency. From the air, horses indicated nearby rebels, and Soviets came to see white horses—and also clean hands and relatively uncalloused soles—as belonging to rebel commanders. Intelligence also improved as KGB and GRU officers built agent networks, which increasingly tipped off the Soviets about arms convoys to the mujahideen. In that connection, Afghan Interior Ministry police, called Sarandoi, and KhAD intelligence service officers frequently accompanied the Soviets in their choppers. (KhAD stood for Khidamat-i Ittila'at-I Dalwati, Pashto State Information Services.) Still, much of the information remained suspect. Pyshkov soon stopped trusting most Afghans in his helicopter, convinced their information was often false because they were unwilling to harm their fellow countrymen.

Pyshkov also grew disillusioned by the conduct of his fellow Soviets. Soldiers traded their cartridges for almost anything they could get: bubble gum, sunglasses, pens, condoms, jeans, sheepskin coats. Although Soviet conscripts looked down at what they saw as medieval Afghan ways, they were often awed by the Japanese boom boxes and televisions they found inside mud-walled *kishlaks*—which many stole in hope of smuggling them back home. They could hardly square propaganda about the high Soviet standard of living with such great luxuries of Afghan life.

Women were also a valued commodity. Since prostitutes often consented to be paid in the Soviet military currency called *cheki*, soldiers dubbed the women *chekistki,* also a play on the nickname for KGB officers. In one scandalous episode, the crew of a transport plane who had sold stolen cases of vodka decided to spend some of the profit on another form of release, and were directed to a house that supposedly supplied it. They barely managed to escape from attack by the "prostitutes" waiting for them, who were actually burka-dressed mujahideen.

XI

"Throughout history," notes Stephen Tanner, a careful historian of Afghanistan's military conflicts, "aggressive military operations, including those that became disastrous, have always been buoyed by initial confidence and enabled by the courage of leaders to ignore the pessimists in their midst. The Soviets looked for a best-case scenario around the Hindu Kush, whereby socialist rule could quickly be reestablished and their forces withdrawn with new laurels and pride. The rest of the world, profoundly unwilling to fight in defense of Afghanistan, signed onto that prospect."

Nevertheless, the Soviet military leadership now knew the Afghanistan campaign would take far longer than it first imagined. The top brass also accepted that its forces were too ill trained and poorly outfitted to subdue the enemy. Reservists drafted to top up the seven motorized rifle divisions in Afghanistan fought ineffectively with twenty-year-old tanks and even older World War II artillery against rebels who made maximal use of their mountainous and desert territory. An overcentralized military command that reserved most decision-making for the top was ineffective for taking quick actions and facilitating the rapid mobility needed for counterinsurgency operations.

Rethinking and restructuring began by June 1980. It included sending home useless antiaircraft missile and other artillery brigades, together with hundreds of tanks. Many divisions were reorganized to make them more flexible. New conscripts were flown in to relieve reservists who had acquitted themselves badly. Muchswelled helicopter squadrons—the number of machines would soar from sixty to some three hundred by the end of the year—may have been even more crucial. They came with greater numbers of jet fighters, mainly MiG-21s, SU-17s, and MiG-23s that flew from Bagram, Shindand, and Herat.

Meanwhile, operations continued until the onset of winter brought most fighting to a stop. Very low temperatures and snow that all but sealed mountain passes left both sides more or less hunkering down to wait for spring. But the persistence of isolated ambushes on convoys and garrisons indicated that both were also adjusting to the prospect of more conflict.

CHAPTER 4

THE MUJAHIDEEN FIGHT BACK

I

Afghanistan had every reason to be a land of closed, hostile clans. Much of its early recorded history, like that of many frontier territories, reads like a log of conquests. Invasions were first mentioned in the sixth century BC, when the Persian Empire was ascending and the Greeks—who would follow the Persians into the territory several centuries later—first recorded history. Cyrus the Great, founder of the Persian Empire and its Achaemenid dynasty, first invaded the region, establishing the empire's border at the Jaxartes River, where he was killed in battle. Called the Syr Dar'ya today, the river waters the Central Asian states of Kazakhstan, Uzbekistan, and Tajikistan north of Afghanistan.

Herodotus chronicled the conquests of the Achaemenid ruler Darius I—under whom the empire's power reached its peak—and of his successor, Xerxes I. Despite their victories, the Persians faced sometimes fierce opposition from local dynasties.

Around 330 BC, the Persian Empire—together with much of the territory that's now Afghanistan—was taken over by Alexander the Great. The Greeks marched up the Panjshir Valley on their way north, fighting hard to reach Samarkand, in today's Uzbekistan. Alexander later married a princess from the province of Bactria, roughly today's Balkh Region in northern Afghanistan, before moving south into India. After Alexander's death in 323 BC, most of the Afghan region fell under the rule of his general Seleucus I, before the Indian king Chandragupta Maurya took control of the southern sections. The northern province of Bactria became an independent kingdom, until its takeover by Iranian nomads called Sakas around 130 BC. Bactria later fell to Chinese Kushans, who adopted Buddhism.

Modern Afghanistan's largest ethnic group, the Pashtuns, are believed to have emerged as a distinct population, along with their language, Pashto (similar to an old Iranian tongue influenced by an early form of Sanskrit and Persian), south of the Hindu Kush during the first centuries AD. In the third and fourth centuries, the Persian Sassanid dynasty, among others, took over, and Arabs invaded the region in the seventh century.

Although the Arab conquerors were Muslims, it took several centuries for Islam to become the dominant religion in a region where local allegiances and political considerations often trumped religious faith. The mountainous territory helped the tribes preserve their independence, and many continued following Zoroastrianism, Buddhism, and shamanism while waves of Iranian and Turkish incursions followed the Arab invasion. In the late tenth century or early eleventh century, a rebellious Turkic former slave raised an army and established the Ghaznavid dynasty, founded at Ghazni, in what's now central Afghanistan. The third Ghaznavid sultan, Mahmud of Ghazni, became one of Afghanistan's greatest rulers, in which capacity he staged raids into India and oversaw a blossoming of Islamic culture.

In 1220, Genghis Khan swept into Central Asia and placed the region under Mongol rule, which would last for almost two centuries. In the fourteenth century, Timur, or Tamerlane—a Central Asian conqueror of either Tatar or Mongol ancestry—took over northern Afghanistan from his base in Samarkand. Timur claimed highly improbable descent from Genghis Khan, virtually a prerequisite for any would-be Central Asian ruler. One of his successors was Babur, who founded India's Moghul dynasty and conquered Kabul around 1504.

Local tribes—of which there were some three hundred, many with a reputation for producing fierce warriors—began gaining power during the seventeenth century. By 1722, the Ghilzai tribe grew strong enough to lay siege to the Iranian capital of Isfahan, but the Persians staged a counteroffensive led by Nadir Shah, who retook most of Afghanistan's territory in 1738. Nadir was assassinated in 1747, after which a *jirga*, or council of Afghan tribes, elected a young member of his guard from the Abdali tribe named Ahmad Khan as their leader. Assuming the name of Ahmed Shah, Afghanistan's first native ruler oversaw its greatest territorial expansion. Ahmed Shah called himself "Durr-i-Durran," or "Pearl of Pearls" (after which the Abdalis renamed themselves the Durranis). From his base in dusty southern Kandahar, Durrani went on to conquer land as far away as Delhi, and many regard him as the founder of the Afghan nation. His dynasty fell in 1818. After a period of anarchy, Dost Mohammed Khan took control of Kabul in 1826 and assumed the title of emir nine years later.

Dost Mohammed's rule provided relative stability for Afghanistan, and it appeared the territory might shake off its reputation for warring and its place as a battlefield of empires. Any such possibility was short-lived, however. The rise of new global powers devoted to expansion of influence, if not always rule, ensured Afghanistan's historical role as a buffer zone between competing empires would continue. The nineteenth-century struggle would become known to the world as the Great Game between the Russian and British empires.

II

The Red Army may have failed to understand the nature of the conflict into which it would thrust itself a century and a half later, but it learned from tactical mistakes. Recognizing the utility of air power, the high command stationed heavy bombers in Turkmenistan in addition to boosting the helicopter and jet fighter count inside Afghanistan. The bombers flew sorties over the border before returning to Soviet territory. And although troop levels remained steady at some 85,000, regrouping divisions and disbanding unneeded units such as antiaircraft brigades—while beefing up those more suited to the fighting—made better use of Soviet manpower. Weapons improved, too. From 1980, the soldier's standby rifle, the 7.62-mm Kalashnikov AK-47 automatic, was replaced with the smaller-caliber, more accurate 5.45-mm AK-74, whose lighter bullets traveled faster and hit targets more accurately, even if many soldiers preferred the more powerful older model, which they continued using.

Better vehicles also appeared. The BTR-60 armored personnel carriers of the late 1960s with which the Soviets began the war were replaced with more heavily armored BTR-70s, whose more easily opened side doors enabled quicker exits than the old top hatches. Still, a greater threat of mines—which struck terror into the Soviets as much as the rebels—prompted most troops to risk sniper attacks by riding on top instead of inside. Those thrown off were sometimes injured but rarely killed or seriously maimed, whereas many mine blasts were fatal to those inside. (The better-armored BTR-80 coming in 1985 would more or less protect occupants from most mines. Its significantly more powerful motor would be another advantage.) The new BMP-2 infantry fighting vehicle also replaced the BMP-1. It had thicker side armor and a 30-mm cannon that fired faster and at greater elevations (fifty-degree elevation as opposed to thirty-three degrees) than the 73-mm it replaced. Many of the lighter, less armored BMD personnel carriers that carried Lieutenant Vostrotin's men and other paratroops were also phased out or re-armored because mines often completely destroyed those hated vehicles.

Larger air squadrons enabled more aerial bombardment during assault operations. Helicopters were increasingly used to land troops for staging surprise attacks against mujahideen groups during the course of battles. The regulation fifteen kilometers, more than nine miles, that reconnaissance squads were required to travel ahead of battalions during offensive operations had been calculated for warfare between mechanized armies. But since ambushes spelled death for most scouts moving that far ahead of their battalions in Afghanistan, new rules stipulated that reconnaissance units had to remain visible to the rest of their groups.

To encircle mujahideen groups, the Soviets also boosted use of mechanized forces as "hammers" that drove the enemy toward the "anvils" of mobile troop units. To destroy rebels' support bases, tanks and artillery were deployed against settlements suspected of helping them. And however ill trained and poorly equipped Afghan government army units remained, the Soviet Fortieth Army became better at staging operations jointly with them.

Yar Mohammed Stanizi, the Afghan Army district commander in Ghazni Province, took part in an early operation in neighboring Paktika Province. A joint Soviet-Afghan force surrounded a mujahideen group before staging a diversionary attack. Approaching from another side, the main Soviet flank then all but wiped out the rebel group in forty-eight hours of fighting. The rarely employed encirclement tactic was one of the few successful maneuvers used against the rebels.

Despite a number of early mujahideen victories, Stanizi believed that infighting among rebel groups would alienate the people, and that their ruthlessness would further diminish long-term popular support. One mujahideen commander who operated around Ghazni was reputed to have killed ten thousand civilians and to have robbed and enslaved many others, forcing some to cook and otherwise care for his men. However exaggerated such stories may have been, Stanizi counted seventeen bodies after a mujahideen reprisal against a local village. A teenage boy had been decapitated; another victim's legs were severed.

At the same time, despite his continued suspicion of the Soviets, Stanizi came to respect them for their apparent fearlessness. They were of course incomparably better equipped than their Afghan counterparts and also had the luxury of following BTRs into battle—but they almost always preceded Afghan units there. While his own men's reluctance to make direct attacks on mujahideen groups often upset him, the Soviets, with their much greater willingness to take risks, usually won handily in the rare cases when they were able to confront rebel units head-on. Despite his admiration for Soviet courage, however, Stanizi was dismayed by the utter contempt with which the troops treated their Afghan allies, and horrified by their tactics against civilians. Most of the fighting in which he participated with Soviet forces consisted of reprisal attacks after mujahideen raids and ambushes. The revenge almost always took the form of indiscriminate bombing.

III

One Soviet problem would grow throughout the war. Rebels became much more battle-practiced because they fought far longer than the many Red Army conscripts who sometimes trained for mere weeks and had a month of adapting to local conditions before serving for two years in Afghanistan. And while the mujahideen were overcoming the great initial Soviet advantage in military knowledge and experience, their ability to obtain modern weapons—through the Afghan Army, raids on Soviet caches, and by trading with Soviet soldiers—dismayed officers like Valery Vostrotin. The increasing store of weapons being captured in battle was also evidence of an even larger problem.

Increasing supplies provided by the United States, Saudi Arabia, Egypt, and other countries usually arrived across mountain passes on the stream of camel and mule convoys moving from Pakistan into the provinces of Khost, Paktia, and Paktika. From caches there, they were distributed north and west. Among the major recipients was the Islamic Society of Afghanistan (ISA).

One of the group's early recruits was an impressionable, sad-eyed high school student from Logar Province just south of Kabul. Mohammed Jan had been influenced by his cousin, a mujahideen commander, but even more by one of his school's teachers—an Islamist who fiercely criticized the Soviet invasion and quietly distributed copies of the rebel publication *Message of the Mujahideen* to students.

The Afghan Army had designated Jan's school as a military checkpoint after the invasion, and it soon came under attack by mujahideen fighters. Jan fled to Pakistan, from where he would return after the spring thaw, a practice he'd continue in later years. Like many Afghans, he came to believe the Soviets had occupied his country partly because they couldn't countenance the thought of an Islamic government on their southern border. He also felt that Moscow, in its old push to acquire a warm-water port, was engaging in imperial expansion. He felt it was his duty to protect his native land.

In 1981, after a year as a rebel foot soldier, Jan became a mujahideen commander like his cousin. He began engineering the most common type of operation against Soviet forces: ambushes near his village. It lay along the flat, fertile valley south of Kabul, an area heavily populated by settlements and farms that raised corn, wheat, and other crops in the shadows of looming mountains on either side. The valley was also the channel for the main road south of Kabul used by numerous Soviet convoys, mainly to Gardez and Khost. When Jan's unit learned of new deliveries scheduled or planned, the men dug foxholes in the sandy ground near the road. When the convoys rumbled by, the rebels let the first two vehicles pass before firing at fuel tankers with rocket-propelled grenades. They then used Kalashnikovs to mow down Soviet troops fleeing the fierce flames.

Other mujahideen bands staged similar attacks. In July, the Soviets struck back. The 108th MRD destroyed several of the mujahideen bases along the road. Air strikes and helicopter-borne troops helped the attackers inflict heavy losses. But Jan's group escaped unharmed.

Elsewhere, more forays were made into the Panjshir Valley, where young commander Massoud had been directing more attacks against Bagram, Charikar, and the Salang highway. And near the town of Farah, south of Herat, the Soviet Fifth MRD had launched a June offensive to pursue mujahideen commander Mohammed Shah. After initiating major clashes, the division turned north toward Herat, where heavy fighting broke out.

Feeling their way ahead, improvising responses to the Soviet offensives, the mujahideen made their own mines and caught some Soviet columns by surprise by ambushing them after the explosives detonated. Another tactic was to rig dummy explosives, then wait to kill soldiers from armored columns who discovered and examined the devices.

At the entrance to the Panjshir Valley, in the village of Gulbahar, mujahideen executed dozens of government sympathizers in a particularly bloody reprisal in August 1981. The deaths prompted another Soviet offensive, dubbed Panjshir-4 in the West. It established a base at the top of the valley. Retaliating against the mujahideen elsewhere in the country, Afghan Army forces conducted a major search for weapons in Herat. The government also mounted a large attack in the northern Balkh Province against a Tajik commander of rising prominence named Zabiullah. Soviet and Afghan fighter jets bombed the area, but Zabiullah held his positions, forcing the Afghan Army to evacuate troops by helicopter.

Reprisal attacks were again conducted against Mohammed Jan's group in Logar Province. Soviet commanders sent infantry to attack rebel bases there, but they were repelled after fierce fighting. Several months later, Jan's base came under more serious attack. The onslaught began when infantry probes entered Jan's Puli Alam District, behind translators using bullhorns to demand surrender. "This is the end!" they shouted to the rebels. "You'll die fighting!"

Jan already had received word of a planned attack. At dawn the following day, he saw Soviet armored columns moving south behind a wave of troops kicking up great clouds of dust as they lumbered down the valley. Ordering some thirty men to take up zigzagging positions along the river next to the road, open desert at their backs, he instructed them to allow the Soviet soldiers to get within thirty feet of their positions before firing. To avoid shooting each other in close-quarter fighting, each man was to engage only the enemy directly in front of him.

Jan counted four jet fighters overhead. They were supporting the ground forces together with six Mi-8 helicopters, which began bombing the valley at eight o'clock. The bombardment was followed by the tanks moving in to surround Jan's fighters near the road—who quickly disabled four of them with rocket-propelled grenades. Fierce combat began when the Soviet infantrymen advancing behind the tanks approached the Afghans. The shooting was at such close range that the fighters were often unable to determine each side's positions—which was the purpose of Jan's zigzag formation.

By evening, bodies were strewn everywhere, but the combat continued. Since the rebels couldn't get close enough to be certain whether fellow fighters were dead or injured, they used ropes to snag bodies and drag them from firing range. Jan sent his wounded—miraculously numbering only three—to the nearest village, whose women sneaked the remaining fighters a dozen ammunition boxes, each containing 750 bullets, when their supplies began running out during the battle.

The fighting saw little respite until after four a.m., when another rebel unit from a mujahideen group headed by the fundamentalist Gulbuddin Hekmatyar appeared to reinforce Jan's group. Together, they beat back the Soviet force, which left seventy dead when it retreated. Although many of Jan's men were injured, only a handful had been killed. The booty included thirty

Mujahideen commander Mohammed Jan in 2006.
(*Gregory Feifer*)

Soviet Kalashnikovs, two grenade launchers, and two sets of two-way radios.

The following day, Red Army loudspeakers were again used to threaten heavy bombardment unless the Soviet corpses were collected and handed over. To back up the message, helicopters and jets dropped some 350 bombs on the valley floor. The mujahideen quickly complied, piling Soviet bodies onto pickup trucks and driving them to the local district military headquarters.

The victory of Jan's men came at the terrible price of countless houses and trees torched. In the Soviet effort to stop the frequent ambushes of their southbound convoys, tank and grenade fire turned the lush green valley to scorched desolation. Anything that moved, including cattle and donkeys, was shot. Red Army units abducted villagers, killing many they accused of being extremists, sometimes making examples of them by dousing them with fuel and burning them alive. But although whole settlements slowly or quickly disappeared, the mujahideen continued staging attacks against the Soviets. The road became littered with the carcasses of tanks, armored personnel carriers, and trucks.

IV

Washington's wariness of openly backing the resistance to the Soviet invasion largely limited U.S. opposition to strenuous vocal disapproval. In 1980, direct aid to rebel groups amounted to only some $30 million. But while that negligible amount would remain essentially steady throughout the next four years of Ronald Reagan's first term, other concerned countries were less hesitant about backing the mujahideen.

Pakistan, Afghanistan's unstable southeastern neighbor, vigorously opposed the Soviet invasion from the start. With its bitterest enemy, India, on Pakistan's other side, Islamabad saw a Soviet-controlled Afghanistan as encirclement by hostile countries and potential isolation. Pakistan's military dictator, Mohammed Zia-ul-Haq, also feared the invasion's success would encourage the Kremlin to push even farther south in a drive for access to Middle East oil and the Arabian Sea. The devout—although not radical—Zia had made himself an international pariah by hanging his predecessor, Prime Minister Zulfikar Ali Bhutto, after taking power in a military coup in 1978. Zia, whose pomaded hair and sweeping mustache evoked an earlier era, further angered Washington by launching a secret nuclear weapons program. Opposing the Soviets now would enable him to make himself useful to the United States, thus delivering even more than geostrategic benefits.

General Akhtar Abdur Rahman Khan, the stern chief of Pakistan's intelligence service—Inter-Services Intelligence, or ISI—helped convince Zia of the feasibility of grinding down the Soviet military machine in Afghanistan. Akhtar prevailed on Zia to supply arms and training to the Afghan resistance, provided the pot didn't "boil over," as Zia liked to say. In addition, Islamabad would allow the mujahideen to establish base camps in its lawless Northwest Frontier Province bordering Afghanistan.

Zia appealed to Jimmy Carter, and the president agreed to help. Aid was not immediately forthcoming, however: Zia turned down as "peanuts" a 1980 offer of $400 million to the mujahideen.

His tactic of holding out for more by drawing Pakistan on a Cold War frontline worked. The following year, the new Reagan administration allocated a total of $3.2 billion for the Afghan resistance (a figure that excluded small CIA funds for providing arms directly to the resistance). But Washington had no real strategy other than to inflict as much damage on Soviet forces as possible. The White House didn't believe the mujahideen could defeat the Red Army.

Zia insisted on maintaining control over the CIA's aid—both weapons and money—to the mujahideen. Pakistan, which also didn't want to openly back the mujahideen for fear of provoking Moscow into open conflict, enabled the U.S. government to deny involvement by funneling its assistance through ISI. But Islamabad's sole discretion would also provide Zia the power to decide which Afghan rebel groups benefited from foreign largesse, the lion's share of which went to hard-line groups, chief among them Gulbuddin Hekmatyar's fighters. Despite his significant successes against the Soviet forces, Ahmed Shah Massoud received almost no assistance from the CIA—and when it was earmarked to him later, most of it was stolen in Pakistan and by the mujahideen leadership, even Burhanuddin Rabbani, to whom he nominally pledged loyalty. The determined ISI chief Akhtar would enforce strict control over the CIA's contacts with the mujahideen. Zia's alliance with Islamist jihadis both inside and outside Pakistan would eventually have serious consequences for his own country, turning the largely secular state into one in which Islamist fundamentalists would wield real power and pose an ongoing threat of toppling the government.

China was one of the first countries to follow Pakistan in providing substantial support to the mujahideen. Beijing, which was also jockeying with the Soviet Union and India, began pouring arms into Afghanistan. Egypt started doing the same, in smaller amounts. But that aid paled in comparison to Saudi Arabia's. Riyadh agreed to double the money Washington provided the mujahideen. The Saudi General Intelligence Department—the GID, headed by the erudite and Westernized Prince Turki al-Faisal—contributed hundreds of millions of oil-profit dollars, and became highly influential among the mujahideen, picking commanders and alliances to favor. More aid would later come from Saudi private sources, including Osama bin Laden. The scion of a major construction tycoon, bin Laden not only would provide millions of dollars and construction equipment with which he built tunnel complexes in Afghanistan's eastern Tora Bora Mountains. He'd also help attract hordes of new Arab and other foreign Islamist fundamentalist fighters to Afghanistan. They would do much to help transform the jihad from a local resistance to the government and its Soviet backers into an international ideological struggle against what they saw as Western decadence and domination.

Afghanistan's other big neighbor and influence, Iran, was harder put to help while engaged in a major open confrontation with the West over its fundamentalist revolution and the seizing of American hostages. Iran was also fighting a devastating eight-year war with Iraq, launched when Iraqi dictator Saddam Hussein attacked in 1980. But although Tehran remained tied up and largely out of the picture, it contrived to aid the isolated and marginalized Hazaras. They were Shias, like most Iranians, who were helping fight the Soviets in the Hindu Kush, where Moscow was largely able to attack only from the air. However, in addition to their antagonisms with Afghanistan's other groups—chiefly the Pashtuns—Hazara tribes were notorious for fighting among themselves, and rarely came together in organized opposition to the Soviet and Afghan government forces.

Increasingly regular arms shipments, mostly through Pakistan, enabled the mujahideen to replace most of their obsolete rifles and other preinvasion weaponry. For concealment, donors supplied Soviet-built weapons, many bought in Eastern European countries of the Soviet Bloc—such as the RPG-7 rocket grenade launcher, whose ability to pierce Soviet armor made it a favorite rebel weapon. The CIA continued buying British Lee Enfield rifles from countries like Greece and India and shipping them through Pakistan. Otherwise, mujahideen fighters now increasingly relied on heavy Czech-built DShK 12.7-mm machine guns, useful not least for firing at low-flying Soviet aircraft, and AK-47 Kalashnikovs.

However, the donor countries had to figure out where and how to distribute their aid, especially after March 1982. That's when internecine rivalries brought down the Islamic Alliance for the Liberation of Afghanistan, formed in 1980 by Afghanistan's six main rebel groups. Rasul Sayyaf's conservative Islamic Alliance split off to become its own party. A former Islamic law professor in Kabul, Sayyaf was the closest mujahideen leader to the Saudis, and he's believed to have received most of the $39 million Saudi supporters sent that month. Twenty-two-year-old Abdul Haq—a Hekmatyar ally before he joined Yunis Khalis's Islamic Party—built up his own resistance group in Kabul. Haq was from a wealthy Pashtun family from southeastern Nangrahar Province and had been jailed for treason under Daoud's government. He now commanded several thousand men, who staged assassinations and attacks in the capital, including the June bombings of the power station and Pul-i-Charkhi prison. Burly, fearless, and outgoing, he was also devout, although less interested in Islamic ideology than other mujahideen figures. He also had close secret contact with the CIA outside ISI's control.

In the southern desert region of Kandahar, a powerful commander called Engineer Esmatullah claimed to command five thousand men. The former army officer—who became a member of Sayed Ahmed Gailani's moderate National Islamic Front of Afghanistan—helped the resistance exercise almost complete control of much of the regional capital. He and other mujahideen commanders elsewhere in the country were continuing to attack not just troops but government officials and Soviet advisers.

V

Lieutenant Vostrotin hadn't fully recuperated from his serious injuries sustained near the Panjshir Valley when he returned from the hospital in Leningrad to Afghanistan in September. Vostrotin had trouble seeing from his left eye, and his arm still moved with difficulty. Nevertheless, he was sent back to Bamian, west of Kabul: the site of the two monumental sixth-century statues of Buddha carved into a mountainside that the Islamic fundamentalist Taliban would destroy in 2001. Company 9's combat duties were supplemented by guarding the statues. When the unit came under fire in the mountain passages, smoke shells helped drive away the ever more persistent mujahideen. After Vostrotin returned to the Bagram air base, he finally received the rank of captain along with his promotion to full-time battalion chief of staff.

Despite the phasing-out of Soviet paratroops' ridiculed BMD fighting vehicles, Vostrotin's men still rode in them in late 1981. They did everything they could to experiment reinforcing their flimsy vehicles' armor, including lining the floor with sandbags. But the personnel carriers remained highly dangerous under attack.

Vostrotin was filling in as duty officer on November 7, 1981, the Soviet Union's Revolution Day holiday. At such times, when the Soviets expected more serious mujahideen attacks, practice called for higher-ranking officers to be on watch instead of their subordinates. On Vostrotin's shift, a motorized rifle battalion came under attack to the north, on the reddish, rocky land just below the entrance to Panjshir. Vostrotin raced to help, joining a column of BMDs heading out of Bagram. Hurrying to reach the men under fire, Vostrotin urged the drivers to move faster. Reconnaissance had been minimal.

Vostrotin was standing inside his BMD, looking forward out of its sights, when the sandbags beneath him exploded, filling the cabin with sand and dust. He landed hard on his knees. The personnel carrier had hit a mine, but the sandbags absorbed the worst of the explosive's shockwaves. Vostrotin was stunned and badly bruised, but he would have to spend only two weeks recuperating in Bagram. BMDs would be phased out of the war entirely by 1983.

VI

The completion in 1982 of the steel-girder Friendship Bridge from the Uzbek city of Termez over the Amu Dar'ya boosted Soviet morale. The road and rail link replaced the ferries and pontoon bridges that had stood—between their frequent destruction—since the invasion. Improving Moscow's ability to provide reinforcements and supplies, the bridge reduced dependence on expensive air cargo flights, until now made mostly by seven-ton payload An-12 and twenty-ton Il-76 planes. The flights also delivered much of the food and other humanitarian aid distributed to civilians in the hope of generating support for the government.

The Soviets continued increasing their military activity, reimposing some measure of control over the cities of Kandahar and Herat, which had bustled with rebel activity. Herat's main rebel group was led by Ismail Khan, who, like Massoud, was a member of Rabbani's ISA. Like the resistance leader's followers, the Soviets called him Turan Ismail, for *turan*, or captain, his former army rank. The city's location in the country's west, far from the main source of mujahideen weapons arriving from Pakistan, posed a major logistical problem, especially since movement in the flat, open land surrounding the city was highly dangerous.

Although the Afghan Army's forces in Herat were overextended, the Red Army's Fifth Motorized Rifle Division was stationed in a Soviet air base in nearby Shindand. The Soviets often engaged in tit-for-tat counterinsurgent offensives after ongoing rebel attacks, but it is hard to determine exactly to what extent because of the difficulty of gleaning facts through the fog of the Afghan War. Soviet and Western media sources reported mujahideen assassinations of some sixty government officials in Herat in the spring of 1982. Reports citing Soviet sources say the Soviet Fifth Division, supported by the Afghan Seventeenth, led an attack that killed thousands while taking the city. But Fifth Division commander Vladimir Leverov denies any such major operation occurred. Soviet statistics are notoriously unreliable: it was common for artillery attacks against an unseen enemy in which it's doubtful anyone was hurt to have been reported as having killed hundreds.

In May, fighting erupted between the Afghan Fourteenth Division and a mujahideen group in Ghazni Province south of Kabul—until a Soviet reinforcement brigade arrived and overwhelmed the rebels. But the Panjshir Valley, where Ahmed Shah Massoud had divided his roughly three thousand men into about a hundred highly mobile attack units and other groups for defending the villages, remained the greatest problem for the Soviets. Although use of small guerrilla bands had proved spectacularly effective against U.S. forces in other insurgent wars, such as Vietnam, the Lion of Panjshir was one of the few rebel commanders to have adopted it, no doubt because few others had his organizational and managerial skills.

Massoud's talents were fully clear to Abdul Nasir Ziyaee, who joined the mujahideen in early 1980, when he was eighteen years old. The following year, the precocious, lanky teenager began training under Massoud in a group of forty-five volunteers, most of whom were at least partly college-educated. The ascetic life was tough. Food was often scarce, as were clothes, which were stolen from the Soviets or taken from corpses when possible. But deprivation did little to dampen the fighters' resolve.

When Ziyaee, at his first meeting with Massoud, expressed his conviction that mujahideen resoluteness and the people's heartfelt support would drive out the Soviets, the accomplished commander indulged him with a smile. "I've heard that from many brave souls," he replied—but only meticulous planning would enable the resistance to win. However, it was more than a flair for tactical planning that made Massoud a threat to the Soviets. The observantly religious leader with the reputation for bravery wasn't above explaining strategy even to the greenest of recruits, like Ziyaee. The trait did much to help earn his men's loyalty.

Massoud established three distinct forms of resistance. In the first, his elite mobile units of ten to thirty men staged simple hit-and-run attacks on artillery batteries and other Soviet targets deployed primarily in the Panjshir Valley. The second involved hitting weak points in areas farther from Soviet control. For that, larger forces of thirty to forty men would target Soviet and government installations, then remain in the area for several days. The third—the most important in the long term—was for working border areas distant from Soviet control: regions like Nuristan, near the Pakistan border. There mujahideen would create zones of solid support in which camps for military training and indoctrination in jihadi thinking would be set up—in other words, fighters would be tutored to spread the tactics elsewhere. Massoud envisioned one such safe area in the Panjshir Valley and another in the Salang Valley.

A supervisory council—later a party—called Shura-i-Nizar, which supplemented Massoud's leadership, delegated work to political, cultural, health, education, judicial, finance, and other committees. More than fighting the Soviets, the rudimentary civil authority sought to attract popular support through political agitation and to show the outside world that the mujahideen were capable of running their own affairs. Thus training in management, social services, and other activities necessary for sustaining life and society in safe areas was perhaps as important as training with weapons. Such skills, crucial when power would be wrested from the government, would meanwhile demonstrate to the people that the mujahideen were a better alternative than Karmal's Soviet-backed rule.

As his plans took shape, Massoud met tête-à-tête with commanders he trusted and involved himself in the smallest details of numerous operations. His subordinates liked him for his ability to command authority without condescension or bullying. He won more points for portraying himself as a man of the people, widely accessible and open to different opinions; his commanders also respected him for shrugging off some of their failures as the will of Allah—and, unlike other commanders, for not crediting himself with their successes. He came to be well regarded by even usually intransigent mullahs. His encouragement of his commanders to act independently when necessary rather than waiting for orders worked all the better because he'd instituted a kind of meritocracy, actively promoting successful and energetic commanders while demoting and punishing others.

In April 1982, Massoud staged a daring night raid on the Bagram air base. The meticulously planned operation, which was aided by saboteurs within the Afghan military, began with attacking more than a hundred checkpoints along the way. Rockets and mortars fired at Soviet aircraft reportedly destroyed a massive twin-tailed An-22 heavy transport plane.

The raid prompted the infuriated Soviets' strongest counteroffensive to date: a joint Afghan-Soviet attack on Panjshir that began the following month, lasted three weeks, and involved some fifteen thousand men of many divisions. After a week of heavy bombing by planes from Bagram, squadrons composed of six helicopters delivered elite airborne troops to selected parts of the valley. While huge Mi-6 transports unloaded the soldiers, Mi-24 gunships—the most feared weapon in the conflict—hovered nearby to provide cover. Each aircraft carried a deadly four-barrel, high-velocity machine gun and pods containing thirty-two 57-mm rockets.

As the mujahideen counterattacked the paratroops and planes, the Soviets launched their main offensive from south of the valley. Massoud allowed the Afghan troops in its vanguard to pass, but when Soviet forces reached the valley's spectacularly narrow entrance, his mujahideen dynamited the sides of the gorge, blocking the narrow dirt road running alongside the Panjshir River and temporarily trapping the soldiers. Elsewhere, Massoud's forces staged several ambushes, one of which, near the village of Doab, destroyed half a dozen BTRs and several tanks.

The mujahideen pinned down one paratroop regiment near the village of Ruha, which Lieutenant Polyakov had helped take in 1980. As the Soviet casualties mounted, the soldiers were rescued by the 108th Motorized Rifle Battalion commanded by Captain Ruslan Aushev, who pushed into Ruha under heavy fire. An ethnic Ingush from Russia's southern Caucasus region, Aushev lost many men and suffered serious injuries himself, for which he was awarded the highest fighting honor: the Hero of the Soviet Union.

Soldiers called Mi–24s "crocodiles" for their fearsome appearance, with their two tandem bubble canopies and stubby wings groaning with rockets and missiles. The helicopters that came to symbolize the Soviet presence in Afghanistan roared up the valley floor to attack hidden mujahideen targets while armored columns, including trucks, personnel carriers, and tanks, followed the valley's dirt path. Red Army units launched a second surprise attack from the north, where they entered the head of the valley and met with the main column, which gave the Soviets control of the entire valley floor for the first time. But they failed to dislodge the mujahideen occupying positions in the mountains above the Soviet airborne troops. All their forces withdrew several weeks later, leaving wrecks of scores of vehicles and destroyed villages everywhere. Three to four hundred of their men had been killed in the fighting.

Staging another attack on Panjshir in late August 1982, Soviet units again took the valley floor while troops engaged mujahideen concealed in the surrounding heights. This time, the Soviet destruction of villages, fields, and irrigation facilities was thorough before the force started withdrawing again on September 10. Although Massoud's forces remained largely intact, Panjshir's civilian population of around eighty thousand may have shrunk by half.

Having failed to dislodge Massoud from Panjshir, Soviet commanders set the simpler task of making his life harder. After the major attacks, Valery Vostrotin's Company 9 remained stationed in the town of Charikar, some fifteen miles from the valley's entrance. To avoid the Soviets, Massoud now had to extend himself farther and risk taking back passages into and out of the valley. Battle-scarred Captain Vostrotin had missed some of the summer because he was in Moscow, attending advanced officer training. Now back with his men, he took some heart in the military command's dropping of what he saw as its "Napoleonic" complex. They could accept that maintaining control of Panjshir would be too costly in

Soldiers from Vostrotin's 345th Division manning a
garrison in the Panjshir Valley. *(Alexander Liakhovskii
archive)*

men and machines, at least for now. Having finally learned the lessons of Afghanistan's geography, they were settling into an almost
predictable pattern of less damaging operations.

The Fortieth Army divided the country into zones. Strategically important areas, such as the famous mountain Khyber Pass
from Kabul to Peshawar and other passes from Pakistan, would
be taken during regular attacks, after which garrisons of Soviet or
Afghan Army units would be left for a year or so—until they'd be
relieved during a new wave of operations. Despite the advances
in tactical thinking, however, Vostrotin's experience in Panjshir
had taught him that small garrisons stationed here and there—by
soldiers driven half-mad by boredom and isolation—would do no
more than make the mujahideen shift their transportation routes
elsewhere in a sweep of treacherous territory much too large for
Soviet or Afghan government units to control. Meanwhile, most
Soviet forces remained tied up guarding major cities, roads, power
stations, and other key objectives.

The relatively few assaults that were mounted were chiefly
against the main rebel groups, including Massoud's and Ismail
Khan's in Herat. Smaller bands were largely left alone. By the time
Vostrotin departed Afghanistan for officer training in July, operations were taking place mostly around resistance strongholds near

Kandahar to the south and Khost to the east, in the vicinity of Kabul, and in the north. As in Panjshir, the goals had been scaled down from eliminating mujahideen commanders to inflicting as much damage as possible on their groups before pulling back to reduce exposure to their attacks.

VII

Life in the Charikar base near the Bagram airfield had turned into a mind-numbing grind for Vladimir Polyakov—the once-idealistic young lieutenant transferred to Afghanistan from East Germany—and his fellow officers. Boredom was alleviated only by moments of absurdity and tragedy, some during long bouts of heavy drinking. One oft-inebriated lieutenant regarded even by conscripts as the unit's village idiot was fond of running around the tents in his underwear, shooting his pistol in the air. Another officer returned from the laundry station so incoherent that a nervous sentry at the gate shot and wounded him after he failed to respond to his challenge.

Binges lasted for days when the men got their hands on cherished supplies of spirit sent from home. Officers' social lives were strictly segregated from conscripts', but no less dependent on drink. From stocks hidden in desert or mountain stashes outside their bases, officers fermented their own brew in metal barrels stolen from canteens, or raided other groups' stores. To obtain the necessary cash, junior lieutenants were ordered to steal diesel fuel, butter, and other goods from military warehouses, which were sold to local shopkeepers. (The money was also used for buying sheepskin coats and other clothes to keep out winter's bitter cold.)

Marijuana was easily available from locals. Initially shocked to find his men smoking it, Polyakov administered a beating so severe he rarely caught his men in the act again. The young officer was even more dismayed by the pecking order and enforced hazing that dominated the enlisted men's lives. The severe, deprived conditions in Afghanistan helped turn the deep-seated tradition of abuse, which extended back to the tsarist military, into a brutal form usually only associated with prisons. With an officer corps too small and not dedicated enough to instill discipline, the task was left to second-year conscripts—*dedy*, as they were dubbed, or "grandfathers"—who spent much of their leisure time beating and torturing their juniors. Only soldiers who'd reached the end of their two years—called *dembely*, slang for having been demobilized—but hadn't yet received orders to return to the Soviet Union were free of the social order. *Dedy* forced their fellow soldiers to work for them, to surrender their rations, and take whatever punishment amused their "elders."

Unable to understand how men who beat each other one day could fight side by side the next, Polyakov soon divided his subordinates into two kinds: the responsible and disciplined and the good-for-almost-nothing—a difference that usually manifested itself most visibly in critical situations. Under fire in Panjshir, he found himself lodged between boulders next to a soldier who was known for flouting the rules and for his disdain for Party lines. Now the man—in contrast to outwardly patriotic soldiers, who were often useless in battle—was stalwart, although shot in his buttocks. "Move over here, Comrade Lieutenant, it's safer," he whispered. Deeply moved, Polyakov ordered the man: "Lie still, you're wounded! And don't worry about me."

During Afghanistan's stifling summer heat, many Soviets spent most of their time in their underwear. Heavy inebriation added to the suffering, often compounded by dysentery from the local water. Some died, but most usually recovered within days, whether or not eating any available cheese helped, as rumor had it. Typhus, cholera, and malaria also plagued Russian troops, if not as much as the routine bouts of hepatitis.

Soviet pop stars such as crooner Josef Kobzon, who was ubiquitous on Soviet stages and television at the time, gave occasional concerts for regiments in Kabul, but lectures about military tactics were more frequent. When a blast went off in the audience during a talk about explosives, it was followed by wild shouts of "Fuck! Fuck! Fuck!" A bored conscript had been playing with the ring of a grenade until it accidentally exploded, blowing off two of his fingers. "Why the goddamned hell am I telling you these things if you're not listening?!" the lecturer demanded.

Polyakov's duties included patrolling sections of Kabul. During the early months, even officers toted Kalashnikovs, which contributed to a macho pride. But officers' high soon dissipated, and Polyakov began violating regulations by leaving behind even his pistol, which he believed would do more harm than good if he found himself in a real confrontation on the streets.

Polyakov and other officers began frequenting a small restaurant near the Soviet embassy compound. The embassy's gardener who owned the establishment and supplied his Russian patrons with the exotic treat of British beer was bold enough to quiz officers about the war.

"Fathers are fighting their sons here," he said one afternoon. "Men are killing their own brothers. What do *you* think you're doing? Whom are you really supporting?" Polyakov replied with the standard officers' view, that Nur Mohammed Taraki had been "our" man and his killer, Amin, was an American agent; that the Red Army was there to protect the gains of Afghanistan's communist revolution. But such explanations rang increasingly hollow even to those most committed to fulfilling their internationalist duties.

The gardener served as a dramatic, disturbing vox populi for Polyakov—who, like most other Russians, was all but isolated from the locals, most of whom spoke only Pashto or Dari, an Afghan form of Persian. His disillusionment with the conduct of the war was advancing toward belief that the invasion itself had been a massive mistake of Brezhnevite imperialism. "What on Earth am I doing here?" he found himself thinking about the country whose landscape and way of life had initially seemed utterly unfamiliar, and in many ways still were.

Polyakov was on a patrol in downtown Kabul with three of his soldiers when an ethnic Tajik conscript from another Soviet unit approached breathlessly. Pointing to an Afghan Army truck parked nearby, he blurted out that several soldiers inside had just tried to recruit him to join the mujahideen by urging that they were all Muslim. Polyakov's disenchantment advanced several notches after his men ran to arrest the would-be recruiters and found, to the lieutenant's near-disbelief, that they weren't Afghan soldiers but Soviet!

The distributing of decorations further incensed him. He learned the truth about how it was done by accidentally overhearing a conversation between two senior officers about an award of the Red Star, a top honor, to a political officer who had apparently delivered a lecture about respecting Afghan traditions while his unit was under enemy fire. The overheard talk revealed that medals were given not as recognition of merit but according to a quota system. Most of the set number allotted to top commanders went to political officers—so-called *politruki*, few of whom faced combat and many of whom were detested by most who did—who served as the Party's commissars within the military. The top honors gave a major leg up to their recipients for selection for further training in military academies back in the Soviet Union.

At the same time, Polyakov saw that serious mistakes were rarely punished. His brigade had been among the last to straggle back toward Kabul after the previous summer's foray into the Panjshir Valley. The men took occasional fire from the mountainsides, but weren't seriously attacked. When the valley's dirt track switched from one side of the river to the other, an engineer unit constructed a small, portable bridge, and remained there to collapse it after the BTRs had crossed. Clattering up from the valley's southern end, a Mi-8 helicopter fired several rockets at the bridge before flying on. The brief attack cost some soldiers their legs and some their lives.

Deeply disturbed by the fatal error and a failure to try to find those responsible, Polyakov tried investigating himself. One of the helicopter pilots he questioned told him that everyone on the ground looks similar to a crew flying a hundred or more feet above. "Except for people with horses—they're definitely *dushmany*," he said, using the derogatory Soviet term for mujahideen fighters. When unidentified helicopters later appeared to Polyakov in Panjshir, he fired red flares he'd made sure to carry with him. Soviet forces without them more than occasionally faced death or maiming.

Still planning to stay in the military despite his disillusionment, Polyakov joined the Communist Party, a prerequisite for speedy promotion and possible attainment of high rank. But he also began misbehaving, perhaps in rebellion or an unconscious desire to tempt fate. He'd violate his base curfew by donning civilian clothes and sneaking out to hitchhike to Kabul restaurants that sold alcohol. Once he took along his battalion commander. Seated at a table, they were approached by several Afghans in civilian clothes who struck up a friendly conversation and suggested moving to a restaurant with better food. Once in their car, however, Polyakov and his battalion commander found themselves being sped to a local Afghan Army station: the Afghans turned out to be members of the KhAD intelligence service. At the station, the commandant ordered the two Russians to spend the night in the building's small jail cell, which was guarded by a single soldier.

Sitting on its little wooden bench, the well-lubricated officers discussed their fate.

"Damn, Slava, we're in here like barnyard animals. No vodka, no beer, nothing!" moaned Polyakov. "It's my birthday soon and I need to start celebrating. We can't just sit here."

"Well, what are we going to do?" replied his ordinarily dour commander.

"You're strong. Why don't we try to break these flimsy bars?"

Waiting until the guard stepped out, they pulled at the bars of their window until they began shifting. Soon, the officers yanked the bars from their concrete bed, jumped from their second-story window, and hailed a taxi to take them to another restaurant. After more drinking, they returned to their base, still feeling restless enough to visit their battalion's medical unit barracks to proposition nurses. By that time, several Afghan officers had hurried to the base to look for the escaped prisoners. When they found Polyakov on a nurse's bunk in his underwear, jumping out of another window was out of the question: a soldier had been stationed outside. Polyakov was escorted to the battalion's detention center to sleep off his hangover.

It took three men to haul him to a session with a major general in the morning. "Don't you know what you're risking?" the senior officer bellowed. "Don't you care *anything* about your Party membership?" Polyakov realized that he no longer did, that the only things he did care about were his deep bonds of friendship with fellow officers and similar feelings he'd also had, in addition to highly satisfying sex, with nurses, secretaries, and other women sent to serve *their* internationalist duties. He'd stopped worrying about his career. As with so many others, his interest in Afghanistan had narrowed to getting home from there.

VIII

The destruction of roads and other crucial infrastructure played a large role in devastating Afghanistan's already desperately ailing economy. Attempting to shore it up, Moscow sent thousands of economic advisers to oversee major new construction projects, including the building of hospitals and power stations and expansion of Kabul Airport. The help coerced from Eastern Bloc countries included trucks from Hungary and credit from Czechoslovakia for irrigation projects, while the Afghan government itself sought to boost agricultural production by easing some of the sweeping land reforms of 1979. But participants in the shattered local economy had already turned to the easiest alternative, and much of the heroin trade from their poppy crops was supporting the mujahideen.

Babrak Karmal's measures to try to stem his flagging political control over the country included a new conscription law enacted in January 1981 that increased the term of service by six months. Karmal also reformed the KhAD security service—formerly called AGSA—which Amin had staffed with his own Khalqi loyalists. (A now-abolished separate KAM secret police had also been subordinate to Amin.) In 1980 and 1981, a new KhAD chief, Mohammed Najibullah, oversaw the replacement of Amin's appointees with Parcham members. He also increased its numbers. By 1982, the security service of an estimated eighteen hundred members—who used torture and summary executions no less ruthlessly than the earlier incarnation under Amin—was enjoying significant success in penetrating mujahideen groups.

The torture was conducted in houses around Kabul controlled by the intelligence services, as well as in prisons and police and KhAD detention centers. The largest KhAD prison, a Kabul institution called the Sedarat compound, served as the main interrogation center. Detainees were beaten, had their fingernails removed with pliers, were sodomized, given electric shocks, and kept awake until they were senseless. Many prisoners confessed to helping the mujahideen and were shot. Starvation as well as sleep deprivation made life hell for those sentenced to prison, some of whose freezing concrete cells contained no bed or blankets. Suspicion and denunciations were rife.

While boosting repression, Karmal tried to increase the PDPA's public support. A new organization called the Democratic Youth Organization of Afghanistan held its first congress in January and formed a youth brigade to deliver hundreds of young men to fight against the "bandits," the government's term for the mujahideen. In June, the PDPA staged another attempt to bolster its legitimacy by holding the first congress of the National Fatherland Front, created as a supposedly nonpolitical body for organizing pro-government activities. But none of the PDPA's jockeying alleviated the party factionalism that had helped bring on the Soviet invasion.

Trying to boost Karmal's support, the Kremlin ordered him to deliver talks in the countryside, where his appearance would be taken for unconcern with his own safety. In fact, he was very concerned, and the initiative brought much worry to Vladimir Redkoborodyi, the KGB officer who headed his security. Even in and around Kabul, which came closer than any place else to a government refuge, shootings and bombings continued to be daily occurrences.

In January 1982, Moscow ordered Karmal to appear in Jalalabad, a mujahideen stronghold half of whose population, by Redkoborodyi's estimate, was connected to the resistance. Although the government exercised nominal control over the city during the day, the mujahideen reigned at night. Redkoborodyi knew he'd need extra guards. Since his requests for more men and BTRs for forays into the provinces weren't always granted, Redkoborodyi went directly to the head of Soviet military forces in Afghanistan, Marshal Sokolov, with whom he had a good relationship.

Redkoborodyi—whose KGB cryptonym was Rubin, Russian for ruby—also made a reconnaissance trip to Jalalabad to prepare for the presidential visit. He usually flew in rattling Mi-8 helicopters, in which his men tried to reinforce thin or nonexistent armor by laying junked BTR hatch doors on the floor. They also tied ropes to flak jackets to hang out the windows for additional if still utterly flimsy protection, and often sat on their helmets to lessen the chances of injury to their genitals during attacks. To keep the time that their craft would be visible to potential attackers as limited as possible, pilots often flew at a height of thirty to fifty feet, where the powerful downdraft from rotor blades made aiming and firing rocket-propelled grenades almost impossible.

This time, Redkoborodyi flew with two large An-10 cargo planes rather than helicopters. The Afghan Army soldiers who went along had never flown before, and sat cross-legged on the floor. Security was such a problem and leaks of information so fast that even army national guard chief Aziz Khassas, who also accompanied them, hadn't been informed about the destination. "You're my older brother, Rafik Stepanovich," Khassas had pleaded before they took off, using the name Afghan colleagues invented for Redkoborodyi. "Tell me where we're going!" The KGB officer's reply was that he had no idea. "Sure, I bet!" Khassas said.

Although Karmal's visit to Jalalabad took place without incident, close calls marked many other trips. During a visit to Kandahar by Karmal, Najibullah, and Marshal Sokolov, Redkoborodyi's men found that a bridge on their motorcade's path between the airport and city had been mined. The explosives were defused. On the way back, an eruption of gunfire near the airport persuaded the visitors to return all the way to Kabul by motorcade—after sending a decoy convoy ahead of them.

During a trip to Herat, also by motorcade, Redkoborodyi saw a fuel tanker convoy in the desert flats destroyed by mines planted near a deserted village. As huge flames billowed from the vehicles, burning soldiers screamed, some until they died. The paratroopers who arrived to help rescue them could do little more than shoot holes in gasoline tanks to reduce the risk of new explosions by enabling burning fuel to seep out—while local Afghans appeared as if from nowhere to try to collect some of the unburned fuel in buckets.

Karmal had learned to cast frequent glances at Redkoborodyi during his talks, watching for a raised hand, the signal for trouble. Doing that during his speech in a Herat government building, the president saw the dreaded sign from the KGB security chief, who had received word of a possible attack. Karmal wrapped up as quickly as possible. On the way to army headquarters, a bad sign confirmed the intelligence: fields empty of farmers. Soon afterward, the government building was blown up.

One of Redkoborodyi's largest and most sensitive operations would come during a 1984 military parade and awards ceremony in Kabul to mark the anniversary of the April Revolution. To minimize their visibility, his men wore Afghan Army uniforms, while soldiers of the Fifth MRD and KhAD intelligence men helped inspect each tank, BTR, and participating vehicle of all other kinds. Since bombs might be concealed anywhere, the main square to be used for the ceremony was cordoned off and Afghan guards were posted on every rooftop. When information reached Redkoborodyi shortly before the ceremony that the mujahideen indeed planned a bomb attack, he informed Marshal Sokolov, who in turn asked whether the parade should be canceled. Redkoborodyi believed it would be riskier to cancel, since it would suggest the government lacked the ability to provide security in the capital.

The parade proceeded as scheduled. Shortly after the participants left, a suicide bomber destroyed one of the platforms on which officials had stood. Redkoborodyi reasoned that his measures had kept the explosion from happening during the event, and that the bomber, determined to fulfill his orders, did so when the dispersal of government guards enabled him to.

Despite the tension of his job, Redkoborodyi found moments of respite. Apprehensive as Karmal was, the KGB colonel found him pleasant to deal with in their daily exchanges, and the president bore himself with appealing dignity. Karmal also seemed to enjoy the Soviets' company. He visited the KGB's palace apartments during the many Soviet holidays, sharing their sausages, herring, and other treats brought back from trips to Moscow, all of course washed down by copious amounts of vodka. Other frequent guests included Interior Minister Guliabzoi and KhAD deputy chief Gulam Faruq Yaqubi.

Like almost all their countrymen, Red Army officers and men were hugely devoted to the *banya*, the Russian version of the sauna. Each rank, from top commanders to conscripts, often had their own, usually built from scrounged or stolen planks of wood. The one Karmal allowed Redkoborodyi to build on the presidential palace grounds was complete with a small pool for cooling off after long sessions in the wood-heated room. Karmal kept a close eye on its construction and asked for a trial session on its completion, then became a regular visitor.

Redkoborodyi also oversaw the construction of a small movie theater for his men, built with the help of a local technician. Unable to understand most of what was shown there—American and Indian films subtitled in Pashto—the Russians watched anyway, the men usually singing and drinking vodka. Karmal often stopped by for vodka shots during walks around the palace compound.

IX

By the end of 1982, the Afghan War showed signs of intensification. Although they had learned a good deal about how to fight it, the formidable Soviet forces concentrated around the Panjshir Valley and west around Herat had managed to do little to neutralize the resistance. Elsewhere, too, the conflict was settling into stalemate. The Afghan Army reversed the tide of desertions and participated in some major offensives. But it nevertheless made even less progress against the mujahideen, whose numbers had grown.

So had the number of refugees. More than 2 million Afghans, mostly Pashtuns, had fled to Pakistan while Tajiks and other Dari-speakers escaped east into Iran. The principal combat zones, such as the Panjshir and Kunar valleys, had suffered major depopulation, and the people who remained were subjected to bombing and destruction, delivered with increasingly less concern about who would die. But in Moscow, Leonid Brezhnev was relieved of any regret about the invasion that he, in his lack of knowledge of and concern about Afghanistan, had been so instrumental in unleashing. The general secretary of the Communist Party of the Soviet Union and head of state as chairman of the presidium of the Supreme Soviet died in November 1982. KGB chief Yuri Andropov, who had initially opposed the Afghanistan invasion, succeeded him.

CHAPTER 5

THE SOVIETS
SEEK VICTORY

I

Russia emerged as a great power early in the nineteenth century, when Tsar Alexander I, newly confident after helping drive Napoleon's invading army back into France, resumed Peter the Great's old push south into the Caucasus Mountains west of the Caspian Sea, and east toward Central Asia. The remnants of Timur's (Tamerlane's) empire there consisted of rival khanates, most prominently in Khiva, Bukhara, and Samarkand. General Alexei Yermolov, an ambitious and outspoken artillery officer who had distinguished himself in the Napoleonic wars, led Russia's expansion into what's now Chechnya and Dagestan, and over the Caucasus into Georgia. Under the reforming Alexander, the campaign sparked a revival of a lengthy struggle with the dying Ottoman Empire. In 1828, Yermolov's replacement, General Ivan Paskevich, beat back a Persian thrust, annexed Armenia, and defeated the Turks in a brief conflict the following year.

Britain was foremost among the powers that opposed Russia's

advance. Increasingly disturbed by the Russians' enduring hunger for a warm-water port on the Indian Ocean, the chief rival for influence in the region watched uneasily from the sidelines. Although myth about Russia's actual capabilities to threaten India inflated the worry by the world's leading naval power, it also had real cause. After the East India Company had spearheaded Britain's subjugation of the Indian subcontinent in the 1830s, the new colony sought protection from the threat of encroachment by Russian forces a few thousand miles to the north. For that purpose, London sent a bright young artillery officer named Alexander Burnes to Kabul in 1837. Burnes had met the Afghan leader, Prince Dost Mohammed, in 1832. The two got on well, and Burnes reported to the Indian governor-general, George Eden, First Earl of Auckland, that Dost Mohammed would agree to an alliance with the British if they would support him in his conflict in Punjab with the powerful Sikhs. Lord Auckland rejected the offer out of unwillingness to cross the Sikh leader Ranjit Singh, with whom he'd previously forged a treaty.

Burnes reported something else about his visit to Kabul: the arrival there of a tsarist army captain. British concern swelled with the news. Although the Russians would also fail to come to an agreement with Dost Mohammed, Lord Auckland, determined to act, ordered an Anglo-Indian army to invade Afghanistan. Thus began the bloodletting of the Great Game in Central Asia between Russia and Britain: a struggle to control the strategic frontier territory that separated the borders of the burgeoning empires. It would bear many of the hallmarks of previous and later campaigns in Afghanistan, chiefly quick victory followed by a long, grinding opposition, then brutal fighting and terrible carnage.

Britain's first Afghan War lasted until 1842. The British forces, eager for conquest and laden with servants and camels (sixty of the animals were required to transport one brigadier's personal belongings), met little resistance at first. Capturing Kandahar and Ghazni in July 1839, they moved on to take Kabul the following month. When Dost Mohammed surrendered, they installed a puppet, Shah Shuja, on the throne, then returned most of their troops to India.

Two years later, the British gains started unraveling. The chain of events began in London. After taking power in August 1841, Robert Peel, the new Tory prime minister, announced cutbacks in the enormous sums required to maintain troops in Afghanistan. In October, the British envoy to Shah Shuja's court announced that some tribal chiefs' annual stipends would be cut. Days later, the Ghilzai tribe attacked a caravan from India, severing the vital British supply line.

Dost Mohammed's son, Akbar Khan, helped lead a revolt against Shah Shuja the following month. After an Afghan mob stormed Alexander Burnes's house and murdered him, fierce fighting ensued. By December, the Afghans had overwhelmed the British forces and forced William Macnaughten, the senior envoy, to negotiate a treaty that required the British to leave the country. However, Akbar Khan tricked Macnaughten, who was also murdered. General William Elphinstone, the incompetent commander of British troops in Afghanistan, was later taken hostage and died in captivity. The British forces withdrew, repeatedly ambushed and brutally massacred during their retreat to India through freezing, snow-covered mountain passes. One group of around 16,500 British and Indian troops made its way toward Jalalabad. Only one person, a severely injured doctor, survived the ninety-mile journey. When the remnants of the British force had finally left in December 1842, Dost Mohammed reassumed the throne.

The debacle, however, did not persuade the losers in the Great Game's first round to throw in the towel.

II

Dost Mohammed set about reclaiming territories lost from his former domain. By the time he signed a peace agreement with British India in 1855, Britain was embroiled in the Crimean War. That conflict had begun in 1853, over a dispute between France and Russia about who had jurisdiction over Christian sites in the Holy Land, then under Ottoman rule. When Russia invaded the Danubian principalities of Moldavia and Wallachia, the British joined the French in fear that the Russians would take control of the Dardanelles—the Turkish-controlled entrance to the Mediterranean Sea—and sided with the Ottoman Empire.

Now it was time for Russian prestige to suffer a humiliating blow. It was delivered by the surrender of its port of Sevastopol and the scuttling of its great Black Sea fleet. The defeat followed a British and French siege that exposed the inefficient Russian military's desperate need for modernization. Nevertheless, Russia soon bounded back under Alexander II, who ascended the throne in 1855, during the war. The tsar revived the push into Central Asia, and his forces took Tashkent in 1865. When Bukhara and Khiva gave way, the British worried again about an invasion of India from Russian Central Asia, called Turkestan.

In Kabul, Dost Mohammed's death in 1878 set off a power struggle among his sons that ended when the third brother, Sher Ali Khan, emerged as the successor. The same year, Turkestan's governor-general, General Konstantin Kaufman, sent a mission to Kabul to enlist Afghan support. Angered by the Russian presence, the British demanded the Afghans also accept a British mission. When the message was ignored—most likely because it coincided with the death of Sher Ali's favorite son—the British issued an ultimatum. Sher Ali accepted, but his notice arrived too late to avert a second invasion of Afghanistan in November.

The British entertained few illusions about involvement in Afghanistan during the Second Afghan War, and their temperamental advance was reinforced by technological and military progress. Rail, steampower, and the telegraph gave their soldiers—who wore khaki and helmets instead of red coats—a huge advantage over the badly equipped Afghan forces. Sher Ali fled when the British retook Kabul in October 1879. In his place, the British installed Abdur Rahman Khan, Dost Mohammed's grandson, who had lived twelve years in Russian-controlled Tashkent. He soon became known as the "Iron Emir" for his moves to break the tribal system's hold over most of Afghanistan's territory.

"It does not disappoint me," wrote of Kabul Colonel Charles Metcalfe MacGregor, the vainglorious chief of staff to the commander of the British force, "it is just what I expected, mean, filthy like an Afghan's heart." Despite their victory, the British were beset by constant attacks from the Ghilzai and other tribes, and controlled only as much territory as their soldiers could defend. Thanks to that, and because they were convinced the Russians would be as unable as they were to conquer Afghanistan, they withdrew from Kabul, retaining control of the country's foreign policy.

In 1885, Russia and Britain agreed to a line stretching between the Hari Rud and Amu Dar'ya rivers as the delineation of Afghanistan's northern border. Further demarcation came in 1893, when the Indian government's foreign secretary, Sir Mortimer Durand, began mapping the country's eastern border. The Durand Line cut straight through Pashtun territory, splitting it between Afghanistan and India. That separation would profoundly affect the country's future by prompting a sustained Pashtun drive to unite their territory and, later still, assuring serious conflict with the new state of Pakistan on the other side of the border. Meanwhile, the British also added to Afghanistan a thin buffer sliver in the northeast between the Pamir and Hindu Kush Mountains. The Wakhan Corridor, as it was called, was intended to ensure that no particle of Russian-controlled territory would touch British India.

The British continued subsidizing the Afghan emir until Amanallah—Abdul Rahman's grandson—launched a jihad in May 1919. Severely drained by World War I and facing a growing Indian national liberation movement, the British nevertheless counterattacked, and a treaty was drawn up at the Indian cantonment town of Rawalpindi. Amanullah lost his British subsidies, but essentially won independence: Britain relinquished control over Afghanistan's foreign policy and recognized Afghan sovereignty. Many therefore regard 1919 as the birth of the modern Afghan nation. Amanallah changed his title from emir to king six years later.

Thus the British left, but with what they thought was reason to believe they'd won the Great Game, especially after Russia suffered another profoundly humiliating defeat, this time by Japan. After the tsar's supposedly powerful Baltic Sea Fleet had steamed halfway around the world to reach the Pacific Ocean in 1905, Japanese guns sank or severely damaged virtually every ship. But Russian aspirations didn't die. Even after the Bolshevik Revolution of 1917, Moscow remained diplomatically engaged with Afghanistan, providing aid and subsidies. Indeed, as mentioned, the Soviet Union became the first country to recognize Afghanistan's sovereignty in 1919, before the British did that same year. Sixty years later, however, history would add to its abundance of ironies when Moscow, now represented by Leonid Brezhnev's supremely misguided Politburo, would go far to destroy what little remained of Afghan statehood.

III

As Soviet forces fought Ahmed Shah Massoud's fighters in the Panjshir Valley, the military also established direct contact with the rebel commander. An intelligence colonel named Anatoly Tkachev met Massoud in the Panjshir Valley in January 1983. On first seeing the mujahideen leader, Tkachev was surprised to find him modestly dressed in traditional Afghan clothes—and friendly. Nothing about Massoud resembled his Soviet propaganda description as the animal-like, evil face of the enemy. The Soviets offered Massoud a cease-fire in Panjshir. For his part, Massoud appeared surprised by the Soviets' willingness to negotiate, a new tactic after two years of strict ultimatums to surrender to Karmal's government. For his part, Tkachev saw in Massoud a serious politician who thought strategically and knew what he was doing. "I'm not an adversary of the Soviet Union or the Soviet people," Massoud told Tkachev. The real enemy, he said, was the Afghan government.

The negotiations worked. In 1983, the Soviets forged a truce with Massoud in the Panjshir Valley. Both sides promised to withhold from launching major offensives, ushering in a period of low-intensity stalemate. The lull served to sharpen mujahideen territorial disputes and other forms of infighting. As rival groups ambushed competitors' convoys from Pakistan with increasing frequency, resort to one of Afghanistan's oldest commercial practices—demanding tolls for passage through transport routes—found new favor. Burgeoning new weapons arsenals helped escalate the infighting.

The supply networks enlarging mujahideen weapons stores became increasingly corrupt as they grew in size. The prospect of profit from American and Saudi funds encouraged some countries to dump their obsolete, unwanted arms surpluses on Afghanistan. While Washington paid for a massive Israeli cache of captured Soviet weapons, Egypt sent broken AK-47s and Turkey sold World War II–era weapons. Even the British contributed an outdated, handheld antiaircraft missile called Blowpipe. The corruption magnified at the lower ends of the supply chains. Officers of Pakistan's ISI were getting rich by selling the mujahideen arms that had been bought by Washington and Riyadh—and some rebels didn't mind paying because they were reselling the weapons for their own profit. By early 1984, Pakistani dictator General Zia resolved to bring Afghanistan operations under tighter control.

Convening a meeting in Peshawar of the seven main Afghan rebel leaders, Zia called on them to form an alliance. The youngest and toughest of the leaders, fundamentalist Gulbuddin Hekmatyar, was ruthless, staunchly Islamist, and volatile in temper, but the Pakistanis saw him as an efficient, effective leader and would continue feeding his Party of Islam the lion's share of the American and Saudi aid they distributed to the mujahideen. Hekmatyar was already disdainful of the United States; he'd soon refuse to meet Ronald Reagan in Washington. Later he would become one of the West's sworn enemies, and would call for jihad against the United States after the U.S.-led invasion of

Afghanistan in 2001. Hekmatyar and Massoud were bitter rivals. After the Soviet withdrawal, their enmity would help tear Kabul and the rest of the country apart in fierce infighting.

Another fundamentalist, Rasul Sayyaf, had maintained his close ties to Saudi Arabia. Yunis Khalis, an elderly Pashtun mullah from the eastern Nangarhar Region who'd split from Hekmatyar, led a group that included Abdul Haq, the CIA-connected commander who staged daring operations near Kabul. Unlike some of the other leaders, who spent much of their time abroad, Khalis had a reputation for being a fierce fighter.

Apart from Tajik linguist Burhanuddin Rabbani and his Society of Islam, the relatively moderate mujahideen leaders included Mohammed Nabi Mahommedi and Sayed Ahmad Gailani, who came from a wealthy family that had connections to the royal family. Western journalists dubbed Gailani's group "Gucci muj" for his well-known love of expensive clothes. Another moderate, Sibgatullah Mojaddedi, was leader of Afghanistan's Naqshbandi order of the mystical Islamic Sufi sect. Mojaddedi's group had a reputation for being ineffectual on the battlefield. Unlike their more radical Islamist counterparts, the four more moderate mujahideen leaders wanted to institute a constitutional government; Gailani even wanted to restore the monarchy. Despite fierce disagreements and deep mutual suspicion, the mujahideen leaders, who came to be known as the Peshawar Seven, formed a fragile alliance.

Although the CIA had been unhappy from the beginning to funnel all its aid to the mujahideen through Pakistan's ISI, it was more practical than having to deal directly with dozens of competing rebel groups, besides helping obscure Washington's role. That role was now taking on a new character under CIA director William Casey. An unrepentant Cold Warrior bent on attacking the Soviet Union, Casey pushed for expanding American aid and other aspects of U.S. involvement in the conflict. One of his operations was smuggling Korans into Soviet Central Asia. The volumes were printed in Uzbek, and their mujahideen smugglers also conducted acts of sabotage on Soviet territory.

Members of Congress enthusiastically supported the jihad in Afghanistan. Chief among them was Texas Democratic Representative Charlie Wilson, an alcoholic former naval officer, who was sometimes accompanied by young models—including a former Miss World USA title winner—when he flew on government-paid junkets, some of them inside Afghanistan.

Trumpeting the Afghan conflict as a crucial fight of good versus evil, Wilson pushed through Congress measures to boost spending on supplying the mujahideen. In time, a growing chorus of conservative voices in Washington joined his criticism of the government for providing insufficient help to the Afghan freedom fighters confronting what President Reagan called "the evil empire."

Washington's $50 million funneled to the mujahideen in 1984 ballooned to $250 million the following year, including CIA funds diverted from the Pentagon. In April, the president dramatically boosted American involvement by issuing a directive requiring "all available means" to be used to force the Soviets to withdraw from Afghanistan.

IV

Despite the propaganda about the American threat in Afghanistan, the Soviets couldn't know then that U.S.—and Saudi—aid would soon turn the mujahideen into an even more formidable force. The daily struggle simply to get by in Afghanistan's grueling conditions was already overwhelming for many troops. "Sand in your eyes, sand in your mouth, sand runs through your veins," went one of the many guitar-accompanied laments Soviet soldiers strummed whiling away time in their barracks when not on training exercises.

The sun was setting when Boris Kuznetsov arrived in his new quarters in southeastern Kandahar in 1982. The surrounding Rigestan desert appeared to him red enough to have been made from crushed bricks. If he'd thought about it, the redness might have seemed a good omen: although Kuznetsov had graduated as an air force pilot two years earlier and volunteered for duty in Afghanistan, he was now a political officer, a *politruk*, whose job would be to enforce the Party line among the ranks of the 280th Separate Helicopter Regiment.

The lieutenant in his mid-twenties lived with two other officers in a trailer next to a row of helicopter hangars. The heat was almost unbearable. The Soviet air-conditioners that were being installed at last often couldn't cope with the soaring temperatures, so the officers covered open windows with blankets and mattresses, then regularly doused them with buckets of water. Evaporation cooled rooms better than the Soviet machinery.

Gunfire erupted outside as soon as darkness fell on Kuznetsov's first night. It came steadily closer until he could make out even the sound of bullet casings hitting the ground. Despite a fenced security perimeter reinforced by sentries and minefields, mujahideen fighters would creep as close as they could before firing their Kalashnikovs and mortars. When the Soviets returned fire, the Afghans would move to new positions and resume their volleys from there, sustaining them for hours on many nights. Since the airfields' landing lights made perfect targets, night flights by helicopters and planes were strictly forbidden. When planes had to take off for emergencies, most risked the considerable danger of doing so in complete darkness.

Later, when Kuznetsov would be stationed in Bagram, two soldiers who'd left their barracks to use outdoor latrines during the night were found dead, their severed heads impaled on sticks in the ground. Either mujahideen had penetrated the base or sabotage had been committed from within.

In addition to accompanying helicopter missions in several regions of Afghanistan, Kuznetsov traveled to various air bases to discuss their condition with senior officers. He shared some of what he learned in "Political Work in the War in the Democratic Republic of Afghanistan," a classified pamphlet of his published in 1985.

Meanwhile, other problems commanded his attention. When he was transferred to the city of Shindand in the western Herat Region in 1983, he found sex between servicemen and nurses, secretaries, and other female workers so widespread that one of his first tasks there was to help set up separate living quarters for women, surrounded by fences and guarded by sentries. Similar "fortifications" would be constructed on other bases throughout Afghanistan.

As the Party's eyes and ears in the military, *politruki* were charged with making certain no one forgot his or her international duty to help the Afghan comrades shore up the Communist Revolution. Kuznetsov believed winning the war was essential for Soviet security too. If the Americans penetrated Afghanistan, they'd be able to set up missile installations in the Hindu Kush Mountains, capable of reaching any part of the Soviet Union (never mind that U.S. intercontinental ballistic missiles could already do the same).

Twenty-five-year-old helicopter pilot Vladimir Kostiuchenko was far less convinced about the rightness of the struggle. The Irkutsk native was in a wave of personnel also dispatched to Kandahar to replace those who'd taken part in the war's initial phase. When he arrived in June 1981, his first squadron briefing was essentially a declaration that all their previous training counted for little.

"Do you know where you've arrived?" barked his battle-scarred squadron commander, an acrid-smelling Soviet Belomor cigarette dangling from his lower lip. "You may be first-class pilots back home, but you're just kids here! As far as I'm concerned, there's no such thing as rank! You're a veteran or a kid. Forget your military manuals. Everything we know here has been written with blood!"

Kostiuchenko's squadron consisted of four Mi-8s and four Mi-24 gunships. On his first trial flight the following day, his copilot, an "old-timer," told him his control dials were almost useless for highly risky operations in dangerous mountain territory. Surviving in Afghanistan required reliance on instinct, he said. Distances were to be ascertained by holding a foot out to the chopper's floor window and using relative size to judge, a method that helped compensate for the lack of a visual horizon and enabled

Mi-8 helicopter pilot Vladimir Kostiuchenko served three tours in Afghanistan and was shot down twice. *(Alexander Liakhovskii archive)*

quicker reaction. Aircraft were pushed as hard as possible, to almost 150 miles an hour. Flying to operations sites had to be done high enough to avoid machine-gun and rocket fire from the ground. But helicopters descended when nearing their targets, and approached as low to the ground as possible. Pilots delivering supplies in the field were to break away immediately, tilting their rotors at angles steeper than regulations allowed. Helicopters traveling toward battlegrounds were to fly in from the direction of the sun to blind the enemy, and fire at anything that moved, including witnesses of possible war crimes.

As with weapons and armored personnel carriers, the Soviets improved helicopter designs throughout the war. Standard Mi-8T models that carried twenty-four troops were replaced with modified types, including the Mi-8MT, which were more powerful, boasted more weapons—including the same rocket pods that Mi-24s carried—and performed better in hot and high-altitude conditions. Infrared jammers and "ears"—attachments that redirected exhaust—to confuse heat-seeking missiles were also added. But Kostiuchenko and other pilots preferred flying without the devices, which added weight and hindered maneuverability.

Although violating regulations was strictly forbidden and often punished, rules were regularly broken. Kostiuchenko's squadron took part in a particularly dangerous mission to evacuate dead and wounded from the Hindu Kush foothills near Shindand in the fall of 1981. Several Mi-8s were shot down. When a doctor on board informed Kostiuchenko one of the wounded would die if the helicopter were to fly at the usual altitude, he violated procedure by flying lower. The soldier survived and Kostiuchenko's helicopter escaped unscathed. But casualties incurred while regulations were broken, even during difficult combat operations, were highly criticized by the regimental command and classified as "unreasonable."

One of Kostiuchenko's first missions was a night bombing raid in the Rigestan desert of southern Helmand Province. While returning to base, the pilots of two Mi-8s spotted a row of headlights below them, moving along the Helmand basin toward Kandahar. Radioing for instructions, the crews were ordered to fire at the vehicles. They unleashed a round of machine-gun fire, noted the position, and continued home. When another pair of Mi-8s flew to the site to inspect the damage the next day, they followed standard procedure by firing at two stationary cars on the flat scrubland below them. As they descended in order to land and investigate, an elderly Afghan emerged from one of the vehicles and fired at the helicopters with an ancient Bora rifle. The helicopters returned fire, but the lone figure below miraculously continued firing and managed to penetrate one chopper's turboshaft before the craft finally dispatched the man and landed. Cautiously emerging to scour the surrounding bushes, crew members saw a grim picture of civilians, mostly women and children, lying dead. Now the Soviets concluded the old man they'd just killed was probably trying to protect his family. Only one person was found alive: a girl of about three years old with a badly wounded hand.

Soon Kostiuchenko's helicopter arrived with parts for the chopper that had been hit. Accustomed to viewing the landscape from a distance, he was dismayed to see civilian carnage close up. Trying to calm the terrified girl, he nervously helped bandage her hand to stop its bleeding. Minutes later, a paratrooper who'd flown in on one of the helicopters took her aside, held a Makarov pistol to her head, and fired. Her small frame slumped to the ground, blood oozing onto the dusty earth. Paratroopers picked up her body and put it along with the others inside the bullet-ridden cars, doused them with gasoline, and set them alight. Later, the strict instructions to keep silent about the incident only deepened the effect on Kostiuchenko. Even after having been shot down twice, the sight of the little girl's murder would haunt him for years as his worst war experience.

Still, Kostiuchenko in time became inured to massacres of civilians. Many took place during looting raids, usually when two Mi-8s would scour roads for vehicles carrying goods. Once a car was spotted, one of the helicopters would stop it while the other circled overhead, providing cover. Drivers and passengers were usually shot before their vehicles were raided for everything that could be pried off and carried away, including radios. On one of Kostiuchenko's first raids, his job was to stop a car identified for looting by firing rounds nearby. He accidentally hit the car's gasoline tank, which exploded, killing everyone inside. Back on the ground in Kandahar, he had to stay out of sight for days because furious "old-timers" threatened to beat him senseless for ruining a promising prospect for profit.

On another flight over the Rigestan desert, Kostiuchenko's crew killed three men on motorcycles, then loaded their bikes through the clamshell back doors of their Mi-8 for sale in Kandahar. "Free hunting," as the rampantly widespread acts were called, provided Soviet pilots and crews with cash to supplement their meager pay and rations, although much of the money went to prostitutes. With little fear of punishment, killing civilians and taking their property soon seemed almost normal. Army officers had more opportunities for raiding than pilots; Kostiuchenko noticed that even some privates were wealthier than he was. Over the years, the spectacle of so many Afghans killed for their possessions would lead him—like so many other participants—to believe looting turned the war against the Soviets.

V

The dusty city of Gardez rises from the Shah-i-Kot Valley, sixty miles south of Kabul near the soaring, snow-covered Gardez Mountains that neighbor a series of extensive mujahideen tunnel complexes. Sergei Salabayev arrived there on December 30, 1984, to join the Fifty-sixth Air Assault Brigade. The young private had studied in a technical vocational school in his native Novokuibishevsk—an oil-refinery city in Samara Region on the Volga River—specializing as a machine-tool worker. Soon after he was drafted, a fight between some young men in the town escalated when police showed up. An officer shot and killed one of the men, who turned on the police, setting their car on fire. All recent draftees from Novokuibishevsk were sent to Afghanistan as punishment.

In Gardez, the brigade's officers were busy scrounging supplies for New Year's Eve the following day. How to greet a new crop of conscripts was far less important than preparing for the biggest holiday of the year; the thirty draftees were taken to a tent that contained a heater, a small supply of coal, and nothing else. The next day, the men were given some bread and canned beef as a New Year's present. That evening, drunken horseplay around the base resulted in firing and several deaths.

The new arrivals were soon assembled by a group of soldiers in their second year of service: the *dedy*, or grandfathers, the Red Army's main instrument of enforcement among the ranks. This contingent told Salabayev's group to respect their superiors and obey their every order, one of the first of which was to wash their socks. Salabayev's refusal earned him a beating. Here, too, the only soldiers exempt from the tyranny of the *dedy* were the "civilians" who hadn't yet been demobilized although their time of service had ended. Exempted from missions and neither issuing orders nor doling out punishment, they did little more than sleep and eat.

Salabayev's first assignment was guarding one of the brigades' arms depots in a small stone warehouse near his tent, which he shared with three other conscripts. Not having been issued winter coats, the soldiers stood duty for twenty freezing nights in light field jackets. Salabayev managed to sleep only standing up and wedged against a wall, his sleeves pulled over his hands for warmth. He jogged in place when his feet began to go numb. Later, the soldiers improvised foot wrappings, *portianki*—which Soviet soldiers wore instead of socks—by cutting material from an insulated tent used for political-education lectures. Salabayev's duty also deprived him of meals. Since leaving one's post was a court-martial offense with severe punishment, soldiers often ate only by sneaking into the canteen to steal what they could find. Salabayev's strength diminished until he collapsed from exhaustion. Carried unconscious to his tent, he awoke two days later and found he'd lost his voice.

He was unable to speak for two weeks, but eventually regained his strength. Then he became so bored with life on the base that he dreamed of being sent on a mission into the mountains.

VI

Despite President Babrak Karmal's ineffectual rule, his government managed to reverse its steady loss of control. The army even began to rebuild its numbers, which may have fallen to as low as twenty thousand by 1983. Stricter conscription was partly responsible, but so was waxing civilian opposition to the often ruthless mujahideen, whose terrorist attacks were wounding and killing innocent people. The KhAD security service, under chief Mohammed Najibullah, swelled to eighteen thousand. Despite the gains, however, when French journalist Edward Girardet visited the Panjshir Valley in mid-1984, he reported seeing ten to fifteen desertions a day by Afghan Army soldiers.

In Kabul, the drive to liberate women from some of their most oppressive restrictions encouraged study and work, even in the military. "Contemporary photos of young women in smart KhAD uniforms performing responsible duties in the capital," writes historian Stephen Tanner, "reveal a stage in Afghan cultural history unique at the time and which has not since been repeated."

In the few parts of the country the Soviets controlled, they set up schools and day-care centers. Soviet officials also provided aid to farmers, then paid generously for their produce. But civilian aid of that kind was small compensation for the growing number of atrocities Soviet units committed elsewhere in the countryside. Most Afghans lived in constant fear of attack. In a conflict with no shortage of horror, the din of approaching Soviet Mi-24 helicopter gunships was perhaps most terrifying to the senses. Appearing as distant specks, the aircraft would grow larger and louder until they roared overhead on their way to pound rebel sites with rockets and bombs—or do the same to villages, often laying waste to them.

Although the Soviets launched no major offensives in 1983, they continued attacking civilian settlements and infrastructure. Since some of the people gave the rebels shelter and sustenance, that was an attempt—when it was not pure revenge or sadism— to destroy their support base. (In the Chechen war a decade later, the same scorched-earth strategy would be used against the civilian population, who in that case were citizens of Russia itself.) Wiping out civilians was also a form of ideological warfare used in the past. Joseph Stalin's policy of collectivization helped create a famine that killed millions in Ukraine in the 1930s. Forcing people from their land appeared preferable to dealing with "reactionaries," be they prosperous landowners or ancient tribes.

Much of Afghanistan's rural population was reduced to subsistence farming or utter ruin. By mid-1984, 3.5 million refugees had fled to Pakistan and another million had crossed the border into Iran. Up to 2 million people were internally displaced, most having fled to cities, whose population ballooned. Kabul's clogged streets and bustling bazaars teemed with provincial newcomers who milled about in the dust, together with rebels, spies, and many varieties of Soviets.

VII

In early 1982, Vladimir Kostiuchenko's helicopter squadron was switched from search-and-destroy and rescue missions to several weeks of desert attack training with other squadrons and paratroop units. In April, orders were given to paint over helicopters' red stars and other markings, remove all insignia from crews' uniforms, and leave documents in their barracks. They were to take part in a secret attack on what they believed to be a mujahideen camp west across the Afghan border in Iran.

Flying low over the ground at dawn one morning, twenty-five helicopters delivered a unit of troops across the border. All Kostiuchenko knew about his Mi-8's passengers was that they were probably *spetsnaz* fighters sent from Moscow. A Tupolev bomber overhead prepared to drop a flare that would illuminate the mujahideen base, but mistaken coordinates had the flare light a village instead. The helicopters unleashed their arsenals of rockets and bombs and destroyed the village. By the time the crews realized their error and located the nearby rebel base, the guerrillas had fled.

When the helicopters landed at the mud-walled base, the troops debarked to inspect the quarters and search for documents and anything else useful for intelligence. Abandoned weapons were hauled to the choppers, which took off heading back to Afghanistan.

Two Iranian F-4 Phantom jet fighters appeared on the horizon, raced toward the helicopters, and attacked them with rocket fire. Kostiuchenko saw a Mi-8 go down in flames before the fighters swooped around for another pass and riddled more helicopters with rocket and machine-gun fire. The helicopters tried to return fire but were more like sitting ducks than a match for the jets. If there's a hell, Kostiuchenko would remember thinking about the encounter, he'd seen it. Several Soviet MiGs were scrambled but not given permission to fire at the Iranian planes when they reached the site. Their presence was enough to make the Phantoms withdraw, however, and the crippled Soviet squadron, still inside Iranian territory, landed to inspect the damage.

Kostiuchenko's craft was unscathed, but many other helicopters not shot down had been badly hit. The crews of those in the worst condition clambered onto others, which reduced their weight by unloading everything possible, including rockets and ammunition rounds. They feared that if they didn't manage to return to Afghanistan, more Iranian jets would appear to destroy what was left of a mission about which no one was supposed to know. But one of the Soviet refuelers, a Mi-6, had been hit, leaving the pilots guessing whether they had enough fuel to get home.

Overloaded with the extra crew members, the flight-worthy helicopters had to take off by taxiing along the ground, then acquiring momentum by bouncing up and down three times, which was what it was supposed to take for Mi-8s to take off using that method. The wheels of Kostiuchenko's chopper touched down a nerve-racking nine times before it groaned into the air.

The maimed squadron drew sporadic light-arms fire from the ground as it flew east. When a bullet hit Kostiuchenko's fuel tank and started a leak, he switched to his three-hundred-liter emergency tank. He knew he'd made it over the border when the flat Rigestan desert appeared below, and he had just enough fuel to get him back to his base at Kandahar, where he was permitted to sleep for a day. The bureaucracy lost the paperwork for his award of an Order of the Red Star for his part in the operation. He received the medal more than twenty years later.

VIII

In the Kremlin, the ailing Yuri Andropov was caught up directing an anticorruption drive within the Soviet bureaucracy. The former KGB chairman knew the rot inside the system had reached an alarming rate. But the hard-liner was also consumed with fighting the Cold War. He ordered many KGB stations around the world to drop their priority operations and concentrate on searching for signs the United States was preparing a nuclear first strike against the Soviet Union.

During a Politburo meeting in March 1983, Foreign Minister Gromyko pressed for an end to the Afghanistan conflict.

"The situation in Afghanistan is, as you know, difficult," he said. "Lately, certain elements of consolidation have been examined, but the process of consolidation is moving slowly. The number of rebel gangs isn't decreasing. The enemy isn't laying down its weapons." Moscow had to do everything possible, he said, to reach a political settlement.

"What do you want?" Andropov replied. "This is a feudal country where tribes have always been in charge of their territories, and central authority far from always able to reach every *kishlak*."

Andropov may have acknowledged the problems in Afghanistan, but he wasn't about to change course. "We're fighting against American imperialism, which well understands that in this part of international politics it has lost its positions," he said. "That's why we can't back off." Still, some believe Yuri Andropov eventually realized Moscow couldn't win a military campaign in Afghanistan. If so, he did nothing about it before he died in February 1984.

Andropov's replacement, veteran Party functionary Konstantin Chernenko, was so debilitated by emphysema, liver failure, chronic hepatitis, and other ailments that he could barely read Andropov's eulogy. Chernenko nevertheless stepped up the war effort, chiefly by ordering more mine-laying, ground attacks, and carpet-bombing of the countryside. On the theory that injured resistance fighters burdened the mujahideen more than dead ones, the mines dropped by Soviet planes included hundreds of thousands designed to maim rather than kill. Although Soviet veterans deny knowledge of any such thing, a UN report also documented testimony about mines intended for children being disguised as toys. The same report also described widespread torture by Soviet and Afghan government forces.

For now, the truce the Soviets had signed with Ahmed Shah Massoud the previous year kept the Panjshir Valley largely free of fighting. Crucially for the Fortieth Army, the rebel leader had agreed not to attack the vital Salang highway supply lifeline in return for a respite from fighting that would enable him to regroup forces that had absorbed the brunt of the Soviet onslaught. Massoud believed the truce would also help make Panjshir a safe area that would play a key part in his plan to wrest control of the country from the government. But many Afghans, especially other mujahideen commanders, derided Massoud for collaborating with the Soviets—in order to enhance his own power, they accused. Whatever the truth of that, the truce did free Soviet soldiers to attack elsewhere. In 1983, the Soviet 108th MRD, which had been previously deployed against Massoud, took part in operations with Afghan troops in the Shomali Valley north of Kabul and against other mujahideen bases near the capital.

Meanwhile, Massoud spent the year retraining his men and replenishing his supplies. The truce enabled him to boost his forces to some five thousand men armed with two-hundred-odd heavy antiaircraft machine guns, several captured Soviet tanks, 120-mm howitzers, and large quantities of small arms and mines. Many residents of the valley—half of whom had fled—returned to rebuild their shattered villages and farms.

But Massoud's many spies in the Afghan military and government informed him that the more the Soviets learned about his plans to build his own civil administration to win over the population, the greater their concern grew. The Soviets were also frustrated with what they now saw as scant results from their large-scale bombing attacks. Indiscriminate raids and other displays of military might appeared to stoke anger more than break the back of the mujahideen's popular support, as intended. The generals were learning the limits of intimidation. Small, mud-walled buildings were easily rebuilt. Bombing into submission a population with little major infrastructure for targets was virtually impossible.

Massoud survived two Soviet assassination attempts. In March, he turned down an offer to extend the truce, then resumed his attacks on the Salang highway the following month.

IX

Massoud had to expect the Soviets would respond with another assault on the Panjshir Valley, and his agents soon confirmed precisely that. The Fortieth Army's generals had begun preparing what would become known as Panjshir-7, their biggest assault operation in Afghanistan so far. The rebel commander ordered most of the civilian population to evacuate the valley along with his own forces. While he hunkered down to wait out the onslaught, one group of fighters went north, including Commander Abdul Nasir Ziyaee, who set up in Takhar Region. Others trekked east to establish a camp in the border area with Pakistan. Radio contact between groups remained minimal.

Meanwhile, the enemy was stationing three squadrons of Tu-16 bombers across the border on Soviet territory. Each plane carried ten tons of ordnance. At the same time, the 108th MRD, reassembling at the foot of the valley, was making ready to take overall command of the offensive, which would include battalions from Jalalabad and Ghazni. Five thousand Afghan Army troops would supplement the fifteen-thousand-strong Soviet force taking part in the attack.

Massoud hit first: a preemptive strike intended to disrupt the Soviet preparations. After blowing up three bridges along the Salang highway on April 16, his forces further narrowed supply channels to Kabul by ambushing a fuel convoy the following day. The day after that, other units struck a Soviet-Afghan garrison near the entrance to the valley. On April 21, the mujahideen attacked Bagram, but the thousands of troops who had collected there repelled them and went on to launch their attack.

Heavy bombing of the valley floor by Tu-16s flying at high altitudes appeared to catch Massoud by surprise and caused a relatively high number of mujahideen casualties. A Soviet ground offensive began soon thereafter, minesweeping vehicles again leading rumbling motorized columns up the narrow valley floor and soon to the village of Ruha, about a third of the way up the valley. More barrages of bombs and artillery destroyed trees, shattered houses, and cleared mujahideen from the armored columns, and Abdul Wahed, one of the mujahideen spokesmen for their cause abroad, was a prize among prisoners taken. By the end of the week, the rolling barrages enabled the Soviets to reach Khenj, about halfway up, where they were stopped by snow that hadn't yet thawed.

Soviet counterinsurgency tactics had improved. This time, troops from the main columns refrained from pursuing rebels retreating into side valleys, where Massoud's mobile strike forces were waiting for opportunities to stage counterattacks. Red Army planners had learned to combine bombing, air, and ground attacks, and increasingly used their own fast mobile forces, usually delivered by helicopter, in the mujahideen rear to block escape routes.

During the first week of May, thousands of elite troops left Bagram in helicopters heading to locations where the Soviets hoped they would intercept mujahideen forces in the branch valleys. Mi-24s accompanied the battalions of airborne troops, attacking resistance fighters flushed out of their positions. One large force

Soviet soldiers fighting in Panjshir, 1984. (*Alexander Liakhovskii archive*)

was deposited above Khenj at the head of the valley; another from Jalalabad obstructed the Alishang Valley leading southeast from Panjshir. With their escape routes cut off, surprised rebel forces climbed ever higher into the mountains to flee multipronged Soviet attacks. Casualties crippled some mujahideen units; others were forced into remote positions unreachable even by the best Soviet *spetsnaz* and airborne troops.

Several weeks later, when the apparent success of Panjshir-7 had the Soviets believing they'd finally beaten Massoud, Kabul Radio announced that "the criminal band of Ahmed Shah no longer exists." For the first time, Soviet forces felt confident enough to leave behind garrisons (that would remain there for four years) to prevent future attacks on the Salang highway. Even the highly cautious Karmal felt safe enough to visit the valley to demonstrate his government's control.

Still, Massoud remained unbowed. From his refuge high in the Panjshir Mountains, he claimed the Soviets had failed to achieve their objectives. While admitting to journalist Edward Girardet that Soviet heliborne troops had become more skillful, he said his men had also learned how to fight at high altitudes, and that the enemy would not achieve a standoff against them. But because he was convinced the Soviets could eventually succeed by destroying the support base of the mujahideen, his main concern was the civilian population. "Failing to crush us by force, they have turned their wrath on defenseless people. Killing old men, women and children, destroying houses and burning crops."

Some of Massoud's men were less convinced. One of his closest lieutenants, a tall, long-bearded commander named Atta Mohammed Noor, and known as Teacher Atta, believed the wholesale Soviet bombardment of villages and farms would only further infuriate the population and jeopardize the government's control with each attack. Atta had been surprised to hear little or nothing about ideology from captured Soviets. Unlike the mujahideen, the enemy soldiers appeared to be merely following orders, and their lack of conviction would never enable them to win the military struggle.

Apart from that, the huge Soviet focus on Panjshir indirectly benefited Massoud by advertising his activities, which helped attract more support from abroad. His mujahideen also drew solace from the knowledge that the concentration of so much Soviet force in the valley prevented the enemy from operating elsewhere. And Massoud's own fighters recovered enough by September to begin attacking the Soviet garrisons. During one ambush, they claimed to have killed 440 Soviets at the cost of only 2 commanders of their own.

In a night ambush on a convoy in the Panjshir Valley, Commander Ziyaee, himself stationed in the hills above to observe, spaced thirty of his fighters along a kilometer of a Panjshir River tributary south of Badakshan Province. When an expected Russian convoy rumbled past, the mujahideen attacked it with two RPG-2 and two RPG-7 rocket grenades, and fired a hundred Kalashnikov bullets rationed among each. Ziyaee claims to have killed more than four hundred Soviets, while other units blocked some hundred tanks and armored personnel carriers farther down the valley.

However, another Panjshir offensive was soon launched at Massoud. Soviet forces also staged an assault in Paktia Province southeast of Kabul and a larger one in the Kunar Valley near Pakistan. While those attacks pushed back mujahideen forces even farther,

Soviet soldiers remove a charred corpse from a disabled
personnel carrier. *(Alexander Liakhovskii archive)*

others also faced serious trouble, and some commanders were hurting. They included Ismail Khan, who was fighting around Herat, most of whose civilian population had escaped to Iran. Short of supplies, many mujahideen groups were forced to lie low against Soviet air and land strikes.

Toward the end of 1984, another top commander, named Zabiullah, who had operated in the country's north, was killed. Zabiullah had been loyal to Rabbani, and some suspected the xenophobic Hekmatyar's fighters of having laid the mine that blew up his jeep. In any case, his death undermined what little unity there had been among Iran-backed Shia forces in the Hazarajat.

X

Vladimir Kostiuchenko was posted to a Siberian air base after his yearlong tour in Kandahar. The helicopter pilot felt too shattered to watch films, listen to music, or kill time in other ordinarily diverting ways. While his response, boosted by spontaneous tears that caused him increasing embarrassment, was to withdraw from people, other Afghanistan veterans he knew became aggressive. One would stand on his apartment's balcony lobbing imaginary grenades at the cars below, then picture dead and wounded swimming in blood. More than anything, Kostiuchenko was traumatized by the civilian deaths he'd witnessed: settlements destroyed by accident or on purpose; soldiers bayoneting babies and killing all the other inhabitants of seemingly innocent villages. An elderly man—one of the several Afghans who flew from a village he'd just helped bomb into a pile of rubble—reminded him of his father. He could not erase that image.

Just after Mikhail Gorbachev succeeded Konstantin Chernenko in March 1985, Kostiuchenko was rotated back to Afghanistan, now to the lush river valley of Jalalabad, where orders to try to avoid civilian deaths when possible put him in a seemingly different war. Rather than fire at anything that moved below, patrol missions were to stop cars and investigate their occupants. But being careful caused more Soviet casualties.

Kostiuchenko participated in operations to flush out rebels in Panjshir, usually after Afghan agents had informed the Soviets of the whereabouts of mujahideen bases or approaching caravans. One 1985 mission in the mountains around the town of Sarawbi east of Kabul was to destroy a large group of rebels believed to be holed up in several caves. Although mountain operations were the most dangerous, with rocket grenade and machine-gun fire coming from seemingly nowhere on the sides of valleys, helicopters rarely blew up. More often, they'd be crippled and forced to land. The crew members of several choppers that were hit during that operation's first day were rescued by other helicopters that landed while still others covered from the air. The commander of one disabled craft whose crew Kostiuchenko's Mi-8 rescued vowed he'd return for a Kalashnikov he'd left behind, despite a face white with terror. When paratroops discovered the cave from which his helicopter had been hit, they saw it had been obscured from the air by a gray blanket covering its entrance. In addition to a kerosene heater and a supply of rifles and grenades inside, they found a kettle that was still warm. The rescued commander was killed the following day.

XI

Newspaperman Mikhail Kozhukhov also arrived in Afghanistan in 1985.

Any illusions the rugged-featured, dark-haired young reporter for *Komsomolskaya pravda* had about his new assignment were quickly dispelled. On the first operation he witnessed, a heliborne attack in the Panjshir Valley, a platoon of paratroopers located a mujahideen weapons cache in the mountains. But what really interested the platoon were the good sleeping bags they also spotted. Their delight at their find, and their poor equipment in general, shocked Kozhukhov. In addition to warm sleeping gear— far warmer and more water-resistant than the Soviet, cotton-filled variety—they were also short of heating fuel and, even that far into the war, edible food. The young reporter often saw soldiers eating rotten potatoes and cabbage. Hospital patients being treated for hepatitis, typhus, and anemia were lucky to get grain cereals. Although many varieties of good, cheap fruit—melons, pomegranates, grapes, apricots—were easily available, the military forbade supplying local produce. Everything in its centrally planned system had to come from the Soviet Union.

Barred from reporting such facts—and the overall conduct of the war, not to mention its ideological paradoxes—Kozhukhov set himself a goal of simply mentioning as many names as possible. That, he comforted himself, would at least provide some satisfaction to the families of the heroes and victims he encountered. Soon he was identifying with the soldiers to the point of violating journalistic codes by picking up a Kalashnikov and taking part in at least one operation he was supposedly covering.

Almost all attempts to foil the censors failed. Even mention of hospitals had been forbidden before 1985, apparently because it might have darkened the required sunny depiction of the war effort. When Kozhukhov mentioned a canteen and a nearby library in a description of a military base in Ugha, west of Herat, a censor returned a draft of the article with the description crossed out for being too specific. The explanation was that "The American enemy would guess that only a regiment would have a library." Summoned to Moscow to explain that and other transgressions to the Central Committee, Kozhukhov was also given a new set of guidelines that permitted him to describe military operations only on the battalion level; anything higher was deemed to provide too much notion of overall operations. And no more than one fatality and three injuries could be mentioned in any one article.

As with many of the soldiers and officers with whom he sympathized, Kozhukhov considered the yawning gap between the war's official version and its reality on the ground only partly responsible for the massive disenchantment with the authorities and the war. While bitterly criticizing Moscow for involving the Red Army in a war it didn't understand, then setting unachievable objectives for it, some veterans still sustained their belief in their international duty to help fellow communists. The higher their rank, the more that was likely. The horror and suffering actually inflicted on the Afghan people may have encouraged acceptance of the propaganda as a way of living with their role in the destruction.

Many young men's more immediate and important problems were abuse from their superiors, on top of their material privations. Perhaps nothing more could have been expected of a political system founded on mass murder and preserved with oppression. But that was irrelevant to those provided barely enough supplies to keep them alive off battlefields where they were risking their lives. Common anguish helped stoke a fierce camaraderie, which reinforced the understanding that each fighting unit would do everything possible to rescue its wounded and recover its dead. Especially since the commands, no doubt in the grip of the old Soviet suspicion that men taken by the enemy were probably traitors, did virtually nothing to try to rescue soldiers taken prisoner by the mujahideen. But in 1989, when dissident Andrei Sakharov—one of the war's most prominent critics from the beginning—would denounce the war as a "criminal adventure," many veterans would take it as criticism of themselves. Most rankling would be his condemnation of the miserable Soviet record on rescuing its prisoners of war, which they would interpret as blaming them for the deaths of their comrades.

Kozhukhov twice occupied barracks rooms next to "Black Tulip" helicopter squadrons assigned to recover dead bodies. The corpses were shipped back to the Soviet Union in zinc coffins, classified as "Freight 200." Kozhukhov heard many stories about soldiers killed while trying to recover the bodies of their fallen comrades, some attempts even resulting in downings of helicopters. On top of the great risks members of many armies in many countries take for the sake of honor and the sacred bond between fighting men, every Soviet soldier knew that families back home would receive no compensation without a corpse to show.

Some coffins returned empty. One purported to contain the remains of Colonel Alexander Golovanov, who commanded the Fiftieth Composite Air Regiment in Kabul. During the war's last days in February 1989, Golovanov would give a final order for the regiment to return to the Soviet Union, then fly back himself in his helicopter, which disappeared. The colonel was extremely popular among his men, who joined an exhaustive search for the missing craft. It was never found.

XII

Six months after his arrival in Gardez, Private Sergei Salabayev was transferred to an artillery regiment and assigned to a three-man group operating a multiple-rocket launcher installed on a truck. As elsewhere, many of its operations were chiefly devoted to destroying civilian settlements. Soldiers too frightened to conduct house-to-house searches for mujahideen—or simply seeking revenge—blew up farm plots and killed livestock. Afghans spotted fleeing were shot, as were the owners of anything worthy of stealing, often no more than wristwatches. Combat operations fighting the rebels were invariably far less efficient. A quarter of the rockets delivered for Salabayev's launcher were duds, and many of those that worked had trouble hitting their targets.

Crippling demoralization helped feed widespread drug use, and not only among the troops. Salabayev's commanding lieutenants regularly sent him to a Gardez kiosk near a military airstrip to buy hashish made from the cannabis raised in many fields outside the city. That was in addition to the drugs provided free, some thrown onto passing armored personnel carriers, by Afghans eager to undermine the Soviet effort.

Salabayev's drinking was limited only by the difficulty of obtaining alcohol or the ingredients to manufacture it. A bottle of vodka cost between ten and twenty *cheki*, prohibitive for soldiers, even if Salabayev's regiment weren't stationed some six miles from the rest of his brigade and the nearest military store. Local taverns, called *dukhany*, sold canned beer but that, too, was usually far too expensive. Buying vodka from helicopter pilots who flew in cases from the Soviet Union was often simpler as well as cheaper, but the best alternative was brewing one's own. Although officers got the vast bulk of the supplies used for that, as with most comforts of military life, enterprising soldiers managed to not stay sober. The most basic ingredient, fermented from yeast and sugar, was called *braga*. Yeast was available from the bakeries on many military bases, and canteens' sugar supplies could also be raided; but medical or industrial spirit, even aviation fuel, were quicker and easier to use. To filter his moonshine, Salabayev used carbon particles pried from gas masks. Anything sweet on hand, such as candy or raisins, was infused into the noxious concoctions to mask their taste.

Brewing was a collective effort, and not always voluntary: *dedy* sometimes forced junior draftees to prepare alcohol—and risk the punishment. Although many *praporshchiki*, the rough equivalent of sergeants in the West, were hard drivers with little sympathy for the men in their units, Salabayev's Armenian *praporshchik* was an exception. He not only stole from the canteen to feed his men but also helped them conceal their alcohol supplies; even assisted in obtaining some of the ingredients.

Soldiers tried to stockpile alcohol supplies for holidays, including a celebration that marked a hundred days of remaining service. For that event, some shaved their heads and, to prevent officers from ruining the festivities, buried or otherwise hid alcohol wherever possible, sometimes in fire extinguishers emptied of water. Marijuana was usually cheaper and more readily available than alcohol, and Salabayev smoked it as often as he could, while others used heroin, some of it left in the barracks by mujahideen who infiltrated in order to hook Soviet conscripts. Salabayev witnessed two fellow soldiers turn into "ghosts" in a few months, after which they were soon discharged. Although he tried to economize by limiting his smoking when not on missions, Salabayev rarely set out on one without getting high. Privates in infantry units usually had the luxury of lighting up only after battles were over, but he was lucky in being able to worry less about his safety because his rocket launcher usually set up at some distance from the fighting.

Marijuana also calmed Salabayev's nerves during convoys, which his little unit's weapon made especially dangerous. Mujahideen ambushers hated the 120-mm rocket launchers almost as much as helicopter gunships, and usually targeted them immediately. Having learned that rebels ordinarily went first for convoys' lead and last vehicles, Salabayev tried hard to stay away from both if he could. Although dismayed at being stuck with a weapon manufactured in the 1960s and designed even earlier, he was relatively happy that his rocket launcher was affixed to the back of a GAZ-66 truck, which was lighter and faster than the usual heavy Kamaz or Ural rigs. Salabayev and his comrades made the vehicle even more maneuverable by removing as much as they could of its armor plating.

They also rarely wore their flak jackets. Salabayev found his heavy and uncomfortable, and positively intolerable during the heat of summer. On one of the rare, coldest days when he did put it on in an attempt to stay warm, his convoy was ambushed near Gardez. Having recently smoked a joint, he had no idea what was happening when gunfire erupted all around him. Afterward, his chest hurt, and he found it badly bruised when he got around to having a look. A later inspection of his flak jacket uncovered a bullet squashed like a rivet, right in front.

The miserable, sometimes depraved conditions weren't pervasive. Experiences differed widely among the units, some of whose officers cared deeply about the men under their command and refused to tolerate hazing. And there was much heroism as well as sadism. Valery Vostrotin became a shining example of the former, at least according to the stories that circulated about him. Vostrotin returned to Afghanistan in 1986 as a colonel to lead the 2,500 men of the 345th Paratroop Regiment. It was said that after two draftees complained to him about having been hazed, he lined up his men as if for a drill before dawn the following morning. Calling out the names of the *dedy* whom the conscripts had accused of having beaten them, he ordered the victims to return the favor. Bunk frames were lugged out and the *dedy* were forced to suspend their bodies by their feet and heads while the abused soldiers used cigarettes to burn "200 days until demobilization" into their skin.

XIII

Despite the tough going and personnel changes that at first appeared unpromising, late 1984 heralded a turning point for the Soviets. When Defense Minister Dmitry Ustinov, one of the chief proponents of the Afghanistan invasion, died in December, he was replaced by one of its chief architects, Marshal Sergei Sokolov. At the same time, Valentin Varennikov, deputy head of the Soviet

General Staff, took over as head of the Soviet Southern Theater of Military Operations and head of military forces in Afghanistan. The promotions were part of a broader movement of Afghanistan veteran officers up the hierarchy. Back in Moscow, the "Afghan Brotherhood," as the writer Alexander Prokhanov called the group, recognized one another by their dress and mannerisms.

After participating in the defense of Moscow against Hitler's invading army in 1941 and the battle of Stalingrad the following year, Varennikov ended the Great Patriotic War—as the Soviets called World War II—commanding soldiers who helped capture the Reichstag in Berlin. Although the mustachioed aging hero was among the many members of the military leadership who initially opposed the invasion of Afghanistan, he would come to symbolize how the top brass were conducting the war. Many blamed years of unnecessary casualties on his rosy biannual reports to the Politburo about steady progress. But the Politburo itself was about to undergo great change. When Varennikov, shortly after his December appointment, delivered his first report in his new capacity to the Politburo's Afghanistan committee, which was chaired by Foreign Minister Gromyko, he described progress in his immediate task of closing Afghanistan's border with Pakistan by building up a force of Afghan border guards. Halfway through his presentation, he was surprised to see another Politburo member enter the room and sit down opposite him at the conference table. After listening to the boilerplate optimism, Mikhail Gorbachev unequivocally delivered *his* opinion: Soviet troops must be withdrawn from Afghanistan.

Months later, Gorbachev would become the Soviet leader. The law school graduate had been Party boss of his native southern Stavropol Region until brought to Moscow in 1978 by a promotion that made him the Central Committee's secretary of agriculture. The following year, he joined the Politburo, where Andropov became his patron. Gorbachev's coming to power as general secretary in March 1985—as the youngest Politburo member and fourth Soviet head of state in three years—would greatly affect the course of the war, the future of Russia, and the condition of the world.

Unlike his ailing predecessors, he planned massive reforms that would transform the Soviet economy and open its society—if he could secure approval, which would be very difficult. Opposition by many Party leaders forced him to seek support where he could find it, including the military. Partly to cultivate it, he decided to give the Red Army a year of full freedom to carry out the war in Afghanistan as it saw fit, before winding down.

American politics would also help change the war's course and seal its eventual outcome. The foreign-policy attention of Ronald Reagan, who won a landslide reelection in 1984, was fixed on opposing communist regimes in Nicaragua and El Salvador. But Congress would soon pressure him to sign his national security directive announcing Washington's unequivocal support of the mujahideen. The quarter of a billion dollars the United States sent Pakistan later in 1985 was more than all aid given in previous years together.

Still, it would be many months before developments in Moscow and Washington would be felt in Afghanistan. In 1985, the Soviets and their Afghan government allies were gaining the upper hand in severe fighting that caused heavy casualties on both sides. In January, the Soviets began several major offensives aimed at flushing out mujahideen groups from their bases. The Afghan Army, its numbers growing and troops better trained, took a prominent part in many of those attacks. After the spring thaw, Soviet forces used newly developed cluster bombs with sixty highly lethal bomblets in an assault on the Maidan Valley south of Kabul. In May, a Soviet-Afghan attack moved up the Kunar Valley north of Jalalabad to Barikot, at the top of the valley next to the Pakistan border, where mujahideen had been attacking a garrison of Afghan forces.

After the successful offensive, Varennikov made his first trip as war supremo outside Kabul. He traveled to Jalalabad, then north to Asadabad and Barikot, where a group of elders promised to withhold support for the mujahideen if he called off Soviet bombing of their villages. Struck by the simplicity of the proposition, which reinforced one of his strongest criticisms of Babrak Karmal,

Varennikov agreed. Whereas Karmal, always trying to increase his control of the provinces, was appointing officials from the Interior Ministry, KhAD, and other central agencies to administrative posts there, Varennikov believed that introduction of outsiders only fed distrust of government. His meeting with the elders further convinced him that his forces would be much better off if locals were allowed to run their own affairs.

Although drought on top of the destruction of Afghanistan's rural economy and infrastructure were making it increasingly difficult for the mujahideen to live off the land, the rebels were aided by the fast-growing support from abroad. New weapons—including shoulder-fired SA-7 missiles and Chinese 107-mm and 122-mm rockets with greater ranges than mortars—would soon be added to the boots, blankets, and radios they were receiving: weapons that would enable them to fire into cities and government outposts. Meanwhile, foreign Muslims were streaming to Afghanistan to help fight the jihad.

Despite their setbacks in the field, the rebels continued raiding military installations and ambushing Soviet columns. In mid-June, Massoud's forces made one of the war's most daring attacks against an Afghan Army garrison in the Panjshir Valley. After the Panjshir-7 offensive, Afghan and Soviet forces for the most part had confined themselves to helicopter patrols. The northernmost army garrison, a battalion of some five hundred men, was stationed at the village of Pechgur. Clearing mines at night, Massoud's fighters stormed the fortress, which a delegation of high-ranking officers happened to be visiting. The rebels killed an Afghan general and colonel and captured some five hundred prisoners, including five more colonels. Massoud was marching about a quarter of them up Panjshir toward a pass leading out of the valley when the Soviets launched another offensive. This one, Panjshir-9, was entirely unsuccessful. Instead of heading off Massoud's men and rescuing the prisoners, helicopter-borne troops found the Soviets' corpses; all 130-odd had been killed—by Soviet bombs, the mujahideen said improbably.

In late August 1985, the Soviets launched their largest operation since Panjshir-7, a drive to flush out rebel bases in Logar Region south of the capital. While troops pushed south from Kabul and east from Jalalabad, heliborne attacks centered on several important mujahideen camps. Moving toward Khost, southeast of Kabul, other troops engaged rebels in the mountains, where in a rare instance of cooperation, four hundred of Hekmatyar's men rescued a group of Sayyaf's fighters under fire from Soviet troops. After reaching Khost, the Soviets moved farther south, toward a large mujahideen tunnel complex, but growing resistance stopped them in September.

Resuming the offensive the following spring, the Afghan Army spearheaded an attack against an important mujahideen logistics base in Zhawar, on the Pakistan border. Guarded by a rudimentary air defense system, the base consisted of an extensive tunnel network run by a fundamentalist commander named Jallaladin Haqqani, of Yunis Khalis's Islamic Party. The complex housed generators, a telephone system, and workshops. Western journalists and foreign officials had been invited to visit the important symbol of rebel independence.

The attack began after more than four thousand airborne troops landed in Khost, due north of Zhawar. In coordination, some eight thousand motorized troops moved southeast from Gardez, while Soviet planes repeatedly bombed the complex of huge tunnels and heliborne troops prevented mujahideen groups from retreating into the mountains at the Pakistani border. After intense fighting in the hills and tunnels killed as many as a thousand mujahideen, the Soviet-Afghan forces eventually prevailed, capturing tons of armaments, including four mujahideen tanks and many thousands of mines, and giving a major boost to the Afghan Army's morale.

XIV

Valentin Varennikov wasn't the only high-ranking Soviet official fed up with what was seen as Babrak Karmal's weak authority, counterproductive policies, and fondness for drink. To buttress public support, Karmal held a *loya jirga* meeting of regional representatives in April 1985, and followed it with elections. But although he also set up a "national reconciliation commission" to draft a new constitution the next year, the Kremlin forced the Afghan president to step down. He was sent to the Soviet Union in April 1986, ostensibly for medical examinations. When he failed to appear at the all-important annual April Revolution parade on April 27, it was clear his days were numbered. A week later, the PDPA's Central Committee dismissed him on health grounds and appointed as general secretary thirty-eight-year-old Mohammed Najibullah, until then the KhAD security service chief. Karmal would retain the title of president until November, when a powerless figure named Mohammed Chamkani would replace him—before he was replaced, in turn, by Najibullah in November 1987.

The Soviets running the Afghanistan campaign, from Varennikov down, got along well with burly, gregarious Najibullah, Karmal's opposite in physique and temperament. Varennikov considered "Najib," who spoke English and a smattering of French, politically astute as well as educated. The founding member of the Parcham wing of the PDPA was a grandson of a Pashtun tribal chief, both important credentials for an authority figure, and this one was very fond of authority. Under Amin, Najibullah was exiled to Iran as ambassador before being sacked and stripped of his citizenship. He returned to Afghanistan after the Soviet invasion. An avid player in Afghanistan's murderous political maneuverings, the security chief was notorious for participating in torture and executions. His influence had grown steadily under Karmal, partly thanks to his successful undermining of rival Sarandoi forces under Guliabzoi's Interior Ministry, a bastion of the PDPA's Khalq wing. After KhAD investigators had begun arresting Sarandoi officers and accusing them of anti-Soviet activities in 1985, the Ministry of State Security was formed in January 1986, to oversee some Sarandoi units. (Guliabzoi's ministry survived those attacks. But President Najibullah would continue seeing Guliabzoi as one of his

(Left to right) Afghan Interior Minister Said Mohammed Guliabzoi, Valentin Varennikov, chief of Soviet forces in Afghanistan, Afghan President Mohammed Najibullah, and Afghan Defense Minister Mohammed Rafi in Kandahar. *(Alexander Liakhovskii archive)*

main rivals. After a series of confrontations, he was sent to Moscow in 1988 to serve as Afghanistan's ambassador.)

Najibullah had also taken advantage of events in Pakistan. In late 1985, the Pakistani government staged attacks against Pashtun tribal leaders in the lawless Northwest Frontier Province bordering Afghanistan. Najibullah boosted his authority among Pashtuns by pledging support and arms to the outraged warlords. Varennikov believed he had a good chance of effecting the "national reconciliation" the Soviet war chief considered key to stabilizing the conflict and withdrawing his troops. In one of the first of many meetings with Najib and his chief Soviet adviser, Victor Polyanichko, the three agreed to exploit Afghanistan's 580 military road checkpoints, each manned by dozens of Soviet and Afghan soldiers. With their direct interaction with much of the population, Varennikov thought they could be used to distribute food, fuel, soap, and other goods for wooing Afghans in a new drive to sap civilian support for the mujahideen. But the ongoing Soviet occupation undermined that effort and others to boost government support.

Najibullah's popularity in the countryside would be little greater than his predecessor's.

However, the Soviets continued gaining the upper hand in the war. Unable to operate under unified command, the scattered mujahideen were on the defensive. Still, Moscow's military dominance did little to help achieve the ultimate goal of enabling a friendly communist government to effectively rule Afghanistan. The war had dragged on for five hard years, and the rebels, with deft use of bravado and foreign help, continued to face down a far more powerful force. The fighting had only become more intense during the year Gorbachev had given the military to wrap up the war. In February 1986, he told a Communist Party Congress in Moscow that "counterrevolution and imperialism have transformed Afghanistan into a bleeding wound."

Three months later, in May 1986, the United Nations, which had brokered faltering negotiations between the Afghan and Pakistani governments since 1982, sponsored peace talks between the Soviets and the mujahideen. At a summit in Geneva in November 1985, Gorbachev had made clear to Reagan he was serious about withdrawing his forces from Afghanistan—in four years, the new Soviet leader offered. However, negotiations ended with no agreement. Soon Gorbachev unilaterally announced a partial withdrawal: from a force that had bloated to 115,000, he would remove 6,000. But American intelligence claimed that while some heavy units were indeed brought home, 9,000 more Soviet troops were dispatched to Afghanistan that year.

Varennikov would later blame Washington for playing the leading role in thwarting a successful resolution of the war by preventing national reconciliation. Surely the CIA was doing everything it could to persuade the mujahideen leaders to continue trapping the Soviet Union in a draining, crippling conflict. Wasn't it obvious that that was sound, highly effective Cold War policy?

CHAPTER 6

THE TIDE TURNS

I

In September 1985, Nikolai Kalita's commanding officer called him into his office inside the sprawling new Finnish-designed headquarters of the KGB's First Chief Directorate. The flagship foreign intelligence division was located in a concrete-block suburb of Moscow called Yasenevo. Twenty-six-year-old Kalita ran a nearby safe house for KGB guests from Nicaragua, Cuba, and other Soviet client states. During his five years with the KGB, the extremely fit, gregarious officer had attracted his superiors' attention.

"How do you feel about joining 'Group A'?" Kalita's boss asked, but wasn't surprised by his subordinate's quizzical look. Like most in the KGB, the younger officer had never heard of it.

"Do you know anything about the storming of Amin's palace in Afghanistan?"

Kalita had heard about the now-legendary operation that had taken place six years earlier, including the leading role played by the *spetsnaz*. "I do know a little something about it," he answered.

"Well, it was Group A that took the palace."

Seeking to break the stalemate in Afghanistan, the KGB was further increasing its *spetsnaz* operations, and Kalita didn't think twice
about accepting the rare offer to be included. He joined a group of
KGB officers undergoing a barrage of tests to determine whether they
were physically and psychologically fit enough to join the agency's new-
est and most elite special forces group, soon to be renamed Alpha.

"You're in the taiga with another officer for three days," Kalita
was challenged during one of his sessions. "There's no water and all
that's left in your canteen is several gulps. Your comrade has drunk
all his, but he still asks you for a drink. Do you give him some?" Yes
he would, Kalita nodded. It was apparently the correct answer.

Routines were constantly varied in an effort to catch candi-
dates off guard. Having relaxed with them in a discussion of family
life over coffee, interrogators would suddenly spring again. "Are
you prepared to die tomorrow?" A *Yes!* deemed too slow brought
dismissal. So did insufficient toughness or lack of inclination for
physical confrontation, for which a record of brawling and even
arrest were considered worthy evidence.

After Kalita made the cut, he entered a rigorous training
course much like the one Valery Kurilov of Zenit had taken six
years earlier before his participation in the taking of the Taj-Bek
palace. This time, the preparation was supplemented by real missions. For one, Kalita joined Interior Ministry officers in freeing the
passengers of a plane hijacked by two soldiers in the Siberian city
of Ufa. They killed one passenger and two policemen before being
captured. Despite the difficulty of his training, Kalita enjoyed the
relatively relaxed relations between the men and their commanders,
since the KGB believed the cream of its special forces need not be
subjected to the usual chickenshit.

The final test would be a two-month stint in Afghanistan
starting in December 1986. Given false legends, or identities, some
Group A officers posed as engineers, while Kalita and others went as
army conscripts. Although their destination was secret, their notice
to family members that they were leaving to train in Soviet Central
Asia was partly true because their first destination was the dusty

Turkmen town of Kerki, forty miles north of the Afghan border. Their arrival in uniforms with no insignias mystified the soldiers of an elite paratroop unit they joined. The new men's average age of around thirty made them too old for conscripts, and they had NATO-issued knives, impressive-looking compasses, and strange spherical helmets with built-in two-way radios. They were also permitted to wear sunglasses and modify their uniforms, which was ordinarily forbidden to Red Army soldiers.

After several days of acclimatization and briefings about the latest happenings in Afghanistan, the *spetsnaz* officers were flown to Sheberghan, in the country's northern flatland, which was littered with burned-out carcasses of planes and helicopters. The men were billeted with a motorized rifle regiment whose chief task was protecting Soviet engineers working in the region's natural gas fields. Walking Sheberghan's streets, Kalita had to stop himself staring at the strange sight of women in burkas and young boys with outstretched hands who pestered, *"Baksheesh! Baksheesh!"* in a hope of cajoling money or a gift. Outside the cities, much of northern Afghanistan was under the control of Uzbek and Tajik mujahideen commanders whose alliances often shifted. An Uzbek named Rasul Pahlawan with a reputation for higher-than-average ruthlessness dominated Faryab Region. In February, the Soviets received intelligence that he was planning to relocate his rebel group to Pakistan after losing a standoff with local Pashtuns. Although Afghan Army and Soviet forces moved in to block his path, there were many places through which he could easily slip.

Later that month, Group A men were sent in to intercept and ambush Pahlawan's column. The Soviets had gotten additional word that it was moving along a dried-out riverbed in desert scrubland. Shortly before midnight, Kalita joined a group of some thirty troops, including a Soviet mortar squad and Afghan Army soldiers. Driving south from Sheberghan for three hours in three BTRs, they set up near a bend in the riverbank. They began with the very hard work of digging foxholes in the pitch darkness. Kalita was preparing to man a machine gun propped up next to a Group A sniper when the major in command ordered him to take a message to the communications unit, dug in a short distance from them. Leaving his foxhole, barely able to see where he was stumbling in the dark, he heard Russian voices as he approached the radio unit. The mortar squad's commander was in an animated discussion with two lieutenants.

"Seryozha, they've got more than two thousand fighters!" he said.

"I don't believe it! Then we're seriously fucked!" another officer replied. The mujahideen group, far larger than expected, was all but certain to overwhelm the tiny band of Soviet and Afghan troops.

Kalita made his way back to his position, where the men, ordered to prepare to fight, crouched in foxholes on both sides of the riverbed. With plenty of time to think while he waited, Kalita told himself it was natural to be scared; he'd learned fear was a constant presence in battle and hoped it wouldn't stop him from using his fighting skills, which he trusted. At the same time, he was prepared for the worst—a good thing because if it came to a battle, he was almost certain not to make it out alive.

The faint sound of steps on pebbles interrupted his thoughts. Vasya, the sniper, elbowed him.

"It's a fucking *dushman*," he whispered. "Let's shoot the fucker right now!"

Kalita peered into his night-vision telescope, which showed nothing: the device required at least a tiny amount of light to work, and there was none. He could make out nothing but a shadow.

"Shoot him!" Vasya urged. "Don't let him come any closer."

"Hold on," Kalita whispered back. "I want to be sure to get him."

The barely perceptible shadow seemed strange as it grew clearer. Somehow, the figure didn't look like a *dushman*. It was holding something—a helmet, Kalita realized.

"That's no *dushman*," he told Vasya. Then he raised his voice. "Who's there?" he called out in a loud whisper.

"Don't fire!" came back a nervous reply in Russian. It was the major, who had lost his way returning from the radio unit. Having found the riverbank, he was feeling his way back in the total darkness, thinking, "Please God, don't let them shoot, *don't let them shoot!*"

After more time passed, two paratroopers dug in next to a sand dune closer toward the bend in the river noticed another solitary figure. This one was a rebel scout. He'd been moving cautiously up the riverbed, periodically clambering up a dune to quickly signal behind him with a flashlight. Several other scouts moved toward him, one after another, and a group of five fighters followed half a mile behind. Their safe passage would mean a still-unseen main column of mujahideen could continue moving.

The scout approached the sand dune next to which the soldiers were dug in. Now they could hear his breathing. Freezing all movement, the Soviets desperately tried to control their own breathing, which their nervousness made very difficult. Sweat trickled down their faces. Stopping right next to their foxhole, he still didn't see them, although they could smell his body odor and could have reached out and grabbed his foot. The paratroopers had to decide whether to attack and try to cut his throat or to allow him to move on, the second option being much more preferable because the other scouts were certain to inform the main mujahideen body of a struggle.

Any sign of ambush would spell failure of the operation. The Soviets' sole hope, tiny as it could only be, was to attack the main column when it was directly in front of them. Otherwise their small force would probably be killed by rebels with plenty of time to attack. Pausing for what seemed an eternity, the lead scout finally moved on, leaving the soldiers drenched in their sweat.

A wind rose from nowhere to whip up dust and produce a characteristic whining sound. Several additional scouts passed on the riverbed, followed by the vanguard group of five more heavily armed rebels moving together. When one stumbled upon a foxhole manned by two Afghan soldiers, the troops sprang into action, but not quickly enough to stop another mujahideen fighter from shouting out as one of the Group A men stabbed him. Leaping up, several other soldiers killed three of his fellows and took the other two prisoners. As they were being dragged away, bound and gagged, Kalita heard the faint rumbling of a diesel engine over the wind. Headlights he made out beyond the turn in the river showed the main column moving toward them.

The continued advance of the lights, as much as they could be seen, seemed to indicate the stabbed scout's yelp hadn't been reported to the column. Kalita steeled himself for the launching of the Soviet ambush, but the lights faded just before they appeared to reach the bend. The rebels must have turned in another direction, he would later reason, after losing contact via two-way radios with their vanguard group.

The little Soviet-Afghan force didn't pursue; in that sense, the operation failed. Whether or not Pahlawan's mujahideen group made it to Pakistan, which Kalita would not find out, he felt his life had been saved by the appearance of the chance gusts of wind that blew away the otherwise fatal signal of the dead scout.

II

Few officers in draftee Sergei Salabayev's Fifty-sixth Brigade in Gardez had much to do with the soldiers they commanded. Interaction with conscripts usually fell to the *praporshchiki*, the Soviet equivalent of sergeants. When Salabayev's commanding lieutenant *did* talk to him, it was often to give an order to pilfer from the regiment's stores. But Salabayev came to despise officers most for confiscating his food and alcohol. Soldiers dubbed them "jackals."

While soldiers who risked their lives fighting *dushmany* smoked rancid Pamir brand cigarettes, officers got Stolichnye and Yava brands, several cuts higher. Instead of the drafty tents that housed soldiers, officers lived in heated wooden barracks, where many ate cheese, paté, canned sardines, and crabmeat. Some of the foul-tasting frozen meat on which Salabayev continued to exist during his first winter bore stamps that read "1942." With rare exceptions, the farther one was stationed from Kabul and other main distribution centers, the more difficult it was to obtain decent food. The military got only what was left after officials had pilfered the best supplies from central warehouses. But Salabayev's situation slowly improved. From his first year's dreams of milk, vegetables, and fresh fish, he went to actually eating mutton, pork, and bread during his second year. Between-meal hunger was sated by pork fat, *salo*, salted and eaten with bread when it was available.

Most of the drinking water was treated with chlorine pills to kill the bacteria, but it remained otherwise dirty. When the pills ran out, the "purification" performed by pouring the liquid through a cloth wreaked havoc on digestive systems. Diseases continued to rage through the ranks. Few servicemen Salabayev met in Afghanistan escaped the crippling bouts of hepatitis he himself endured—together with malaria, which put him in the hospital for a month. Many he knew also suffered dysentery and typhus, and lice attacked constantly, especially during the days and weeks on operations, away from the bases, when the worst outbreaks prompted soldiers to burn their uniforms and douse themselves in gasoline. Although that brought some relief, the smell would cling for days.

Officers had much easier access to carnal pleasures. Salabayev's buddies said they overheard their brigade commander claim that as insurance against gay sex among his officers, he made sure to provide employment for at least forty women as secretaries, canteen workers, and other assistants. When women were permitted to fire automatic rifles and pistols during officers' parties, shots and laughter rang out for hours. Sessions with them cost twenty-five *cheki*, the internal currency paid to service personnel—a prohibitive price on a conscript's monthly wage of ten *cheki*, even if there had been private places to go for coupling. But draftees did sometimes manage to obtain sex. Despite the often coercive nature of the prostitution, some soldiers tried to observe a few niceties, such as sharing preliminary swigs of vodka and bites of canned meat.

Green lieutenants, many still steeped in Marxist-Leninist ideology and ignorant of the realities of the war they were fighting, earned Salabayev's lowest opinion. Not that many such officers in his regiment willingly participated in the fighting itself. Having been nowhere near bouts of combat, they'd appear afterward to shout commands. Conscripts were convinced such commanders' inexperience, incompetence, and regard for the men as cannon fodder significantly increased casualty rates, and the brutal hazing system made their lives worse. Soon life came to be defined by two classifications. "Getting" meant successful stealing, often by means of well-planned schemes involving creating diversions. "Getting fucked over" meant missing an opportunity for theft or being robbed oneself.

Stealing from Afghans meshed with thieving from the brigade's warehouses. The farmers in the mountainous countryside surrounding the Gardez base worked devilishly hard to eke out their hardscrabble livings, starting with digging rocks from the ground and hauling fertile soil by hand from valleys below to enrich their little plots. But Salabayev and his ravenous fellow soldiers tripped over themselves to steal cucumbers and tomatoes growing there, when they spotted them. The tripping was often literal: the men trampled much produce underfoot, demolishing annual crops of grapes, cantaloupes, and watermelons. After farmers began planting mines on their fields, Salabayev saw several comrades die from stepping on them.

The supply of clothing was little better. New arrivals of conscripts were often relieved of boots, gloves, and hats—anything warm. With little chance of obtaining timely replacements for flimsy fatigues that quickly wore out, older soldiers also forced new draftees to hand over theirs in exchange for threadbare, dirty ones—a switch made easier by a general lack on uniforms of stencils and emblems identifying the various units. Fuel supplies were also high on Salabayev's list during his frequent sneaks from his barracks to scrounge. After relatively easy bribery of guards who had no love for their duty, a barrel of kerosene could be exchanged for the equivalent of a couple of warm sheepskin coats, a pair of jeans, and a Japanese-made cassette player. Double-cassette recorders on which tapes could be dubbed for selling were especially valued. Little Sanyo Dictaphones sold for two hundred *cheki*, almost a year and a half of Salabayev's pay.

Men of the Fifty-sixth Brigade joined the mass of Soviet soldiers throughout Afghanistan who sold the mujahideen arms and ammunition, often pilfered during combat operations, sometimes for big profit. Some of the soldiers who engaged in that trade sought to save or steal enough to return home with a pair of Western jeans, but a friend of Salabayev's earned so much that he constantly worried about where to conceal his cash. Eventually, he used spent casings of 150-mm shells, burying them with great care so as not to be seen. As for Salabayev, his qualms about thieving quickly disappeared, leaving him convinced that man's natural state is animal-like; civilization is a thin veneer that wears off at the first serious inconvenience. Having settled in that belief and on his own gain as his highest priority, he achieved a degree of calmness, even aloofness, that appeared odd even to his fellow conscripts, who nicknamed him "Bummer."

III

Operating from its base in northern Sheberghan, Nikolai Kalita's Group A force often provided security for clandestine meetings with Soviet agents in the mujahideen. Flying out well in advance to sites picked by KGB and GRU personnel, the *spetsnaz* men dug foxholes and prepared to provide cover if needed. One such meeting netted the valuable information that a group of local mujahideen field commanders was planning to meet in a nearby village.

The Soviets prepared an ambush around the mud-walled compound. When the mujahideen commanders gathered in one of its houses, they fired two mortars, the second of which was a direct hit.

Snipers forced escaping rebels to retreat through a bottleneck where Group A marksmen picked them off. The operation was spectacularly successful. Most of the rebels were either killed or captured. Still, Kalita had no idea whether the mission changed the situation even for a few weeks in the area it had been carried out.

Group A also protected gas engineers and workers. To stop the mujahideen from blowing up pipelines and attacking teams sent to repair them, the KGB officers flew to the sites to set up security perimeters. Other units took part in frequent *zachistki*, or "cleaning-up" operations, meaning searches for rebels in *kishlaks*. Like so many other Soviets, Kalita found that work the most frightening, especially in the abandoned villages that heralded almost certain attacks. (The presence of women and children was an invitation to breathe a little easier.) When they had to pass *kishlaks* showing no signs of life, BTRs usually sped by as fast as they could.

Kalita's suspicion of Afghans increased after he befriended an Afghan government soldier who had been kidnapped by a local mujahideen group and forced to fight the Soviets before its commander switched loyalties and began cooperating with the Afghan military. Kalita came to believe that most Afghans saw such deals as one of the few means of surviving the ubiquitous death and suffering, and that the only certainty was betrayal because no allegiance would last longer than it seemed to serve the purpose of escaping the daily horrors. The brutality shook even hardened combatants. Arriving at a battle scene shortly after the fighting had ended, he came across a Soviet soldier who had been completely skinned. He was still alive, sitting next to a tree, covered in flies.

As if trying to match that kind of cruelty, the Afghan Interior Ministry's Sarandoi meted out ghastly punishments, perhaps because rampant nepotism within the service created a sense of security and impunity. Kalita stopped one group of Sarandoi officers from cutting off the ear of a teenage boy they were questioning. Partly to save them from torture at the hands of Afghan officials if they were captured, Group A officers took prisoners with them when they could. They prided themselves on their relative compassion toward locals—one of the main reasons, Kalita believed, that his KGB group didn't lose one man during his first two-month stint.

Kalita believed the Kremlin was wrong to try to impose its version of modernity on a thoroughly foreign culture. He accepted that the mujahideen were fighting against foreign invaders and would continue doing so as long as the occupiers remained. While Soviet soldiers fought to stay alive, the enemy was fighting for its beliefs. He also respected the rebels' accuracy with weapons and other fighting skills, developed without the rigorous selection process and training he and his KGB comrades had undergone.

IV

Alexander Rutskoi flew fighter planes for the Fortieth Army. The thirty-one-year-old colonel, the son of a tank officer from the southern Kursk Region, had been assigned in 1985 to train three squadrons of mostly young lieutenants to fly the Su-25. Two of the squadrons would be based in Bagram, the third in Kandahar.

Decades earlier, Nikita Khrushchev had directed the Soviet Air Force to focus on strategic bombers and supersonic fighters instead of ground-attack aircraft. The recent arrival of the Su-25 marked one of the first major advances in the development of close air support of infantry since its prominent role in World War II, when Soviet pilots had provided vital help to infantry units facing the Wehrmacht. Rutskoi liked the new plane. Nicknamed *grach*, or crow, the squat, low-flying Su-25 was armed with a twin-barrel 30-mm cannon and had ten pylons under its wings that could carry thousands of pounds of weapons, including thousand-pound RBK cluster bombs, and 57-mm to 330-mm rockets. In addition to being well armed and armored, and configured for providing very close support of ground forces, the plane took rough handling well.

Compact, mustachioed Rutskoi, whose prematurely graying

hair improved his good looks, had a reputation for independence and speaking his mind to his fellow officers. Rather than hold him back, those qualities had served him well, rare as that was. Now he'd been trusted to develop tactics to maximize the new fighter's effectiveness in the dusty and otherwise adverse weather conditions often encountered when flying in hazardous mountain terrain. It was a dangerous task; Rutskoi's predecessor had lost twelve pilots.

Fighter pilots, like their counterparts flying helicopters, rotated through Afghanistan every year, and although only parts of regiments were often deployed, there were many units. Even though helicopters were the Fortieth Army's main air weapon, fixed-wing planes had played an important part in the war, and not only the long-winged Tu-16 and pointy-nosed Tu-22 bombers that carpet-bombed the Panjshir Valley and other areas in preparation for ground attacks. Agile MiG-21 fighters had been used as attack planes early in the conflict, but the aging craft had primitive radars, carried relatively light weapon loads, and had not been designed for close ground support. Heavier MiG-23s, which were more effective in that role, replaced many of them over the years, as did Su-17s, which carried large weapons loads.

When Rutskoi landed at the Bagram air base, it was under attack. Incoming mortars and rockets were severing heads and limbs in a battle raging on the green plain between the base and Charikar at the foot of the Panjshir Valley. "Where the hell have I arrived?" the young colonel thought. Rutskoi took some revenge later, when he came to command the base. He gathered local Afghan elders in order to warn them he would obliterate any areas used to attack the base. "I'll turn it into the Gobi desert," he vowed. When the next attack came two weeks later and he delivered on his promise, the attacks ceased, at least when he was known to be on the base.

Rutskoi's squadrons were among the first to fly at night, when most caravans moved through the Hindu Kush passes, and rebels planted mines. But the cover of darkness was also useful for the Soviets: *spetsnaz* fighters carried out many of their ambushes and other operations at night. Highly dangerous as it was, night flying could also be highly effective. When nervous mujahideen unleashed volleys of antiaircraft fire, it was relatively easy to see from the air where it came from, then destroy the rebel positions.

Rutskoi developed a reputation for dependability. During a 1986 attack on the Panjshir Valley led by Fortieth Army Chief of Staff Yuri Grekov, mujahideen counterattacked the Soviet command center from several sides. After air squadron commanders had rebuffed Grekov's order for air strikes because the weather was too cloudy, Grekov radioed Rutskoi in Bagram.

"How fast is the wind blowing?" the colonel asked. "And from what direction?"

Although Grekov didn't know, he pressed a reluctant Rutskoi to bomb the mujahideen. Rutskoi relented. Flying into the valley, he dropped four massive cluster bombs and listened for the result. The explosives went off dangerously close to the Panjshir command point. It now maintained radio silence—until he heard a stream of swearing. "You fucking bastard! What the hell do you think you're doing!?" The fury came from Grekov. "How close did you have to drop those things? We're scraping ourselves off the ceiling!" However, the general later sent Rutskoi a case of Armenian cognac for saving the command point from immediate danger.

Helicopters rarely flew at night, when Rutskoi's squadrons were often called on to support *spetsnaz* pinned down in narrow valleys. The pressure was intense; pilots wore special camel-hair jumpsuits to help wick away rivers of sweat. On long missions, they violated regulations by flying on one engine to conserve fuel. Attacking caravans in mountain passes, they sought to hit the first and last vehicles, then swooped back to finish off the others. Rutskoi's squadrons sometimes flew up to eight sorties a day, far more than earlier units had. His own plane was hit often. Parts of it were burning during four very tricky landings at his base.

In 1987, mujahideen fighters shot down six Afghan Mi-8s close to a major rebel base in Zhawar near the Pakistani border. The Soviets had taken the complex at great cost from rebel commander Jallaladin Haqqani two years earlier, only to surrender it again when the attacking force withdrew. Rutskoi was given a reconnaissance mission to attract fire to himself over the rugged mountain terrain while another pilot photographed the source of the attacks. Five miles east of Zhawar, a U.S.-built Stinger missile found his right engine while he was flying at 150 feet. The aircraft started spinning, but with its left engine still working, Rutskoi regained enough control to clear the valley from where the missile was fired—but only until a burst from an antiaircraft gun sent the plane crashing to the ground in a no-man's-land between mujahideen and Afghan Army positions.

His back was broken and his head and a hand were injured, but Rutskoi managed to crawl from his cockpit and see mujahideen and Afghan soldiers making for him as quickly as possible from opposite sides. An Afghan BTR got there first under heavy fire, some of which caught a captain in the back during the rescue.

Hospital doctors told Rutskoi he'd be confined to a wheelchair for the rest of his life. He began physical therapy three months later, using a course developed to prepare Soviet cosmonauts—and made fast progress. He was back in the air within months. Promoted to deputy head of Soviet Air Force training in late 1987, he planned to make himself eligible to join the top brass by enrolling in the General Staff Academy. But the following year he was sent back to Afghanistan as deputy head of the Fortieth Army air forces.

V

The skirmishing in the first half of 1986 was less intense than it had been during the previous year. In August, a mujahideen rocket attack lit up the night when it hit an Afghan Army ammunition dump outside Kabul, exploding tens of thousands of rockets and mortars among forty thousand tons of ammunition. Such success was increasingly rare, however. Despite the mujahideen's unrelenting resistance, the Soviets appeared to be cementing their upper hand in the semi-stalemate.

Valery Kurilov, the Zenit *spetsnaz* officer who had taken part in storming the Taj-Bek palace in 1979, believed then that Soviet troops would be out of Afghanistan within a year. But in 1984 he was back, now in a six-man KGB antiterrorism detail protecting Soviet advisers and specialists in Kabul. Their number was considerable. Significantly higher pay than back home continued to attract a steady stream of Soviet volunteers—not only KGB, military, and embassy staff but also doctors, mechanics, teachers, architects, and technical specialists of all kinds, some charged with building factories and infrastructure and otherwise trying to stimulate the civilian economy and society. There were also a large number of Party activists. Many lived in the capital's concrete-slab suburb called Microrayon, or micro-district—from a generic Soviet term used to describe residential areas. Although its six-story buildings were indistinguishable from similar shoddy structures throughout the Soviet Bloc, from Prague to Vladivostok, they were prestigious enough in Kabul to house a number of top Afghan officials in addition to the Soviet specialists.

Many of the staff were accompanied by their families. Wives and children often escaped the worst of Kabul's stifling summer heat—unrelieved by any air-conditioning in their concrete apartments (hot water was provided only one day a week)—by returning to the Soviet Union for a month or two. Otherwise, vans delivered many of the Soviets to and from work, while buses—sometimes accompanied by troops when mujahideen shelling was heavy—took children from Microrayon to the Soviet embassy school.

In an attempt to make life as normal as possible despite the inexorable security threat, the Soviets had built a movie theater, a concert hall, and a sports complex. At the same time, the Komsomol (Communist youth organization) and various Party committees helped the KGB keep watch on the community. In fact, life was far from normal. In the resumption of hostilities after the spring thaw, rebel shelling of the city increased to up to fifty times a day. Much of it came in the form of rockets with time-delay fuses fired from the surrounding hills. The missiles were far from accurate but served their purpose of intimidation. Soviet civilians, enjoying few breaks in the sound of gunfire, often kept their own weapons in their quarters. During one typical attack, a rocket hit a wall and destroyed the living room of three nurses living together in a Microrayon apartment. They saved their lives by following instructions Valery Kurilov had given them shortly before: "Get down on your bathroom floor." Farthest from the building's outer walls, it was the best-protected spot in most apartments.

Despite all their efforts, it was very difficult for the Soviets in Kabul to adjust to the constant violence. All the more because determining who the enemy might be on the city's bustling streets was all but impossible. The Soviets had no monopoly on disguising mines as toys: Kurilov saw one explosive device hidden in a thermos blow up when a young Russian child picked it up. Such violence was aimed at provoking anger against the government for not being able to provide elementary security to residents of the capital. Abductions and killings regularly occurred on the city's streets, adding to the circumstances that kept life from being even remotely normal.

Soviets' spirits ebbed. Many advisers complained of having to do "everything" themselves because their Afghan instructees were either unwilling or unable to complete tasks on their own. "How's the situation supposed to improve under such conditions?" was a common refrain around Soviet kitchen tables. Many already knew Afghans' answer: "You came here for this, you do the work." Still, many Kabul residents welcomed or tolerated the Soviet presence as a guarantee of some kind of stability and cosmopolitanism in the capital. Although many blamed Moscow for the country's problems, to Kurilov at least they appeared fewer than those who feared what would become of their lives if fundamentalist rebels took over the city.

Kabul's central hospital, the country's biggest, reflected the general circumstances. Seriously understaffed and undersupplied with drugs and anesthetics, it was also overcrowded with military and civilian patients. Soviet soldiers with relatively light wounds preferred to stay away to help keep space free for those with amputations and other serious conditions.

Mikhail Zheltakov, another KGB officer, spent much of his free time taking photographs for medical journals. Amputations were among the most frequent procedures, even though many mine-blast victims didn't survive. They often died from shock or loss of blood, especially if wounded far from medical help. Zheltakov found officers to be the most philosophical about losing limbs, probably because they could hope for desk jobs back home. However, amputations were quite another matter for young conscripts facing uncertain futures. In one operation he observed, surgeons spent hours cutting below the knee of a soldier's leg shattered when he'd stepped on a mine. Cutting above the knee would have been much easier, but would have made walking with a prosthetic limb more difficult. The procedure eventually went well and the head surgeon was in good spirits when Zheltakov accompanied him on a visit to the amputee the following morning.

"How are you feeling?" the smiling surgeon asked the patient, who had had the benefit of anesthesia, unlike many amputees with limbs sawed off in field hospitals. "Are you doing okay?"

The soldier burst into tears. "Doctor, what's happened to my leg?" he moaned. "I want to die!"

The surgeon frowned. "I don't want to hear that!" he barked. "Next time we'll cut off your head!" For Zheltakov, it was a jarring lesson in war's brutality.

Kurilov would remain in Kabul with his wife and two sons for three years. He returned to Moscow for good in late 1987. Well before then, he'd joined the great number of Soviets who came to believe the war was futile.

VI

Eight Mi-24 gunships approached Jalalabad on September 25, 1986, on their return from a routine mission. As they neared their base, a rocket streaked toward them from the ground, slammed into the lead helicopter, and exploded. When a second craft blew up seconds later, the frantic pilots of five of the remaining six helicopters brought them down hard enough to cause damage and injure passengers. Only one of the choppers turned to fire its cannon at the attackers, and it too was destroyed as it swooped toward a group of rebels near the airfield. Another rocket had scored, followed by yells of "Allah akbar!"—God is great—from the ground as a handful of mujahideen fighters raced to retrieve their spent rocket tubes and escape before Soviet tanks from Jalalabad gave chase.

Ronald Reagan would soon watch footage of the event, videotaped by the rebels themselves, in the White House. Stunned helicopter crews in the Jalalabad base had a harder time trying to make sense of it. How had the mujahideen targeted the helicopters with such deadly precision and effectiveness? Although many Soviet handheld surface-to-air missiles had fallen into their hands, they had to be fired from behind because they used heat-seeking technology to home in on hot exhaust. However, the September missiles that had done so much damage so quickly had been fired from various sides, including head-on.

The Fortieth Army grounded all aviation except for the most essential flights, and investigators rushed to the strike scene, already convinced they had the answer: the mujahideen had got their hands on American Stinger missiles.

VII

William Casey intensified his campaign to heighten American efforts in Afghanistan throughout 1985 and much of 1986. The CIA director's wish for a high-stakes, all-out game against the Soviets was clear in his instructions to Milton Bearden, the CIA's new Islamabad station chief, early in 1986. Meeting in his Langley office, the agency's director told Bearden that he wanted him "to go out there and win."

Huge amounts of weapons and American money—almost $500 million in 1986—were now pouring into Afghanistan. The CIA imported thousands of mules, some from as far as Texas, to help carry the burgeoning cargo over the mountain passes from Pakistan to Afghanistan. To bypass the Pakistani ISI's strict control over the flow, Langley also began recruiting its own agents in Afghanistan and paying top mujahideen commanders up to $100,000 a month.

Washington had long debated whether to include Stingers in its supplies. During the war's first years, when the United States did little beyond buying Soviet-designed weapons for the mujahideen, many, not wanting to escalate the conflict by providing American versions, believed bleeding the Soviets would be sweet enough revenge for Moscow's underhanded participation in the Vietnam War. But the longer the rebels were bogged down, the less satisfactory many believed propaganda to be—compared to helping the mujahideen win outright.

Still, weapons purchased through third countries were one thing, and brand-new, highly advanced Stingers with their infrared tracking systems were another. Providing them to the rebels would do more than signal Washington's open entrance into the conflict. The Pentagon was also loath to expose its technology to capture and copying by the Soviets. And Washington was wary of supplying Islamic fundamentalists with the missiles soon after the blowing up of several civilian airliners. Islamabad joined the general concern.

Nevertheless, Stingers would surely make a significant military impact by enabling a challenge to the Soviets' total air supremacy. Congressional and CIA voices eager to step up the fight argued it was wrong to withhold a potentially devastating weapon from rebels fighting and dying in the battle against America's Cold War enemy. A series of escalating battles in 1985 finally helped them prevail over the doubters. Pakistan's General Zia was among those who'd long opposed introducing Stingers, fearing they would escalate the conflict. His relenting in January 1986 opened the way for their supply to the mujahideen.

Washington insisted on strict safeguards. Trainees were carefully vetted for skill and reliability. New missiles would not be sent without proof from the resistance fighters that they had fired those already supplied. With such rules in place, U.S.-trained Pakistani ISI officers were soon teaching mujahideen units to operate the weapon in training camps near the Afghan border.

Although some question whether Stingers truly exerted a decisive impact on the course of the war, their psychological impact is undeniable. By giving the mujahideen a major boost that helped demoralize Soviet forces, Washington began tipping a balance whose angle would prove crucial in the coming years.

VIII

At least one of the Pentagon's concerns was moot: Soviet military intelligence, the GRU, already possessed a blueprint for the Stinger. Still, the Fortieth Army promised the highest Soviet honor—Hero of the Soviet Union—to anyone who captured and delivered an actual missile and launcher. Meanwhile, a week after the first Stingers downed the three Mi-24s in Jalalabad, the Soviet command issued new flying regulations. Gunship armaments were rendered much less accurate because the craft could no longer be used for close-quarter support. In addition, airplane pilots had to fly well above the Stingers' 12,500-foot ceiling, fire deception flares, descend by zigzagging, and make sickeningly steep spiral approaches when coming in for landing and after takeoffs. They also regularly had to maintain radio silence in order to prevent eavesdropping by mujahideen, and fly much more often by night. All that made Soviet bombing and airpower in general far less effective.

Mi-8 helicopter pilots like Vladimir Kostiuchenko, who now had to fly as fast as his aircraft would allow, ripped out what they could from their cabins to make their craft as light as possible. Knowing the first chopper in formation was the most likely to be hit, they quickly came to consider flying first a deadly assignment.

Komsomolskaya pravda correspondent Mikhail Kozhukhov noticed the effect almost immediately. However bad life for the Soviet forces had been, morale now sharply dipped. A large number of Soviet planes, including most of the ubiquitous An-12 cargo craft and smaller An-24 turboprops, weren't pressurized. Breathing during many flights had been difficult, but now the air at the required twenty thousand feet was so thin Kozhukhov sometimes felt he was suffocating, and the even more dangerous night flying caused the atheist journalist to cross himself before takeoffs.

Not that the revised measures made the Stingers less than a roaring success. Pressing their sudden advantage, the newly confident mujahideen dramatically increased their taste for combat and shot down 270 Soviet aircraft during the following year. Even if the CIA's estimation of their success rate at 30 to 40 percent was more accurate than the 75 percent the rebels themselves claimed, it was still remarkable.

IX

If the Cold War showed few signs of abating in Afghanistan, that didn't mean no change was taking place. For one thing, Gorbachev had kick-started an anticorruption drive begun by Andropov, and that forced some of the most notoriously corrupt Party bosses to resign. When a reactor exploded in the Chernobyl nuclear plant in the Ukraine in April 1986, and radioactive material spewed from the world's worst nuclear accident, Gorbachev chose to publicly announce the catastrophe. Although the decision took some days to make, it heralded a new level of openness on the part of the Soviet government.

Gorbachev maneuvered quickly to secure his power. His main rival, a military-industrial complex chief named Grigory Romanov, who many had believed would succeed Chernenko, was forced to retire from the Politburo after rumors circulated about his alleged alcoholism. A day later, Foreign Minister Andrei Gromyko, who had served since 1957, was promoted to the honorary post of president. The following year, Admiral Sergei Gorshkov, another member of the old guard who had commanded the Soviet Navy since 1956, was forced to retire. Prime Minister Nikolai Tikhonov, who was closely tied to the Brezhnev circle, also stepped down in September, citing poor health.

Greater upheaval would come in foreign affairs. Gorbachev's October 1986 summit with Ronald Reagan in Reykjavik was seen as a failure at the time. But relations between the two would soon dramatically improve, boosted by British Prime Minister Margaret Thatcher's declaration that the Soviet leader was someone she could "do business" with. Relations at the highest levels thawed despite an increasingly tense security standoff partly caused by American misreading of the Soviet economy. U.S. analysts, not least those in the CIA, failed to see the Brezhnev stagnation had so thoroughly corrupted the system that it was teetering on the verge of collapse. The military-industrial complex was swallowing a quarter of the gross domestic product, compared to about a sixteenth in the United States. As oil prices headed to new lows, the exports that had propped up Brezhnev's tottering administration were now bringing in far less.

Society's increasing derision of the Party's authority was no less significant. Gorbachev's loosening of administrative repression unleashed a backlash that would quickly go from cautious to relatively daring. *Ogonyok* magazine—a very rough equivalent of *Life* magazine—began publishing scathing reports written by a young journalist named Artyom Borovik, about conditions endured by Soviet forces in Afghanistan. *Ogonyok*'s exposés of official corruption would help bring about a revolution in Soviet journalism.

Gorbachev had no intention of abandoning communism, however. On the contrary, the social democrat believed the Soviet Union could be reformed and saved. Freeing government control would help revitalize the economy by enabling local decision makers—factory managers and regional politicians—to run their own affairs instead of following orders about almost everything from Moscow. "Those who don't intend to adjust and who, moreover, are an obstacle to the solution of these new tasks simply must get out of the way, get out of the way and not be a hindrance," Gorbachev warned Party officials months after his appointment.

The war in Afghanistan was among the biggest hindrances to Gorbachev's plans to streamline the state's machinery. Addressing members of the Politburo on November 13, 1986, he reminded them that the fighting there had already dragged on for six years, and "In general, we haven't found the key to resolving this problem. What, are we going to fight endlessly as testimony that our troops are unable to deal with the situation? We need to finish this process as soon as possible."

However far-fetched, the Politburo clung to the hope a political solution still lay in a friendly regime in neutral Afghanistan. One of the hardest problems was how to save face. There were serious worries that a quick exit from Afghanistan would deal a body blow to Moscow's global authority, particularly over other Third World client states.

The next speaker at the Politburo meeting was Andrei Gromyko, the long-serving foreign minister who, although he had nominated Gorbachev for the Soviet leadership the previous year, was soon afterward banished to the largely ceremonial post of chairman of the Presidium of the Supreme Soviet. Now he pushed for concrete goals in Afghanistan. "It's necessary to establish a strategic target," he said. "Too long ago, we spoke about the need to close off Afghanistan's border with Pakistan and Iran. Experience has shown that we were unable to do that because of the area's difficult terrain and hundreds of passes through the mountains. Today it's necessary to precisely state that the strategic assignment concludes with moving toward ending the war."

After Gorbachev repeated his insistence that the war end in not more than two years, Gromyko continued by arguing that the "rather wide spectrum of steps" recommended by Najibullah deserved attention and should not be spurned. "One path is to draw in the peasant masses to support the government's authority. Another is negotiations with those Islamic parties and organizations inside Afghanistan and beyond its borders that are ready to compromise. The third path involves relations with the former king." The veteran diplomat who had signed the United Nations charter and spoken with President Kennedy during the Cuban Missile Crisis insisted no settlement could be achieved without involving Pakistan. However, the Americans "aren't interested in a settlement of the situation in Afghanistan. On the contrary, it's to their advantage for the war to drag out."

Gromyko was followed by KGB Chairman Victor Chebrikov, who, after succeeding Andropov when his old mentor became general secretary in 1982, had sustained his predecessor's anticorruption drives. For now, at least, Chebrikov supported Gorbachev's reforms. Contending that the Soviet Union hadn't done everything in its power in Afghanistan, he proposed inviting Najibullah to Moscow for a first visit because telephone conversations with him through intermediaries weren't enough. "A direct conversation is necessary. It could clear up a great deal. It's important not to put off such a conversation; a day or two should be found for the purpose."

Gorbachev had picked Eduard Shevardnadze, Georgia's wily former Party boss, to succeed Gromyko as foreign minister the previous year. Shevardnadze would go on to become one of the strongest supporters of Gorbachev's policy of *glasnost*, or openness, and to play a key role in ending the Cold War. When his turn came to speak, he called for "Afghanization": leaving the conflict to local forces to battle out. "We must regard Afghanistan as an independent country and entrust Najib to make decisions independently," he said. Najibullah's new government had made noticeable progress stabilizing the country and he needed practical support, "otherwise we'll bear the political costs."

Marshal Sergei Akhromeyev, the military's chief of staff who'd been one of the top planners of the invasion seven years earlier, gloomily disagreed about visible progress. "There's not a single piece of land in that country that hasn't been occupied by a Soviet soldier," he said. "Nevertheless, the majority of the territory remains in the hands of rebels." And although the Afghan government had "a significant military force" at its disposal—160,000 people in the army, 115,000 in the Interior Ministry's Sarandoi, and 20,000 in state security organs—"there's no single military problem that has arisen that hasn't been solved, and yet there's still no result."

Akhromeyev said Moscow had lost the battle for the Afghan people; only a minority of the population supported the government. "Our army has fought for five years. It's now in a position to maintain the situation on the level that it exists now. But under such conditions the war will continue for a long time."

First Deputy Foreign Minister Yuli Vorontsov, a former ambassador to France who would soon head the Kremlin's negotiations over Afghanistan, agreed. Only 5 million Afghans of a population of 18 million—just several hundred thousand families outside the country's main cities—were under the government's control. "The peasant hasn't received significant material benefit from the revolution. . . . The party and the government haven't inherited from the previous government precise plans on how to quickly raise the standard of living of the 300,000 to 400,000 peasant households under the government's sphere of influence."

Agreeing to meet Najibullah and other Afghan leaders, and also agreeing about the need for talks with Pakistan, Gorbachev closed the meeting by repeating his insistence that the war end in two years. "In 1987, we should withdraw 50 percent of our troops, and another 50 percent in the following year. . . . Most important, we must make sure the Americans don't go into Afghanistan. But I think the Americans won't go into Afghanistan militarily."

Shortly after the Politburo meeting, Shevardnadze told U.S. Secretary of State George Shultz that the Kremlin was serious about withdrawing from Afghanistan. Surprised by the revelation, Shultz kept it to himself for weeks. But even though Gorbachev would soon make clear his intentions directly to Reagan, even though the American goal of pushing the adversary out of Afghanistan appeared to have been achieved, Washington's suspicious Cold Warriors would continue ignoring the message. They were among the last to understand that the Soviet Union, where Gorbachev would fully launch his policies of *glasnost* and *perestroika* (restructuring) in 1987, stood on the cusp of political revolution.

In Afghanistan, Najibullah was trying to force change. In November 1986, a new constitution formally provided for a multiparty system, an Islamic legal system run by an independent judiciary, greater freedom of speech, and the election of a president by a *loya jirga* assembly consisting of parliament and tribal and religious leaders. The following month, Najibullah announced a national reconciliation program that proposed dialogue with opposition leaders and a possible coalition government. The plan also called for a six-month cease-fire to begin in January 1987. But mujahideen leaders rejected the program, which was never implemented.

In December 1986, a month after the critical Politburo meeting, Gorbachev summoned Najibullah to Moscow to inform him that withdrawing Soviet forces from Afghanistan was now official policy. Negotiations between the Afghans and Soviets on one side and Pakistanis on the other would begin in earnest the following year—and run into immediate trouble because the Afghans would offer a Soviet withdrawal in four years while the Pakistanis wanted it to happen in months. Nevertheless, the Kremlin had made its decision. Implementing its new policy would be only a matter of time.

CHAPTER 7

ENDGAME

|

Still not fully aware that ending a war is usually more difficult than starting one, the Kremlin ordered a stop to all offensive combat operations in Afghanistan after January 1987. From then on, the Fortieth Army was to fight solely to defend itself from mujahideen attacks—which were increasing, thanks largely to American aid. Washington would spend some $630 million on the arms flow that year, and at least an equal amount would come from Saudi Arabia. If that didn't make the situation grim enough for Moscow, the weapons streaming in were increasingly sophisticated ones. Among new hardware introduced by the CIA, the French Milan antitank missile was much more precise than any of the old arms used by the rebels, including their RPG-7s, the shoulder-launched, rocket-propelled grenades of Soviet manufacture that had already knocked out so many Soviet tanks.

Most of Washington saw Gorbachev's promises of withdrawal as bluff. The CIA was at the forefront of such thinking. Its surpassing suspicion of the Soviet leader's statements about his reform plans reinforced an ideological position that ensured the agency would be caught completely off guard by the collapse of communism a mere five years later. Another reason was William Casey's focus elsewhere, especially after he became engulfed in congressional hearings about the Iran-Contra scandal. In late 1986, the combative agency director suffered a seizure in his Langley office. A brain tumor caused his death in early 1987.

America's rebuff of support for a Soviet withdrawal from Afghanistan prompted Gorbachev to look elsewhere. Using the atrophied UN negotiations framework established in 1982 under Ecuadoran Diego Cordovez, he appealed to Pakistan to help draw up a timetable for pulling out. But Islamabad's help would be little greater than Washington's. Pakistan promised to stop supplying the mujahideen only if the Soviet Union agreed to end its support of Mohammed Najibullah: a quid pro quo negotiators called "symmetry." Islamabad wanted nothing to interfere with its main goal of bringing down Najibullah's government as quickly as possible.

The Politburo's eagerness to negotiate with the Americans and Pakistanis incensed Valentin Varennikov, the commander of Soviet ground forces and the defense minister's personal representative to Kabul. Twenty-six years later, the general determinedly described the 1979 invasion in the old terms of fraternal help. In his sprawling office in central Moscow, a grandfatherly Varennikov insisted that the Red Army had first entered the country with the agreement only of the Afghan government—therefore the Kremlin in 1987 needed no one else to tell it how or when to withdraw. Varennikov believed Gorbachev and Foreign Minister Shevardnadze were currying favor with Washington for the sake of their own agenda: to help shore up their *glasnost* and *perestroika* reforms. If the Americans *were* to be involved, they too must make sacrifices. For every one of the 183 Soviet bases in Afghanistan to be shut down, the same should happen to a mujahideen training camp in Pakistani territory. Later, during the Soviet withdrawal, Varennikov would insist that teams of UN observers should travel to Pakistan. When one eventually did, Islamabad apparently refused to permit it to inspect any installation of ISI, the Pakistani intelligence agency. Varennikov could do nothing about it; the Soviet Union had no real bargaining power outside Afghanistan.

In the effort to negotiate the difficult withdrawal inside the country, Varennikov met with Ahmed Shah Massoud. But the mujahideen commander pressed his growing advantage too far, and the initial contacts produced scant results. Massoud had formed a new political group, the Supreme Council of the North, in order to strengthen his hand as the end of the Soviet occupation loomed and jockeying between mujahideen groups eager to take power increased.

The Red Army's new reliance on solely defensive tactics helped Massoud tighten his grip on the Panjshir Valley during the summer and fall of 1987. In July, he staged a number of attacks against Afghan Army outposts in Kalafghan, in the mountains east of Kunduz. In a daring attack, 300 men fired rockets and mortars at the base in the first phase of their assault. They also peppered a nearby Soviet base with mortars to prevent it from supporting the Afghan forces. In October, Massoud staged another assault, against a base at the top of the Panjshir Valley in Koran-va-Monjan. The rebels took more than 250 prisoners. More important, they opened an easier northern route into the valley. At the same time, the Afghan Army withdrew a 500-man garrison at Pechgur.

||

Dmitri Lekarev knew he didn't have to serve in the military. If an escape from the draft was wanted, his father, a KGB colonel in charge of spying on British and American correspondents in Moscow, could have provided it easily. But the father, a disciplinarian by nature, would countenance no such thing. Instead, he packed Dmitri off to a military academy, where he trained as a paratrooper before being sent to Afghanistan—not as a paratrooper, however, because he was assigned to a regular infantry battalion in a transport base on his way there. But ties between paratroopers, who considered themselves the ablest of Soviet soldiers, were very strong, and a paratroop lieutenant, noticing Lekarev's light blue beret and blue-and-white-striped paratrooper's vest, offered to engineer another transfer. Claiming Lekarev as his cousin, the lieutenant asked a battalion commander to authorize a change, and when the commander agreed, the young "cousin" was assigned to be a machine-gunner in a paratrooper assault storm battalion attached to the Seventieth Separate Motorized Rifle Brigade. Lekarev arrived in Kandahar in that capacity in September 1987.

The next day, a young officer took him around the base to meet other privates from Moscow. That they were from Moscow was important. *Zemlyachestvo*, friendship between servicemen from the same region, was an essential element of soldiers' lives, affording networks for procuring food and clothing. It also provided crucial support for surviving *dedovshchina*, which Lekarev saw drive conscripts to suicide or being shipped home as psychological wrecks. Bonds were especially strong among ethnic minorities, including those from the Baltic States and Ukraine—and probably strongest of all among Uzbek, Tajik, and other Soviet Central Asian soldiers who usually received the most brutal treatment.

The old-timers in Lekarev's brigade learned not to pick on him because he could defend himself: he was lucky to have learned to fight well at his military academy. But he would see many other paratroop privates broken by their slavery to the veterans, just as in less elite units. After days of doing their laundry, washing their dishes, and running their errands, the most downtrodden were sometimes made to feel even worse by being left behind during combat operations. Resistance to the oppression often brought even harsher treatment.

Lekarev's first duty, loading bullets into automatic rifle magazines, continued for several months, enabling him to grow accustomed to the difficulties of life in Afghanistan. Most of what he ate was stolen from the brigade warehouses or from Afghans. Even when hungry soldiers left the base to shoot local farmers' sheep, as they often did, the cooking was usually on tin trays pilfered from the mess hall because pots and pans were as scarce as most other essentials. Still, he learned that other brigades' rations were even worse, perhaps because their officers were more ruthless.

Travel around Pashtun-dominated Kandahar seemed very dangerous. Sealing the border with Pakistan sixty miles from the regional capital fell to border guards from the Afghan Army's Fifteenth Division. But the caravans that passed freely into Afghanistan suggested to Lekarev that the border was practically open. He saw his first combat while escorting a supply convoy, one of the Seventieth Brigade's main tasks. The ambush took place along a narrow road in the Hindu Kush foothills. The convoy stopped. Lekarev rolled off his BMP and cowered on the ground, terrified of raising his head until he heard a scream above the hail of automatic fire. It came from a *praporshchik* who had crawled up behind him. "Fucking hell! Don't you hear where the shooting's coming from?! Fire your gun, goddamn it!" Even with that encouragement, Lekarev could barely bring himself to follow the order. Nevertheless, he escaped unscathed and soon, to his surprise, became used to fighting. During hand-to-hand combat near Shindand shortly afterward, he was even more surprised to find bayoneting people easy, as if he were slicing into butter.

Despite the military's ban on offensive operations, Lekarev's brigade often took part in *zachistki*. The old "cleanup" missions were now deemed necessary to protect Soviet convoys. Troops searching for rebel fighters usually rode two BMPs into *kishlaks*—which, however, were almost always empty when the soldiers arrived because the vehicles were seen kicking up dust miles away. Detaining suspected mujahideen was easier when heliborne troops arrived first to seal off the perimeters of the villages chosen for attack. Most suspected rebels were killed. The Soviets sometimes drove prisoners into the desert, where they shot at them with rocket grenades for amusement.

When they weren't killing or stealing from Afghans, Soviet

soldiers relied on locals near their bases and garrisons. The dependence was often mutual. Many Afghans' only source of fuel was from soldiers who'd siphoned it from their units' supplies. That kind of cooperation saved Lekarev from possible death when his battalion was making a rendezvous near its base with a motorized rifle battalion from Shindand. As the BTRs approached, Lekarev was surprised to see no soldiers sitting on top as they usually did, a mystery that was resolved when the personnel carrier drew up. The men had taken cover from snipers, and came under fire again the minute they opened the hatches. Several were killed and injured—but apparently no one from Lekarev's battalion was targeted. Lekarev asked why of a mujahideen fighter taken prisoner in the ensuing gun battle. "Those other guys came here from somewhere else to fight us," the Afghan replied. "But you're *our* guys."

Although battalion commanders issued orders about where and when missions would take place, sergeants—the *praporshchiki*—controlled virtually everything else, including operational details. That arrangement swelled battlefield chaos by reducing communication between units to near-nothing. But since most officers tried to avoid duty in the Kandahar desert, the Seventieth Brigade had fewer commanders than usual, a circumstance Lekarev believed reduced some of the confusion and helped increase coordination during battle operations. The downside was fewer soldiers, too. The number of men in Lekarev's company increased slightly twice a year, after the spring and winter draft cycles, but then sank back down to an average of usually no more than half its regulation of thirty-four.

Deafness was another cause of the lack of coordination between infantry and artillery units. After two or three booms from the 152-mm barrel of a Hyacinth artillery vehicle, anyone nearby could hear nothing but ringing for a good twenty minutes. Shouted commands had to be repeated and repeated. Central Asian soldiers were often assigned to man the loudest artillery pieces, and almost always without the required earphones because most of that kind of equipment was stolen higher up the supply chain. Distrust between Tajiks and Uzbeks and their Russian comrades further increased chances for miscommunication when weapons were fired.

Lekarev saw a BTR destroyed when a soldier mistook a *praporshchik*'s command to rotate his turret fifteen degrees for an order to move it *five* degrees. That little mistake cost twelve lives, but if coordination on the ground was bad, there was *none* with the air force, as far as Lekarev could tell. The proof of that was an attack on his unit by Mi-24 helicopters during an operation in Helmand Province.

Lekarev's first brush with death came about halfway through his tour. He was sitting on top of a BMP escorting another convoy when it came under rocket-grenade fire. While he was loading his automatic rifle, a grenade exploded some twenty feet away, knocking him from the vehicle. When he woke eighteen hours later in a hospital, he had a heavy concussion and bad bruising but was otherwise not seriously hurt. During his stay, a girl about seven years old sat on the floor not far away. Lekarev offered her some of his precious supply of chocolate and a tin of condensed milk. She returned for more the following day, and with her father the day after that.

"You can take her now," said the bearded, turbaned man in broken Russian.

"What do you mean?" asked Lekarev.

"You've paid your bride-money, she's yours now." Dumbfounded, Lekarev explained that he expected nothing in return.

Later, a young private driving a Kamaz truck near Lekarev's base hit and killed a small boy. Soon after, the father showed up demanding to speak to the brigade commander. The Afghan insisted on payment for his son's death: a bag of rice and another of flour.

In some areas, the Soviets began negotiating truces with elders and mujahideen commanders to establish "peace zones" through which soldiers and rebels would usually pass without reacting to each other. There were many exceptions, however, including when Lekarev's company fired on what it believed to be a mujahideen caravan that turned out to be a wedding procession moving between *kishlak*s. The threat of revenge attacks by Afghans after such incidents made moving nearby much more dangerous, and visiting local shops highly inadvisable.

III

Lekarev's BMP was escorting a convoy of spare machine parts in January 1988 when it came under fire outside Kandahar. Regular intervals between shots made it immediately clear that experienced, well-armed snipers were conducting the ambush. The convoy stopped and the troops rolled from their personnel carriers onto the sandy ground underneath their vehicles. They waited until dusk, after which the convoy proceeded without incident—but Lekarev's commanding lieutenant wanted revenge. "Let's find those snipers!" he ordered, and led eight soldiers to a *kishlak* near the site of their ambush. Armed with Mukha antitank grenade-launchers and a flamethrower, they approached the village from two sides. When a dog began barking as they were crawling toward its mud walls, the men panicked. But the barking soon stopped and they continued surrounding the settlement.

Then they began firing. To the soldiers' surprise, the inhabitants quickly returned fire. Lekarev would remember little of the raging battle: another soldier would later tell him he'd seen him digging in the sand with both hands, apparently to make a ditch in which to hide, a reaction the experienced Lekarev couldn't explain. After the Soviets prevailed, thanks partly to their flamethrower and grenades, the sniper rifles they found inside the *kishlak* led them to assume they'd killed the sharpshooters who'd pinned them down earlier in the day.

Walking single-file to reduce the danger of mines, the exhausted soldiers returned to their BMPs. Lekarev was next to last. Behind him, *praporshchik* Nikolai Pleshakov tripped and fell. When

Lekarev turned around, "He's a paratrooper and can't even walk on level ground!" was barely out of his mouth before he saw that Pleshakov was lying still. Something was seriously wrong. Bending down to help, Lekarev registered irregular breathing but could see no blood. Then he saw Pleshakov had been shot in the head right behind the ear, a wound that had blinded him. Lekarev and other soldiers picked him up and rushed him to the BMPs, but he was dead before they reached the vehicles.

IV

Valery Vostrotin, who helped storm the Taj-Bek palace as a new lieutenant in 1979, graduated from Moscow's prestigious Frunze Military Academy in 1985. Now a colonel, he spent a year leading a paratrooper regiment in the Moldavian capital Kishinev before returning to Afghanistan in 1986 to command the Bagram-based 345th Separate Paratroop Regiment, of which his old Company 9 was part.

Vostrotin, his already rugged features now scarred by his battle injuries, had become highly popular, thanks not least to the pains he took to entertain his men. The notorious skirt-chaser with seemingly never-ending family problems back home organized many drinking bouts and parties with the base's female staff. His hero was Denis Davydov, a nineteenth-century hussar and minor poet famed for leading guerrilla attacks against Napoleon's invading army. Unlike Davydov, however, Vostrotin was on the receiving end of a resistance force, one he recognized as noticeably more experienced and well armed than when he'd last left in July 1982. The largest difference he found on the Soviet side lay not in fighting ability but infrastructure: instead of crammed tents, officers now lived in barracks with electricity and running water. But if bases were far better equipped, as far as he could tell, fighting tactics hadn't perceptibly changed apart from a decision to stop mounting large-scale operations and to cut back the size of units sent on missions.

Commanders also had new orders to recruit mujahideen into the Afghan Army, but Vostrotin quickly dismissed that as a senseless task. The main purpose, as he saw it, was submitting reports that would further pad the Fortieth Army's illusory statistics about progress, on the order of: "As a result of such-and-such operation, 125 mujahideen were killed, 22 taken prisoners, such and such number of weapons found . . . and such number of mujahideen joined the DRA military." In fact, enemy casualties were much overblown and men coerced into agreeing to join the Afghan Army usually deserted upon receiving their uniforms and weapons.

On one of the first operations of his new tour, Vostrotin found himself bivouacked near the village of Khasankheyl, in the green flatland just south of the Panjshir Valley, very near where he'd been seriously wounded by a rocket-propelled grenade while riding in a BMD six years earlier. He asked an interpreter to scrawl MUJA-HIDEEN MUST DIE in Dari on a red cloth he found, then fashioned it into a flag around which he commanded his soldiers to lay a minefield. When he returned to the spot three days later, the flag was gone. Hoping the mines had caused the enemy suffering, Vostrotin felt he'd taken revenge for his wounding. His bravado also earned him more respect from his troops.

The colonel's reconnaissance chief was a fit, fair-haired captain with a Roman nose. Franz Klintsevich headed a thirty-man "special propaganda group" within the 345th Paratroop Regiment. He'd joined the 345th in 1986 and became close to Vostrotin. Code-named Chameleon, Klintsevich's group had been formed to run agents inside the mujahideen, but it was soon conducting other types of operations. Twenty-eight-year-old Klintsevich had studied Dari, the Afghan form of Farsi, at Moscow's Military Institute of Foreign Languages. His assignment was not to seek out operational intelligence but to take the measure of mujahideen ideology and political activities.

Captain Klintsevich found the mujahideen to be well-organized, canny strategists, and excellent psychologists. "You can buy an Afghan," he liked to say, "but you can't beat him." He also confirmed the importance the rebels placed on Stinger missiles by identifying them as a mark of status. The weapons often accompanied commanders wherever they went, borne by subordinate fighters. Three men lugging three missiles were a serious show of a commander's power.

Colonel Vostrotin relied heavily on reconnaissance and negotiations with Afghan civilians. Whenever possible, he informed local residents of planned convoys and search and offensive operations in the area. "We won't touch you if our soldiers are allowed to pass by on the main road," he'd communicate to local elders. "But we'll retaliate if we're attacked." Vostrotin believed he was saving his men countless skirmishes that way.

In 1987, Captain Klintsevich's group was ordered halfway up the Kunar Valley near Aserabad to aid the Sixty-sixth MRD, pinned down by relentless mujahideen shelling. The heavily mined mountain pass was accessible only by helicopter. Landing in bad weather, Klintsevich helped pinpoint the rebel location and direct artillery fire there. He did that by monitoring mujahideen radio traffic with the help of a Western two-way radio he had appropriated from an intercepted caravan and always carried with him.

But most of Klintsevich's time, at least early in his tour, was spent organizing missions to intercept caravans from Pakistan and Iran, now one of the main Soviet activities in Afghanistan. The caravans were legion, except after winter snow clogged the mountain passes, which decreased their number by about two-thirds. The Chameleon group often traveled in a helicopter squadron of eight Mi-24s and eight Mi-8s, which usually flew dangerously low for observation. When they spotted caravans of camels, horses, and mules, the choppers landed and the animals' loads were inspected, occasionally after battles broke out.

Risking punishment for disobeying regulations that forbade captains to participate in certain dangerous operations, Klintsevich sometimes went along on such ambushes. Those operations

Two *spetsnaz* Mi-8s after having attacked a camel caravan moving from Pakistan. (*Alexander Liakhovskii archive*)

began with helicopters first landing in several locations. The dust kicked up by their rotors would obscure the view of mujahideen, making it nearly impossible to tell where the Soviets debarked. Klintsevich's unit usually lay low until nightfall, then trekked up to fifteen miles to planned ambush locations. The work was often disheartening, if only because intercepted supplies and medicine were of far better quality than the Soviet variety. But the eight Stingers on which Klintsevich soon got his hands were a welcome reward.

V

The 345th Regiment helped Afghan forces carry out annual operations to resupply and relieve a large Afghan border-guard garrison in eastern Paktia Province. The isolated stronghold stood on a series of cliffs called the Parachinar ledge, just west of the Pakistani town of Parachinar. During one such operation in May 1987, Vostrotin's friend Colonel Ruslan Aushev led his 108th Motorized Rifle Regiment up a parallel valley. The charismatic ethnic Ingush with rakish good looks, a bushy dark mustache, and green eyes had been awarded his Hero of the Soviet Union after a major offensive in Panjshir in May 1982.

The men had to make their way through thick forest, unusual in Afghanistan, and more dangerous for Soviets trying to defend themselves from well-hidden mujahideen. Vostrotin made good progress at first, moving forward from one rocky strategic height to another. Although the Soviets were still there ostensibly only to aid the Afghan forces, they bore the brunt of the fighting, following the same path they'd taken in previous years. This time, however, the combat was fiercer.

As the Soviets neared the garrison, the mujahideen began tenaciously attacking their positions from the bushes and trees on all sides of the rocky heights, often several times a day. Colonel Vostrotin ordered his men to affix bayonets at all times. Attacks usually took place between dusk and dawn. What was not at all usual was Vostrotin taking part himself, fighting off attackers with his fists and Makarov pistol, once after he was ambushed while making his way to a reconnaissance unit. At one point, the mujahideen pinned down two companies for three days from surrounding high ground while they engaged soldiers in hand-to-hand combat.

The attacks caught Vostrotin completely by surprise because close combat was unusual. The mujahideen usually avoided it at all costs. The explanation came with the Soviets' first prisoners: the rebels were Arab volunteers, giving Vostrotin his first sight of a black African fighter in Afghanistan. Most of the rebels wore black uniforms, fingerless gloves, and were equipped with American M-14 rifles.

Aided by air attacks and supplied with reinforcements and 240-mm Tulpan self-propelled mortars, Colonel Vostrotin finally broke through to the border, where he met his friend Aushev. Vostrotin had lost fifteen men. He estimated his forces killed six hundred resistance fighters and heard reports that more than two thousand were hospitalized across the border in Pakistan. Seven years after having lost his first Hero of the Soviet Union award, Vostrotin finally got one he could keep.

Still, he was reminded of the great difficulty of maintaining control over the mountain passes. Despite the Soviet efforts, the area remained under mujahideen control. One of Paktia's two main cities, Khost, lies forty-five miles southeast of the larger Gardez across some of the region's most treacherous territory. Khost's forty thousand residents and garrison of eight thousand Afghan soldiers had long been cut off by local mujahideen tribesmen led by rebel commander Jallaladin Haqqani. The city was supplied by airlift, but the appearance of Stingers had made flights much riskier.

Haqqani had attracted considerable support from Arab fundamentalists, and he hosted many Arab volunteers, some of them convicts sent from Egypt, Jordan, and other countries to take part in the jihad. They were among the thousands of foreign fighters pouring into the country, some of whom clashed with Afghans who were far less religiously observant. Arab money was also being used to carve roads and cave complexes from the region's mountain rock. Among those building in Paktia and Nangarhar provinces was Osama bin Laden, who had opened his first training camp for jihadists in 1986.

The Soviets estimated about fifteen thousand mujahideen were active in the area. Haqqani had positioned some of his forces high above the lush, tree-filled Satukandav mountain pass along the Khost-Gardez road. They were well armed with high-caliber machine guns and antiaircraft weapons, including Stingers and British Blowpipes.

In 1987, the Soviets decided to mount a show of force to open the road. It would be the biggest offensive of the entire war and involve a large part of the Fortieth Army. Vostrotin's Kabul-based 345th Paratroop Regiment would be among five Soviet and Afghan divisions, amounting to ten thousand Soviet troops and eight thousand Afghan soldiers, that would take part in an operation overseen by the Fortieth Army's new commander, Lieutenant General Boris Gromov. He'd been appointed in July, and is said to have attempted

Map 3: Gardez-Khost Road

to convince the general staff the operation would be a folly. Nevertheless, the assault began in mid-November.

A force of mostly Afghan soldiers moved along the road southeast from Gardez while Soviet air and artillery units provided support and sappers cleared mines along the Kanay Valley south of Gardez. Even the initial push down the relatively open part of the road to Khost was extremely slow going, since the way was heavily mined and mujahideen waited in ambush. Before sappers could begin demining, often by scraping off a layer of road to get to the fuses, the Soviets had to take control of high points within striking distance on either side. Many soldiers of the 345th Regiment were familiar with the area from previous operations along the Gardez-Khost road, but if Vostrotin's men had sometimes covered up to twelve miles a day there, they were now lucky to make a single mile. It took a month to get to the Satukandav Pass, about twenty miles east of Gardez, where the real fighting began.

VI

By the time of Operation Magistral, Vostrotin had come to trust Klintsevich more than some of his higher-ranking deputies. When the reconnaissance chief was sick in Bagram that November, Vostrotin insisted he transfer to a Gardez hospital, then that he return to duty two weeks later. The haste paid off when Klintsevich received intelligence about a well-hidden mujahideen arms cache in a cave complex in the Srana District along the Gardez-Khost road. After scouring the countryside, the Soviets found the abandoned hoard near two helicopter landing pads in a thoroughly mined area, through which sappers required six hours to clear a path. The complex was also well protected by antiaircraft guns that could be retracted into a cave. Inside, Klintsevich found a great store of Soviet weapons, and other materiel and supplies, including Pakistani sleeping bags. Reams of documents provided information about the

Franz Klintsevich *(right)* with two of Vostrotin's other
deputies in the 345th Regiment—political officer Major
Valery Samsonov *(middle)* and Lieutenant Colonel Yuri
Lapshin—near the Satukandav Pass during Operation
Magistral on January 20, 1988. *(Alexander Liakhovskii
archive)*

rebels' ties with Chinese intelligence agents and proof that some of
the weapons had passed through Czechoslovakia and Yugoslavia.

A popular television correspondent named Mikhail Leshchinskii, who reported for the most-watched Channel 1, was flown in
to trumpet the important find back home. But the Soviets soon
came under fire again, and Vostrotin gave the order to evacuate.

On December 19, Soviet paratroopers joined Afghan forces
to battle for the Satukandav Pass, the site of Haqqani's most important defenses, manned partly by rebels loyal to the hard-line
mujahideen leaders Sayyaf and Hekmatyar. After moving toward
the foothills on personnel carriers, units of the 345th continued to
climb on foot. Clambering up steep, rocky Janghulegar Mountain,
which the soldiers dubbed "the Hooligan," they came under enemy machine-gun and rocket fire that forced them to retreat. With
a large number of companies advancing and retreating in various
directions compounding the usual communication problems, the
345th Regiment found itself under fire not only from the mujahideen but also from other Soviet forces and from the "greens,"
Afghan Army units. Vostrotin dispatched Klintsevich to coordi-

nate operations with the Afghan 8th Division, whose commander Klintsevich ordered to act only with Vostrotin's approval.

A company of the 345th staged a nighttime operation to storm one of the heights, and achieved a rare initial success. But even when the Soviets managed to take such strategic positions, mujahideen attacking from other high ground still forced retreats. Vostrotin began using a new tactic, in addition to air sorties given him by Gromov. Advancing soldiers laid mines as they went—and lured rebel fighters to them when they were pushed back. Used together with the artillery, the "hunting system," as Vostrotin called it, proved highly effective.

The Soviets also used deception in the form of dummies with parachutes thrown out of helicopters, which prompted the mujahideen to fire and expose their positions. Soviet planes bombed the sites before heliborne troops staged a series of nighttime attacks to seize Haqqani's positions. Those operations—flying at night through the passes under the constant threat of Stingers—were more treacherous than merely very dangerous.

Paratroop units were flown to strategic heights to cover the armored columns making their way up the road. One of the most important such places was a cliff top marked 3234—its height in meters—on Soviet maps. After being delivered there to hold a small, isolated garrison overlooking ten miles of the road, Company 9's thirty-nine men came under relentless fire from machine guns, rockets, and mortars on January 7. While the huge, mixed barrage provided cover, rebels crawled toward the soldiers from several directions. Dressed in black, they yelled, "Allah Akbar!" and, in Russian, "Russ! Surrender!" The Soviets surmised that the force was actually composed of hundreds of Pakistani commandos. Klintsevich and others had seen them parachuting from helicopters during the night. A Pakistani videotape of the operation he later confiscated from a captured officer seemed conclusive confirmation.

The fierce assault proceeded, threatening to overwhelm the Soviet soldiers. They responded to their attackers' taunts by calling out their hometowns before lobbing grenades: "For Kuibishev!" "For Borisov!" Despite their far smaller number, the men of Company 9 stood their ground while the rebels launched wave after wave of bloody attacks that lasted into the night. From the garrison's crude stone quarters, Senior Lieutenant Ivan Babenko called in artillery strikes that were highly risky because the volleys from below arced toward Company 9 as well as the rebels. A private named Andrei Fedotov ordinarily operated the radio, but he lay in a corner, wounded from shrapnel. When the radio's batteries began to fade, he crawled over to wire together several weak spare batteries before he died, the wires still clutched in his hand.

Ammunition almost ran out, but before it did, reinforcements arrived with more supplies. They came in a helicopter that unloaded and took off just before a fog rolling rapidly toward the cliffs isolated the little band of Soviets. Having flown in with the reserves, Klintsevich saw a blood-drenched soldier wheezing through a hole in his chest made by shrapnel that had punctured his trachea. When Klintsevich asked a young medic to do something about it, he replied that he had nothing to bandage the wound. In desperation, Klintsevich found a discarded biscuit wrapping and pressed the wax paper against the private's chest so he could breathe through his mouth. Vostrotin was now refusing to allow helicopters to take off for the cliffs to collect dead and wounded, and Klintsevich radioed his commander to beg him to change his mind. "People are dying! Let's save some of them!" The soldier died soon after the colonel refused.

Casualties mounted. Disobeying orders, a pilot took off for the cliff top in the heavy fog, but with landing on hill 3234 no longer possible, the best he could do was put down his Mi-8's front wheel. Ammunition was quickly unloaded and Klintsevich helped three soldiers carry several heavily wounded and dead men to the helicopter. When the exhausted men couldn't muster the strength to load the last body, the helicopter's engineer jumped off to help. "Quick! Quick!" screamed the pilot as a new dark cloud of fog approached the cliff. The chopper took off just in time, but the

Soldiers of Company 9 on hill 3234 after having fended
off rebel attacks during Operation Magistral, January
1987. (*Alexander Liakhovskii archive*)

pilot would be given a serious reprimand, despite petitions from
Klintsevich and even Vostrotin. Back on hill 3234, the fighting
continued until morning, when the rebels finally abandoned their
attacks. The cost of Company 9's valiant holding of the garrison
was six men killed and ten wounded.

Klintsevich remained on hilltop 3234 for two weeks, during
which the garrison came under frequent tracer fire, but saw no
more serious fighting. One night, two mines connected to tripwires
simultaneously detonated at a sentry post manned by a fresh-faced
private. Expecting another assault, the Soviets unleashed a barrage
of machine-gun fire. No attack came; Klintsevich believed rabbits
may have set off the mines.

The massive effort of Operation Magistral as a whole pushed
on, and the Soviets eventually opened the road to Khost. Vostrotin
cheered his men, who'd missed New Year's, by decreeing they'd celebrate on January 31 back in the relative comfort of Bagram. But
when the 345th Regiment and the other Soviet forces returned to
their bases, the mujahideen promptly retook their positions in the
hills. Many Soviet soldiers subsequently saw Operation Magistral

as no more than a completely unnecessary demonstration of toughness to the rebels. Had soldiers given their lives for that empty cause, that worthless reason? What was the sense of launching a major operation when it was clear the Soviet Union would be withdrawing its forces as soon as it could—and along a road that was used relatively little? As much as any other battle of the past years, Magistral begged the kinds of questions that lie at the center of any "limited" counterinsurgency struggle. It came to be a symbol of the futility of the entire war, not merely its last years.

Soon after Magistral, Vostrotin finally received the Hero of the Soviet Union medal he'd been awarded in May. Fortieth Army commander Gromov received another. Vostrotin would soon be promoted to general.

VII

By the beginning of 1988, extracting the Soviet forces from Afghanistan had become more important to the Kremlin than the nature of the regime that would remain in place. But Moscow was bogged down in talks with Islamabad, unable to agree over how the withdrawal should proceed. Finally, in February, Gorbachev unilaterally declared that all the Soviet Union's 100,000 troops would begin pulling out on May 15. He stipulated only that some kind of understanding be reached. Half the troops would return home within three months, the other half by February the following year. But the question of who would hold power afterward remained a sore point. While Gorbachev hoped Mohammed Najibullah would cut deals to enable him to remain in control, Pakistan prepared to topple him as quickly as possible.

On April 14, Gorbachev signed a peace accord in Geneva that gave Moscow nine months to pull out its forces. The agreement, whose other signatories were the Afghan government, Pakistan, and the United States, included "noninterference" articles supposedly protecting Afghanistan's sovereignty and right to self-determination. The country would have the right to be free from foreign intervention or interference, and its refugees would have the right to a secure and honorable return. Moscow could continue giving the Afghan government billions of dollars in aid. But Pakistan, the United States, and other mujahideen-backers would have to stop providing the rebels support. Those provisions, and the document in general, were intended to salve Moscow's humiliation for having to reverse its Afghanistan policy after a decade of brutal war. Although Moscow purportedly *would* have secured a friendly government—the goal envisioned in 1979—the Geneva Accords finessed the main sticking points in the standoff with Pakistan. In fact, American funding and Pakistani training of the mujahideen would continue, and would help ensure that whatever remained of Afghanistan would teeter on the verge of disintegration.

Several days before the agreement was signed, a giant explosion devastated ISI's central arms warehouse outside the Pakistani town of Rawalpindi. More than ten thousand tons of rockets, mines, shells, Stingers, arms, and ammunition earmarked for the mujahideen blew sky-high, sending up a large mushroom cloud. However, the incident was apparently an eerie coincidence that reflected no change in Moscow's plans. On May 15, 1988, twelve thousand Soviet troops began withdrawing garrisons from Jalalabad, Gardez, Kandahar, and other cities. Logistics, supply, and nonessential units were the first to pull out, and the Fortieth Army further restricted combat to the most essential missions, chiefly to keep roads open along mujahideen ambush positions and to resupply garrisons and outposts.

Jalalabad was the first Soviet garrison handed over to the Afghan Army, on May 14. The Sixty-sixth Separate Motorized Rifle Brigade left the base in fully operational condition, having repaired facilities and equipment, and handed it over with a three-month supply of ammunition, food, and fuel. By the afternoon, the base was completely stripped of equipment—air conditioners, radios, even doors and window frames—which were sold to Jalalabad shops. The commander who'd signed for the base asked for new supplies. From then on, the Soviets would videotape their handover procedures.

The Geneva Accords incensed General Varennikov. Worried that Hekmatyar and other fundamentalist rebels might follow the Soviets north, taking their jihad to Soviet Central Asia, he continued railing against American funding of mujahideen bases in Pakistan. At the same time, he felt the Afghan Army had become significantly more effective, giving Najibullah at least a chance of remaining in power. That put him at odds with even the Afghan president himself, whose growing frustration with the Soviet pullout the general did his best to calm.

Varennikov based his hopes on his experiences during extensive tours of Afghanistan. He'd spearheaded the construction of several new roads, an asphalt factory in Kandahar, and the digging of water wells. Even at that late date, he believed those and other projects had won the support of some locals. He'd also negotiated with a number of mujahideen commanders in addition to Massoud, among them fifteen commanders in Herat who promised to allow safe passage to Soviet columns moving along the main highway from Kandahar northwest to Kushka on the border with Turkmenistan. In return, Varennikov promised to stop targeting mujahideen trading with Iran, mostly in opium and hashish.

Fortieth Army commanders received copies of a memo listing six discussion points for negotiating cease-fire agreements with hundreds of local mujahideen groups. The Soviets promised not to launch offensive operations and to ignore mujahideen looting and drug trade, in return for which the rebels would have to agree to stop ambushing convoys returning to the Soviet Union. The Soviets also issued vaguely worded promises of political power in an effort to encourage rebel leaders to back the government during negotiations that appeared to proceed relatively well, at least in the beginning.

As Soviet troops withdrew, the standoff with the mujahideen became more relaxed. Soldiers and officers flocked to bazaars to buy as many televisions and other electronics as they could haul back to the Soviet Union. Even obvious mujahideen fighters interacted with the Soviet soldiers, selling them tobacco and other goods in addition to the usual drugs.

Private Dmitri Lekarev's Kandahar-based Seventieth Separate Motorized Rifle Brigade was among the initial group of forces that left on May 15. After turning over its barracks, tents, warehouses, and other installations to Afghan Army forces, his regiment pulled out in columns of armored personnel carriers, trucks, and tanks that rumbled slowly northwest toward Herat. Despite Varennikov's claim of safe passage on the highway, the column was ambushed as it reached the Shindand Pass south of Herat. Lodged in the craggy cliffs above the valley road, the mujahideen fired rounds from two heavy 12.7-mm DShK antiaircraft machine guns. Unable to maneuver their BMP cannons high enough to counterattack, the Soviets were forced to turn back.

When a second attempt in June put the Seventieth Brigade under fire in the same pass, it again retreated to Kandahar. On a successful third try, however, Lekarev crossed the Friendship Bridge over the Amu Dar'ya River into Uzbekistan on August 8. Expecting a wave of relief for having left the conflict behind them, many troops felt only little more than their accustomed exhaustion. When the column stopped and Lekarev jumped off his BMP, a young lieutenant instinctively yelled, "What the hell are you doing?! There are mines everywhere!" Lekarev gently reminded him they were finally back on unmined Soviet soil.

VIII

Air Force Colonel Alexander Rutskoi, who'd been shot down near Zhawar in 1987, returned to Afghanistan in early 1988 as deputy head of the Fortieth Army's air forces. He had become critical of military policy, and believed much more should have been done to build infrastructure and employ locals to win their support. Still, he came to enjoy serving in Afghanistan—as did Valery Vostrotin, Ruslan Aushev, and many other professional warriors—for the fierce loyalty the war fostered among fighting men. Like it or not, Afghanistan was the central part of their so-far-successful military careers. Rutskoi's warm feelings for Afghanistan itself were boosted by Mohammed Najibullah's special affinity for pilots. On seeing Rutskoi, the president several times unbuckled an expensive watch from his wrist and presented it to him. What the colonel *disliked* was the paperwork that took up most of his day, the greater part of it from his command of the Bagram air base. So he began finding opportunities to take part in operations, an exploit made easier by his reputation as a crack nighttime flier who had trained many pilots during his first tour. Since their yearlong stints were coming to an end, Rutskoi now trained more pilots, and soon his squadron was attacking mujahideen bases that threatened the Soviet withdrawal around the Salang Pass, Jalalabad, Shindand, Khost, and Kandahar.

In late July, the Soviets learned of a large delivery of supplies from Pakistan. Reconnaissance flights noticed heavy activity at a Pakistani air base in Miram Shah, across the Afghan border in the country's northern tribal areas. On August 4, Rutskoi took off in a MiG-23 to enter Pakistani air space and photograph U.S. planes unloading supplies. After spotting as many as sixty trucks being loaded, he made a second pass and saw even more, then, while still in the air, ordered planes back at Bagram to prepare for an attack.

After nightfall, eight Su-25s and four MiG-23 escorts took off in pairs from Bagram and headed for Pakistan. Rutskoi's account of what happened next differs from other testimony. He says the Soviet planes were intercepted by Pakistani F-16s after they crossed the border. He says he would later learn one of his pilots was a spy who betrayed the mission. Meanwhile, his radar system began beeping a warning of an incoming rocket. It hit his right engine, setting it on fire. When the beeps sounded again, he could do nothing to maneuver the plane. He ejected seconds before the next rocket hit. Launched from the plane, he managed to glimpse his disappearing aircraft below before the second rocket pierced the cockpit.

His parachute opened and he floated down, burned from the explosion caused by the first rocket, smelling his incinerated mustache, and peering at the Pakistani land below him. "Fuck!" he thought. "Here we go again, just what I need."

He saw trees. That was good, his landing wouldn't be hard—and indeed, the parachute caught in some branches, breaking his fall. Cutting its cords and lowering himself to the ground, he took stock of the supplies in a box under his seat: a snub-nosed AKSU automatic rifle, a small Makarov PM pistol, two grenades, two bars of chocolate, and four shots of morphine.

The land was hilly and forested. Nearby, a river flowed northwest toward Khost, across the border and back into Afghanistan. Easing himself into the water, he let the current take him four kilometers. When day broke and his wounds began burning from the sun, he hid in some undergrowth, where he quickly used all his morphine. Judging the risk of being seen as too great, he waited out the day, then repeated his river travel the following night until he saw Soviet helicopters searching for him by dropping flares some distance away. That was bad: it would alert the enemy that no ordinary pilot had been shot down.

The next day, Rutskoi was within a mile of the border when he saw a woman and a small child leading two cows. The child spotted him and pointed in his direction. Aiming his rifle at them, Rutskoi didn't pull the trigger. Instead, he jumped back into the water. He felt certain he'd soon be discovered, all the more when a large bend in the river took him away from the border. Sure enough, a group of mujahideen found him by nightfall. Defending himself with his rifle and pistol down to one bullet he left for his suicide, he says he heard a grenade explode very near him before he could pull the trigger a final time. A piece of shrapnel hit him in the head, shearing off some of his scalp and knocking him unconscious.

He woke hanging from a pole that was being carried by two men while a third chanted. His arms and legs were bound; the best he could hope for his future was a quick death, with minimal torture. The mujahideen fighters—of Hekmatyar's force, he would find out—brought him to a base carved into mountain foothills, where he was handcuffed and interrogated. While flies and mosquitoes fed on the flesh exposed by his burns, he identified himself as "Captain Ivanov"—which brought further retribution. His hands were cuffed behind his back, then tied to a rope that was hung from the ceiling. He lost consciousness from the pain.

Rutskoi was still hanging when he awoke from a loud din. He saw American Cobra helicopters landing outside the cave. Uniformed soldiers jumped out and began yelling at the rebels while an officer struck one of the mujahideen fighters, who did not try to return the compliment. Entering the cave, the arrivals took down Rutskoi and gave him water. He was wrapped in a sheet, placed on a stretcher, and flown away.

With no idea exactly who'd rescued him, Rutskoi was delivered to a military base and interrogated in English and broken Russian. He refused to answer, which resulted in more punishment. He was lowered into a concrete hole in the ground, its bottom filled with water, and a metal grille was placed over his head. He remained there a week. Then he was removed, given medical treatment, and taken to a small bungalow, by which time he had concluded he was in the hands of the Pakistani ISI. In any case, his conditions were incomparably better: although guards stood at the door and outside every window, he was dressed in a clean Pakistani *shalwar kameez*, treated respectfully, and even shown videos of action films and pornography, which he'd never seen in the Soviet Union. Rutskoi believed the Pakistanis had worked out who he was. "Anything you see," he was told of the women in the videos, "you can have—Asian, European, you name it." He was more interested in food, which was also choice. Having had almost nothing to eat for two weeks, he was somewhat overwhelmed to be instructed to select what he wanted from a menu.

That was part of a determined recruitment effort that now began. Although Rutskoi would never know exactly who was questioning him, some of his interrogators who spoke English and used Russian interpreters clearly weren't Pakistanis. Handing him a felt-tip marker and a map of Afghanistan, they told him to "Just mark where the Soviet air defenses are." He was also asked where major Afghan bases and weapons caches lay and questioned about details of the Soviet withdrawal schedule, for which he was offered $3 million, a Canadian passport, work as a flight instructor, and the rank of general. When that didn't work, the interrogators took to making lighthearted arguments about the superiority of the U.S. Air Force, reinforcing his suspicion they were actually Americans. He says he refused to take the bait because he knew that almost any rejoinder by him would reveal something about the Soviet military.

One interrogator who had spoken in English suddenly switched to Russian. "Why are you treating us as if we don't know the score?" the man asked. "You know your career will be over. You know you'll be sent to Siberia if you go back." That was a reference to the Soviet tradition of suspecting their own men who fell prisoner of being turned into spies by the enemy, even if they hadn't been traitors in the first place.

On August 16, Rutskoi was blindfolded and driven to a nondescript concrete building. The blindfold removed, he was shown a suitcase—containing money, he believed—while someone handed him a Canadian passport. "We understand your concerns," he was told. "You don't have to tell us anything now. Just sign this paper and we'll discuss everything later." Still refusing, he was blindfolded again and driven away. Soon after, the cloth over his eyes was removed again. Blinking in the bright light, he made out a bustling city street. He was in Islamabad; in the distance, he could see a red flag fluttering in front of the Soviet embassy. Weeks of dread and apprehension turned into relief.

Inside the embassy, Rutskoi stood in a room facing a foreigner—an American intelligence officer, he believed—for whom he was told he'd be exchanged. Passing each other after they were given the signal to cross the room toward their respective countrymen, they shook hands, after which the Soviet staff flew Rutskoi to Karachi. There they hid him in a kind of storage closet on a passenger jet until the plane crossed into Soviet airspace. When it landed at Moscow's Sheremetyevo Airport, a reunion with Rutskoi's wife, who was waiting there, was slightly delayed because she failed to recognize the stick of a man who had lost so much weight.

Rutskoi had twice previously been nominated a Hero of the Soviet Union. This time the medal was awarded, while a rich addition was made to the war's ironies: his belief that he owes his life to the CIA. If it weren't for American intervention, he was convinced, he'd have been left to die hanging in Hekmatyar's cave.

Alexander Rutskoi would return to Pakistan and Afghanistan after the Soviet collapse in early 1992, then as the Russian vice president under Boris Yeltsin. In Kabul, Mohammed Najibullah would ask him for more aid, which Rutskoi would help deliver.

Fortieth Army air force Colonel Alexander Rutskoi in 2007. (*Gregory Feifer*)

IX

CIA Islamabad station chief Milton Bearden would soon fly to Washington to head the agency's Soviet and East European division, the success of his two years fighting the Soviets from Pakistan having had much to do with his promotion. But even after two years there, he could not have been prepared for what an ISI officer told him over the telephone one day in August 1988, shortly after Rutskoi had been downed. "There's been an aircraft shot down near Parachinar," the officer said of the Pakistani town near the Afghan border. ISI knew the CIA was keen to get its hands on any example of Soviet weaponry, and this prize—a fighter with a nose full of intact avionics instrumentation—would be huge. For delivery of an aircraft that could save the Pentagon millions of dollars in research, the mujahideen were asking the fire-sale price of some ten Toyota pickup trucks and as many rocket launchers.

The ISI intermediary followed Bearden's rapid agreement with an offer of a bonus. "There's one more thing," he said. "They also have the pilot"—for whom the charge would be two more trucks and rocket launchers. It would be a matter of bemusement for the CIA officer when, five years later, Russian Vice President Alexander Rutskoi would turn against Boris Yeltsin and lead a nationalist revolt in Moscow.

Another twist of aviation fate occurred two weeks after Bearden rescued Rutskoi. General Zia's plane crashed near Islamabad, killing everyone on board, including General Akhtar—ISI's chief during most of the Afghanistan War—and eight more Pakistani generals as well as U.S. Ambassador Arnold Raphel and his military attaché. Although the cause was never found, witness statements that the Pakistani leader's plane dipped seriously, then regained altitude before plummeting to the ground fed contradictory rumors. Some blamed Soviet sabotage, supposedly performed in revenge for Pakistan's role in the Afghan War. Others pointed fingers at the CIA on a theory that Washington wanted Pakistan to cut its support of the mujahideen who were obstructing the Soviet withdrawal.

X

The Afghan government pleaded for increased Soviet aid to shore up its army. In August 1988, a senior Soviet Central Committee official named Oleg Baklanov flew to Kabul to discuss the requests. When his Tu-154 passenger jet was taxiing down Kabul Airport's runway to take off for its return to Moscow, it was attacked by rebel rocket fire. Although the plane escaped unharmed, the episode could not have boosted Moscow's hope for stability in Afghanistan.

The waves of Soviet evacuation continued. As the 345th Paratrooper Regiment packed up, reconnaissance chief Captain Klintsevich kept in constant contact with the mujahideen. Hoping to minimize casualties in as many operations as possible, he also took part in talks with those who controlled passes through which the Soviets continued to supply their remaining garrisons. One particularly difficult round of negotiations concerned a biannual convoy that passed through Alikheyl, southeast of Kabul just above the Black Mountains into which bin Laden had dug his massive cave complex. The supplies were for a garrison of "reds" and "greens"—Soviets and government Afghans—near an area firmly under mujahideen control. The talks succeeded and the garrison was resupplied.

Klintsevich and Vostrotin also tried to exploit rivalries among the mujahideen. When negotiations failed with one commander, they approached a rival with a promise of his adversary's territory. The second rebel commander's attack of the first group served to tie up his forces, relieving another headache for the 345th, at least for a time.

Klintsevich usually traveled to meetings with mujahideen on a BTR accompanied by a driver, a translator, and a second officer. Arriving at a *kishlak*, he and his translator would debark while the second officer remained behind. The captain made a point of taking off his coat to show he carried no weapons—which, in any case, he knew would provide little help if trouble arose. But he came close to being shot when his interpreter took off *his* coat on one occasion, and a grenade fell to the ground.

Once inside the usual venues of mud-walled *kishlak* buildings, Klintsevich kept in radio contact with the second officer, and his interpreter would leave to make visual contact every fifteen minutes. If the interpreter failed to appear, the second officer had orders to activate a company waiting nearby to storm the building and evacuate Klintsevich's corpse. For his additional security, the captain pretended to understand only Russian. When his interpreter stepped outside during one negotiation session and two mujahideen fighters began debating in Dari about killing him and stealing his BTR, Klintsevich tried to remain calm. When his interpreter, an Afghan Army sergeant named Murat Sharipov, returned, Klintsevich used Russian to describe their plight.

"So what do we do?" Sharipov asked.

"I don't know."

Sharipov didn't either, but something told him to ask for a guitar he'd spotted under a bed in the room. He began playing a popular Indian pop song that lightened the mood enough for the two men to leave unharmed.

Negotiations went well enough during another meeting for the Afghans to propose a toast to seal their deal. The Hennessy cognac they poured—Klintsevich's first taste of Western alcohol—so appealed to him that he forgot to send Sharipov on his regular little assignment. When he stepped outside to relieve himself some time later, Klintsevich noticed Soviet troops preparing to attack the building. Half an hour had passed since the last contact had been made, and he had only minutes to spare.

XI

The first half of the Fortieth Army's 100,000-odd troops crossed back into Soviet territory by October 15 relatively unscathed. But mujahideen groups were debating whether to ambush the combat units moving north. Although many wanted to exact revenge on an easy target, others argued for letting the Soviets leave as quickly as possible. Despite the efforts of Klintsevich and other Soviet officers, the desire for vengeance triumphed; Soviet units had to fight increasing attacks through the winter.

Developments elsewhere did not bode well for the Afghan government. Many Afghan Army soldiers abandoned their garrisons as soon as the Soviets left, especially in the farthest-flung regions, but even some populated areas fell quickly. After the 201st MRD withdrew from Kunduz, hundreds of mujahideen fighters looted the city. On Najibullah's request for help, General Varennikov flew to the city to coordinate its successful retaking by the Afghan Army's Eighteenth Division, backed by Soviet forces and heavy air support.

The Soviets were forced to periodically halt their withdrawal to carry out operations to protect their columns. They began using new weapons, including a tank-based heavy flamethrower, named Buratino, or Pinocchio, which soldiers said incinerated anything up to a quarter of a mile in front of it. The Soviets also introduced SCUD surface-to-surface missiles and low-altitude MiG-27 fighter jets.

To try to help smooth the withdrawal, the Kremlin sent First Deputy Foreign Minister Yuli Vorontsov to Pakistan to negotiate with mujahideen leaders about the ongoing pullout and a possible coalition government to replace the Najibullah regime. Foreign Minister Shevardnadze also flew to Islamabad in 1989. But the mujahideen were increasingly distracted by a power struggle of their own over who would come out on top after the Soviet withdrawal. The fundamentalist Hekmatyar, backed by ISI, was already assassinating rival mujahideen commanders and taking other brutal measures to try to eliminate his opponents around Afghanistan.

Ahmed Shah Massoud was well aware of the uncertainty into which Afghanistan would fall after a Soviet pullout. In 1987, he had told Atta Mohammed Noor, one of his top commanders, that although he believed the Fortieth Army would leave within a year, "I hope the Russians stay another four years."

"We've been fighting them so long, and now you want them to stay?" Atta laughed.

Massoud replied that he was concerned about the yawning splits within the mujahideen, especially between Hekmatyar and the other leaders. "We're experts in guerrilla warfare, not government," Massoud said. "Jamiyat and Shura-i-Nizar"—Rabbani and Massoud's organizations—"should never join the government." Atta says that was the only promise he ever witnessed Massoud break.

XII

The bulk of the Fortieth Army withdrew along the serpentine Salang Pass, winding up the flat plain north of Kabul into the barren rock-faced mountains, where huge snowdrifts slowed the withdrawal. Then through the pitch-black, exhaust-choked Salang Tunnel, and down the north side, treacherously slick with ice, toward the flat desert leading to the Friendship Bridge into Soviet Uzbekistan. Massoud agreed to a cease-fire with General Gromov, then had his fighters establish posts along the roads between Soviet and Afghan Army checkpoints to stop other mujahideen groups from attacking the rumbling convoys belching their black diesel fumes. Still, ambushes continued, often staged by looting rebels, mostly along the treacherous Salang Pass.

Helicopter pilot Vladimir Kostiuchenko—back on his third tour to support the withdrawal—was moving north toward Uzbekistan when a burst from a DShK machine gun took out the tail rotor of his Mi-8, which was loaded with bombs and flying on a full fuel tank. Kostiuchenko was unable to steer his craft or to stop it from spinning horizontally. But the highly experienced pilot instantly switched off his engine and the helicopter fell to the ground. It tipped over, but Kostiuchenko, his crew, and his passengers escaped without serious injury.

In late 1988, Vostrotin and other Soviet commanders were

ordered to break their cease-fire with Massoud. Najibullah had pushed for the directive, fearing Massoud would quickly topple him. The revered rebel leader had declined Najibullah's offer to become defense minister, made in a hope of neutralizing him. The Defense Ministry's order was not well received by Vostrotin and other high-ranking officers who opposed it as not only dishonest but also dangerous for Soviet forces.

General Gromov unleashed Operation Typhoon in January 1989. Three days of heavy fire followed from Buratino flame-throwers, Grad rockets, planes, and helicopters south of the Salang Tunnel. The fiery display prompted the mujahideen to increase their own attacks in response—and to display the corpses of Soviet soldiers along the sides of the road. Operation Typhoon was the final hurrah. According to Soviet records, the last soldier killed in Afghanistan was a paratrooper from Vostrotin's 345th Regiment, shot by one of Massoud's snipers. On February 15, 1989, a BTR carrying the blanket-draped body of Igor Liakhovich crossed the Friendship Bridge into Uzbekistan.

Shortly thereafter, a tank stopped in the middle of the bridge and the last Soviet officer officially to leave Afghanistan jumped off: Fortieth Army commander General Boris Gromov. As a large group of Soviet and foreign journalists looked on, he began walk-ing to the other side until he was greeted by his fifteen-year-old son, who clutched a bouquet of red carnations. They embraced and walked the last fifty yards together.

Najibullah acknowledged the formal withdrawal with a short statement: "I express my appreciation to the people and govern-ment of the Soviet Union for all-around assistance and continued solidarity in defending Afghanistan." The carefully scripted scene at the Friendship Bridge had pleased no one for its neatness. Hav-ing spent the previous week across the Soviet border in Termez, Gromov prepared for the drama by quietly crossing back into Af-ghanistan the previous night. Nor was he actually the last to leave: a few combat units would continue crossing the Friendship Bridge during the following weeks. Besides, hundreds of Soviet advisers would remain in Afghanistan. Among them was General Makhmut Gareev, Moscow's new chief military representative in Kabul. He'd arrived on February 7, by which time the mujahideen were stepping up their bombardment of the capital and the war appeared to be turning decisively against the government.

Gareev was a former deputy chief of the general staff, whose short physical stature belied his combativeness and fierce pride in his Tatar background. When he visited Najibullah shortly after February 15, the usually fearless-seeming Afghan president was frantic. Having pleaded with the Soviets not to withdraw, then to delay their schedule, and finally to leave some units behind, he evacuated his family to India. Gareev now advised him to return them to Kabul.

"You've got hundreds of advisers and subordinates working for you, not to mention the rest of the country," Gareev lectured. "Who's going to put any faith in your leadership if everyone suspects you're planning to leave the country yourself? Do you want those closest to you to be thinking about how to replace you?"

"There used to be 100,000 Soviet troops here," Najibullah replied defiantly. "And together with our army they couldn't neutralize the enemy. Now your forces have gone. What can we hope for?"

Gareev trotted out one of his favorite sayings in reply: "A good commander can make a column of three out of one Tatar soldier. You've got at least one Tatar here. Hold on, fight back. Otherwise, why did I come to Kabul?"

Soon Jalalabad was under siege by rebels, and Gareev flew out to organize the Afghan Army's defense.

Valentin Varennikov had already said his good-byes to Najibullah. When he and Yuli Vorontsov flew out of Afghanistan on the last plane to leave Kabul Airport on February 15, the general felt he was betraying the Afghan people. Like many other top officers, he was convinced the Red Army hadn't been defeated by the mujahideen. The fight had ended only because Gorbachev, Shevardnadze, and their like had given it up.

Some 620,000 Soviets served in Afghanistan. Officially, 13,833 died—although that number is still the subject of debate between various Russian government agencies—plus some 650 from affiliated units. Another 469,685 were sick or wounded; 10,751 of them became invalids. But many who fought in Afghanistan believe the real number of those killed was closer to 75,000. Among the equipment lost were 118 jets, 333 helicopters, 147 tanks, 1,314 APCs, 433 artillery pieces and mortars, 1,138 communications vehicles, 510 engineering vehicles, and 11,369 trucks. Even the unofficial figures are tiny compared to the Afghan deaths the conflict caused, along with a society left in utter ruin by the decade of bloody warfare. Few in Moscow truly believed Najibullah would be able to hang on without Soviet military support. It would be an irony of history, or another lesson about the unintended consequences of using force, that his regime would outlive the Soviet Union that was convinced it had a duty to teach the world how to think and live.

CHAPTER 8

AFTERMATH

I

Although most of the world believed the Soviet withdrawal meant Afghanistan's decade-long war was over, conflict of that nature rarely ends so easily or without lasting damage to all parties. The "host" country's losses were staggering. Roughly 1.3 million Afghans were believed to have been killed. About 5.5 million people, a third of the prewar population, had fled abroad and another 2 million were internally displaced.

The massive destruction did not seriously concern the CIA, whose officers celebrated the Soviet exit with a champagne party in Langley, then turned their attention elsewhere. Although the United States would continue funding the mujahideen, the amount of its aid plummeted from almost $500 million in 1986 to some $40 million in 1989. Washington's refusal to restock weapons lost during the massive warehouse explosion near Rawalpindi incensed the Pakistanis, who began turning against their former allies. ISI's new chief, General Hamid Gul, claimed Washington was breaking its promises by abandoning Afghanistan. Many in Islamabad believed the United States didn't want a mujahideen victory. Now that the Soviet Union was out, stalemate there would suit both superpowers.

In fact, Washington more or less matched its lack of worry over the population it had helped ravage with disinterest in the implications of a victory by fundamentalist Islamic mujahideen over the Soviet-backed government. The United States would begin earnestly perceiving the threat to regional—and global—security it had unknowingly nurtured only after the terrorist acts of September 11, 2001. Having blocked the Soviet advance south, most Americans believed there was no longer a strategic need to care about Afghanistan.

Matters were very different among the people most involved, however. In Peshawar, the mujahideen leaders formed a new alliance they called the Afghan Interim Government, or AIG, to take control of the country after what they hoped would be Najibullah's quick ouster. No less eager to see him go, Pakistan encouraged the Afghan parties it wanted to return home as quickly as possible. The mujahideen decided to begin by taking Jalalabad and making it a temporary capital and main base for operations until Kabul could be seized. In March 1989, thousands of fighters streamed toward the regional city seventy miles east of Kabul and thirty-five miles northeast of bin Laden's mountain cave complex near the village of Tora Bora. The Arab millionaire was said to have promised up to $200 a day to fighters taking part in the siege.

Preparing for the assault, the Afghan Army had reinforced defensive positions with new bunkers. The city's perimeter was surrounded with barbed wire, minefields, and pillboxes as far as twelve miles away. Soviet chief military adviser Makhmut Gareev flew to Jalalabad to help coordinate the defense.

Surprisingly, the measures worked, at least enough for the mujahideen coalition to begin tearing itself apart. With the Soviet enemy gone, infighting broke out almost immediately, and the Jalalabad siege disintegrated. In July, one of Hekmatyar's commanders, Sayed Jamal, ambushed a unit of Massoud's fighters near

Taliqan in the northern province of Takhar. Thirty-six men were killed, including seven of Massoud's top commanders. Attack units Massoud dispatched to hunt down the assailers found Jamal hiding in a basement. They delivered him to an Islamic court, which sentenced him to death by hanging. In August, Hekmatyar—by far the biggest beneficiary of ISI's ongoing largesse—withdrew from the AIG.

Spending some $300 million a month in 1989, the Soviets continued sending thousands of planes packed with weapons and staples—most important, tons of flour—into Afghanistan. In April, General Varennikov met several Afghan ministers in Khairaton, just across the Soviet border, for a pep talk. The following month, he traveled to Kabul to meet Najibullah and even flew to Kandahar. Varennikov found the Afghan president far more confident than when he'd last seen him, indeed now bearing himself as if he felt he had a real chance to hold on to power.

Two years later, Varennikov would be in a Moscow jail for helping direct a coup d'état attempt against Gorbachev. General Gareev, who would remain in Kabul until the end of 1990, would go on to become president of the Russian Academy of Military Scientists and the military's chief strategist and ideologue. Later he would use that position to help express Russia's new opposition to the West.

||

The Afghanistan War wasn't a trauma just for the survivors. For many Soviets, it represented a last senile folly of the Brezhnev era. Gorbachev's "bloody wound" highlighted the system's bankruptcy and undoubtedly to some degree helped speed the collapse of the Soviet Union.

Sympathy initially ran high for the soldiers and officers of the Fortieth Army who returned home after their protracted nightmare.

During the first weeks and months, troops were hailed as heroes and the government rewarded them with generous retirement benefits and allocations to perpetually scarce apartments. But the Afghan veterans would very quickly become just another group of victims. The whole of Soviet society was beginning to implode, leaving it unable to properly treat the men's physical injuries, let alone address their psychological scars.

The centrally planned economy was nearing collapse from increased demand as well as massive inefficiency and theft. And while store shelves were becoming ever emptier, it was no longer risky to buy coveted jeans from the growing number of Westerners who visited the Soviet Union. That was but one result of a transformation that also fed disillusionment in the old slogans and promises. Bold new television programs and newspapers that openly criticized the authorities were supplanting media that once consisted of state propaganda mainly recounting Soviet leaders' official pronouncements. In that heady time of crisis and uncertainty, few Soviets truly cared about their government's ten-year fiasco in Afghanistan or wanted to hear about the suffering of the soldiers.

The first relatively open interviews with veterans drew attention to two main complaints: cold and hunger. Conditions had been so bad military authorities in Afghanistan had restricted information about the straitened circumstances even from the KGB. Mikhail Zheltakov, a KGB officer posted to Kabul, had been warned then not to mix with military personnel. But he could not be stopped from seeing trucks of soldiers' supplies and rations stolen—or from noticing their contents stacking the shelves of local shops. The top commanders knew what was going on but took no effective action to stop it because even if they weren't directly profiting from the pilfering, the privations of their subordinates were low on their list of priorities. Zheltakov concluded that corruption forced soldiers to steal. Living as they did, they were unable to suppress the temptation to loot local houses, farms, and caravans—and kill their owners.

Returning to Moscow, Zheltakov joined the Committee of

Internationalist Soldiers—founded by Ruslan Aushev, the former commander of the 108th MRD—which was one of several new groups that had sprung up to assist veterans and to locate those missing in action. Zheltakov soon came to believe the war's worst damage to the Soviet Union wasn't the dead in Afghanistan, but the severe psychological injury suffered by those who returned. Many had great difficulty adjusting to civilian life. Having endured the war's horrors, they were upset by the seemingly trivial trials and squabbles of daily life. Of the tens of thousands of young men who had learned to steal and kill civilians with equanimity, some now easily turned to crime.

Veterans called themselves *Afghantsy*—literally, "Afghans." The Soviet collapse of 1991 left many adrift and unable to cope with their new lives. Just as some who had been hooked on drugs in Afghanistan succumbed to addiction, skyrocketing inflation wiped out most of their savings, like those of almost everyone else. Some former soldiers with missing limbs went out to the streets to beg; other veterans joined the vast mafia that was spawning in Russia's post-Soviet chaos and lawlessness.

In the postwar downsizing of the Fortieth Army, older officers were pushed into early retirement. Pilot Vladimir Kostiuchenko, who had barely escaped with his life when his helicopter crashed in November 1988, left the military soon after returning to the Soviet Union the following year. He faced a common problem: having served more than a decade, he wasn't registered to live in Moscow—a Soviet requirement extended by the government— even though his parents had lived there. Their deaths left him with nowhere to live as well as almost no money. Kostiuchenko appealed to acquaintances in the Party for help, and was lucky enough to be given a job in the customs agency. He soon helped organize the Russian Union of Afghanistan Veterans, another of the new networks that sought to benefit from the influence of the Afghan brotherhood's highly placed members.

The new veterans' organizations went into business. Well equipped to provide their own security in the dangerous conditions of the "robber" capitalism of the early 1990s, former military men soon learned to profit from tax breaks ostensibly aimed at providing assistance to invalids. Exempted in 1994 from paying duties on imported goods, veterans' groups quickly made huge profits, mostly from selling alcohol and tobacco. But the new wealth created bitter rivalries and fierce battles over the control of commercial activities netting hundreds of millions of dollars. It also nourished organized crime.

Among the loudest fights, one took place within a group called the Russian Fund for Invalids of the War in Afghanistan. When its chairman, a paratroop colonel who'd lost both legs, was ousted in 1993, he refused to relinquish control and took over the fund's Moscow branch. The new chair, Mikhail Likhodei, initiated a criminal case against his predecessor, after which Likhodei soon found himself targeted by assassins. The following year, he was killed when a bomb exploded in his apartment building's elevator. Two years later, Kostiuchenko was attending a memorial service at Likhodei's grave in Moscow's Kotlyakovskoe Cemetery when another bomb exploded, killing Likhodei's successor and twelve others.

Kostiuchenko was among the few who escaped without injury. He would serve as deputy head of the Russian Union of Afghanistan Veterans until his less-violent ouster from that post.

III

When the Soviets withdrew from Afghanistan, thousands of Afghans who had cooperated with them fled the country, fearing for their lives. Those who settled in Moscow and elsewhere had as little notion as anyone else that Najibullah would manage to sustain his tenacious grip on power. Almost a year later, in March 1990, Najibullah's Afghan Army fought off a coup attempt by Defense Minister Shah Nawaz Tanai, who had joined forces with Hekmatyar.

To attract support, Najibullah attempted to liberalize the government's policies. To signal that he was changing his ways, he had already altered the country's name from the Democratic Republic of Afghanistan, DRA, to the Republic of Afghanistan, RA. He'd also changed the PDPA's name to Hizb-i-Watan, "the Homeland Party."

But Najibullah could not survive without the lavish Soviet funding that would cease soon after August 1991, when Soviet hard-liners mounted their attempted coup d'état against Gorbachev. Shortly thereafter, the Soviets and Americans agreed to stop funding both sides of the Afghan conflict before the end of the year. When Gorbachev resigned on Christmas Day and the Soviet Union was formally disbanded, the Republic of Afghanistan was left to fend for itself.

Little more than a year later, in February 1992, General Abdul Rashid Dostum, who had fought the mujahideen in northern Afghanistan, turned against Najibullah. A stout Uzbek warlord with a bristling crew cut who had carved out a fiefdom around Mazar-i-Sharif, Dostum now allied with Massoud, and their combined forces took Mazar. Not long after, Herat and Kandahar also fell to them. Three years after the Soviet withdrawal, the mujahideen began closing in on Kabul, and Moscow advised Najibullah to resign.

The United Nations had been advocating a plan to transfer power peacefully from the government to the mujahideen. That solution failed when Najibullah fled on April 15. Stopped at the airport from leaving the country, he took refuge in Kabul's UN compound. His KhAD chief, Farukh Yaqubi, committed suicide.

Now mujahideen leaders turned on each other to battle for control over the capital. Hekmatyar's men snuck into the city to take key installations, but Massoud's forces, which had far superior training and a much more reliable command structure, pushed them back to the city's southern outskirts. In an effort to break the deadlock, the Peshawar Seven leaders formed an interim government called the Islamic Jihad Council. Mojaddedi was named president, Massoud defense minister, Gailani foreign minister, and Sayyaf interior minister. Hekmatyar declined to become prime minister as long as Massoud was defense minister.

The new council was fatally flawed. Kabul was put largely under the jurisdiction of Tajik and Uzbek forces from the north. Their ascendance struck a psychological blow to the country's majority Pashtuns, who lost control of the capital for the first time in three hundred years. Civil war broke out almost immediately.

Tajik scholar Rabbani soon took over the presidency from Mojaddedi, who was almost unanimously perceived as power-hungry by the others. In December 1992, a special assembly confirmed Rabbani in office for a two-year term. In response, Hekmatyar began mercilessly bombarding the city from the south to dislodge Massoud, who took command of forces fighting for the Rabbani government. They were no less ruthless killing civilians and demolishing buildings than their mainly Pashtun rivals.

Most of Kabul had largely survived the Soviet War's relentless attacks. It was now almost systematically destroyed as the rival mujahideen groups fought each other house-to-house. While refugees streamed from the crumbling city, an estimated eighteen hundred civilians were killed between May and August.

Meanwhile, the countryside reverted to medieval warlordism, with Pashtuns essentially ruling Kandahar and Ismail Khan taking over Herat with Iranian help. Dostum subjugated Mazar-i Sharif and fought Massoud for power over Kunduz. The independent warlords who controlled various roads demanded tolls for passage and fought rival groups for surrounding territory. To help finance their fiefdoms, the mujahideen increasingly looked to poppy cultivation, which had already become many people's sole means of survival. Afghanistan became the center of the global opium trade.

IV

The mujahideen took almost no Soviet prisoners during the first years after the 1979 invasion, but they later reconsidered. They used the four-hundred-odd Soviet personnel they captured during the rest of the war to extract intelligence and as slaves. Hundreds remain missing in action. Some of the Soviet personnel captured had deserted, hoping to either join the rebels or make their way to the West. Many were seized by mujahideen posing as traders, or drug dealers lured them from their comrades. Some prisoners were tortured and forced to convert to Islam in order to save their lives. Living in the mountains for years, the captives had little idea of where they were, let alone of how to escape. Some fought with the mujahideen against their own Soviet forces.

After questioning a handful of former Soviet prisoners, the CIA resettled a number of them abroad, where most led troubled lives. Many of those who remained in Afghanistan did so because they were psychologically, and in some cases physically, unable to return home. Marrying and settling down rarely helped them restore their minds and bodies to anything resembling normalcy.

The reluctance of the Fortieth Army command to take measures to rescue prisoners of war—largely based on the old Soviet suspicion that if prisoners weren't traitors to begin with, their captors later "turned" them—of course worsened their lot. Some families of prisoners were informed that their missing loved ones had died, and the relatives buried empty coffins believing they contained their remains. Although a few captured soldiers managed to smuggle letters to their families, almost all that reached the Soviet Union were intercepted and withheld by the KGB.

Hospital doctor Ada Semyonova was living on the outskirts of Tbilisi, the capital of the Soviet republic of Georgia, when her athletic, musically gifted son Konstantin Gabarayev enlisted in the army. While undergoing training in Turkmenistan to become a *praporshchik*, he was ordered to Afghanistan. A colleague of Semyonova who was serving as a military doctor hinted to her that he'd be willing to contrive a diagnosis that would excuse eighteen-year-old Kostya from service, but when she conveyed the offer to her son, he refused. "Is that the kind of thing you've taught me to do?" he asked his youthful, mild-mannered mother. She did not persist. At that point, just a year after the invasion, Afghanistan didn't seem dangerous enough for great worry. Kostya left for Afghanistan in May 1981 to serve as commander of a BMP infantry vehicle in the 201st MRD.

From his base in Kunduz, Gabarayev wrote his mother regularly, describing his generally boring guard duty at an electric power station. She knew him well enough to know he was withholding information about his combat operations, and only later learned he was wounded in the leg. After a year and a half, the young man began writing about his plans for returning to civilian life, which centered on his intention to get a university degree.

Semyonova started worrying when Gabarayev, due home in October 1982, failed to show up and no one explained why. After two months of anxiety, she contacted their local *voenkomat*, the military draft office. Getting no help there, she wired the Defense Ministry for information, again in vain, except this time without so much as a reply. Increasingly frantic, she sent more telegrams, now to every possibly relevant office she could think of. And as 1983 approached, she sought help from her hospital's head doctor, whose nephew happened to have been discharged from his Afghanistan tour in October.

When Semyonova met the former private and mentioned her son's name to him, she noticed his face turning white. Then she fainted. He was gone when she came to, after which another doctor told her he was crazy. "They all go crazy in Afghanistan," he said. Her burning requests to speak to the ex-soldier again got her no further than an insistence that he and her son had really never met, that the "crazy" young man had made a mistake.

Four days later, Semyonova was summoned back to the office of the head doctor, who had had a change of heart. Now the apparently sympathetic man confirmed that his nephew, who wasn't there for the meeting, had indeed known Gabarayev. Konstantin's BMP, the doctor further explained, was escorting a water truck near Kunduz, in the Samangan Region town of Kholm, when it broke down on September 19. Although the standard procedure was to fire a flare and wait for help, an inexperienced lieutenant ordered Gabarayev and another *praporshchik*, named Yuri Puch-kov, to walk to a Sarandoi police outpost about a mile away. Fif-teen minutes after the two set off, each carrying a submachine gun, the crew who stayed with the stalled vehicle heard gunfire and explosions. Their searches for the two *praporshchiki* uncovered no trace of them.

Although Semyonova had tried to prepare herself for the worst, the news was devastating. Fighting despair, she devoted most of the next two months to searching for a contact in the KGB who might help her find out what was known about her son's whereabouts. In Moscow, a Defense Ministry colonel agreed to speak to her, but only to declare, tersely, that discovering the fate of a single private was virtually impossible. In Tashkent—to which Semyonova flew to speak to commanders of the Turkestan military district where Gabarayev's 201st Division had been based before the Afghan in-vasion—she was handed a chit. It stated, even more tersely, that her son was missing in action.

Military MIAs prompted almost as much suspicion among Soviet bureaucrats as POWs. Were they missing because they'd de-fected? Had they gone as far as fighting against the Motherland? Even if not, no one could know what anti-Soviet ideology they'd heard and swallowed. A dead Gabarayev would have been buried with honors. A live one was a possible traitor.

During the following years, Semyonova wrote countless let-ters to officials of all ranks and heard various versions of her son's disappearance, including that he and Puchkov had died when their ammunition ran out after killing two mujahideen fighters. Occasionally, the local *voenkomat* phoned with urgent requests for Semyonova to bring photographs of Gabarayev or samples of his handwriting. The calls boosted her spirits until a sympathetic ac-quaintance told her they were no more than a bureaucratic show of taking action that went no further. Four years after Gabarayev's dis-appearance, *perestroika* allowed more access to official information, and Semyonova learned she hadn't initially been informed about her son's death because military officials were negotiating with local mujahideen to release him. She was also told blood and a helmet had been found at the scene of the abduction. Several Afghans had been arrested for possible exchange for the missing soldiers or their remains. Knowing that the mujahideen took prisoners to trade for captured rebels, the news gave Semyonova another infusion of hope. More optimism came from new information that after Gabarayev's disappearance, his commander had dug up a nearby garden rumored to contain his remains. The search yielded no buried bodies.

But Semyonova also learned that the Soviet government had made it clear it wanted no part of negotiating with the "bandit" mujahideen about missing military personnel. Worse still, prosecutors opened criminal cases against missing soldiers, including Gabarayev.

Semyonova was determined not to give up her search. In December 1988, she happened on a small notice in a crusading newspaper called *Literaturnaya gazeta*. It announced that relatives of soldiers missing in Afghanistan were planning to hold a demonstration in front of the Pakistani embassy, on a main thoroughfare in central Moscow. Although Pakistan was officially uninvolved in the Afghan War, Soviet citizens had heard some Red Army captives had ended up imprisoned there, across the Afghan border. Semyonova flew to the capital to join the protest, organized by a journalist named Iona Andronov. During the demonstration, Andronov was invited inside the building. He emerged to announce that the ambassador had agreed to speak to him and three mothers of missing soldiers, Semyonova among them.

The son of one of the other mothers had disappeared without a trace from a Soviet garrison. The third mother related that her son went missing a mere week after he'd arrived in Afghanistan. It happened during a night operation to free several PDPA activists jailed inside a mosque. When the soldier's unit prepared to leave the grounds, his Kalashnikov fell off the back of a truck and he jumped off to retrieve it. That was when he was captured—and, his mother had heard, tortured, after which his injured body was dragged by a mule. The Pakistani ambassador agreed to help by bringing up the matter with the recently elected prime minister, Benazir Bhutto.

In 1989, Semyonova attended a news conference with Defense Minister Dmitri Yazov, during which he was asked about prisoners of war in Afghanistan. "There are no such prisoners!" he barked in reply; all personnel missing in action were actually dead. But Bhutto had recently agreed to facilitate a trip for relatives of missing Soviets to Islamabad, and Yazov, despite his outburst, also agreed to meet them. Early the next morning, in his office inside the sprawling Defense Ministry near the Kremlin, he showed Semyonova and others an official list of 314 Soviets missing in Afghanistan.

The Defense Ministry flew the relatives to Islamabad. Although Semyonova had few expectations for the trip, being close to where her son had disappeared gave her a small measure of comfort. During its week in Pakistan, the group met a Belarussian prisoner of war named Andrei Lokhov. The distant-seeming young man with a ghostly white pallor described his conversion to Islam, but all he could reply to a question about whether he wanted to return home was "I don't want to fight." Handing a letter for his parents to the group, he told them to "Forget about me, my life is over." Bhutto had said she wanted at least one Soviet soldier to be released during the trip. But despite the group's attempts to bring Lokhov back home with them, he wasn't free to go for reasons the Soviet mothers couldn't ascertain.

As well as meeting Bhutto twice, the relatives also saw mujahideen leaders, including Rabbani, Mojaddedi, and Hekmatyar, the Afghan foreign minister at the time. During the first of their two meetings with Hekmatyar, he promised to provide information about the fates of at least some missing soldiers. At the second session, he said he'd failed to find out anything. That prompted Semyonova to say she believed he hadn't even tried to help them, to which Hekmatyar retorted angrily that "Gorbachev hasn't even met with you once!"

The relatives did meet Gorbachev after returning to Moscow. In late 1989, the Soviet leader closed the criminal cases against missing soldiers and declared an amnesty for all Afghan veterans accused of wrongdoing. Although Semyonova by then had lost all hope of finding her son alive, she wanted at least to recover his remains. She made two trips to Afghanistan with other missing soldiers' relatives, to tour prisons. They made another visit to Pakistan, during which they finally secured the release of Andrei Lokhov and another soldier. In Islamabad, Semyonova met a *Pakistan Times* reporter who had covered the war. Looking through stacks of photographs the Soviet relatives had brought with them, he picked out Gabarayev as someone he had seen. He could say nothing more about him, however.

Back in Moscow, Semyonova continued picking up scraps of information. Alexander Oleynik—a journalist for the trailblazing *Ogonyok* magazine, which had been among the first publications to print honest accounts of the war—directed her to a letter published by one of Gabarayev's commanders in *Literaturnaya gazeta*. The officer described Gabarayev's bravery during an attack against Massoud's fighters who had pinned down a group of Afghan Army soldiers.

Then Semyonova learned from a Red Cross report that Gabarayev had been sent to Pakistan. Although no destination was given, *Ogonyok* reporter Oleynik had been conducting research about a prison camp in Pakistan where Semyonova thought her son might have been taken. The jail was part of a U.S.-supplied mujahideen base some twenty miles from Peshawar. Now controlled by Rabbani, the Badaber camp had been a CIA air base—the one from which Francis Gary Powers had taken off in 1960 in his U-2 spy plane that was shot down over the Soviet Union.

A dozen Soviet prisoners had taken part in an uprising in Badaber on April 26, 1985. Semyonova would later see KGB documents claiming Rabbani himself had appealed to the Soviets to give themselves up, but that they had refused. After Pakistani army soldiers surrounded the base, fierce fighting raged throughout the night. When a shell hit the base's arsenal the following morning, it set off a massive explosion that destroyed much of the complex. All the Soviets are believed to have been killed in the fighting.

Semyonova received a letter from the Soviet embassy in Afghanistan saying a Soviet agent had confirmed having seen her son in Badaber. A former Soviet prisoner of war also contacted her in order to report that Gabarayev had been one of seven Soviets in the Badaber camp. (American correspondents reported twelve Soviets had been held captive there.) But Semyonova continued meeting with top officials, including Shevardnadze, Varennikov, and Boris Yeltsin, then a member of the Russian Republic's parliament. Franz Klintsevich—the reconnaissance officer from Valery Vostrotin's 345th Paratroop Regiment—took part in the effort to find missing soldiers, and compiled a list of Soviets in Badaber. Gabarayev wasn't initially on it, but Klintsevich later included him.

Another letter from the Soviet embassy in Afghanistan declared that Semyonova's son had been seen on December 21, 1985—eight months after the Badaber uprising—in another mujahideen camp in Pakistan. But she was no closer to discovering his fate, and while the Russian Defense Ministry said it was still finalizing a list of Soviets missing in the war, her pain is unrelieved. She now believes her son would be better off dead than still suffering somewhere.

V

In December 1982, another eighteen-year-old driving a tanker truck joined a regular convoy heading north from Kabul. Private Alexander Olenin had arrived in Afghanistan from his native Volga River city of Samara the previous year. He had only months left to serve—a comforting thought because many days, like that one in particular, could be debilitating. Steadily falling snow made the road winding up toward the Salang Tunnel treacherously slippery. Olenin's truck was last in the convoy, behind another tanker. After traversing the pitch-black tunnel, they descended the rock-faced mountains on the north side, where he refrained from stopping despite a desperate urge to relieve himself after ten hours of driving because the territory was unfamiliar and forbidding.

At last, he saw a likely place in the shape of a small restaurant by the side of the road. Olenin urinated nearby and was about to get back inside his truck when a young man approached. Olenin waved him away, but as he climbed back into the truck's cab, the Afghan slipped onto the passenger seat from the other side. Olenin kept a loaded pistol and a Kalashnikov inside. He grabbed his handgun, but when it misfired, more men attacked the cab.

Olenin managed to hold them off until he passed out from exhaustion, after about an hour. When he awoke, four Afghans were carrying him up a mountain path. They put him down when he began swearing and struggling, then delivered kicks to his side and dropped heavy stones on his legs. Resuming their march, they dragged him by the arms.

At a stop, Olenin produced a tiny wad of Afghanis, the local currency, from a pocket and screamed, "If you're robbers, take my money!" That made no impression, and the tramping resumed to a hilltop, where the mujahideen sat down to wait. Soon a rebel commander arrived together with some forty fighters. Olenin's anger turned to terror. He would later learn his captors belonged to Hekmatyar's Islamic Party of Afghanistan, and that they had prepared an ambush for his entire convoy—but waited to begin attacking for the arrival of BTRs. The bigger prizes never came.

Taken to a nearby rebel camp, Olenin was ordered to write a letter to his regiment commander. In it, he used Russian slang, *mat*, for a primitive code. Drawing on the worst and most confusing profanities he could devise, he described the route he'd taken to the camp and asked to be rescued. Help never came. Olenin was taken on a longer trek across mountain passes and valleys to another camp. Utter uncertainty over what would happen virtually paralyzed him. Escape seemed pointless. Even if he weren't always escorted by several men, he wouldn't know where to go if he somehow managed to break free.

Day after day passed, during which he did almost nothing apart from occasionally collecting firewood. After two attempts to hang himself to relieve his fear and boredom, his captors confiscated the rope. Most were ordinary peasants who ranged from teen-age boys to elderly men. Rotating shifts every ten days, they took turns returning to their villages. While in the mountains, they had little to do besides cleaning their weapons, on which they spent a good deal of time. Meat occasionally supplemented their meager diet of dried fruit and potatoes.

Olenin met the son of the local rebel commander, who had studied at Kabul University and could speak some English. Olenin had a minimal grasp of English, but the two managed to com-municate with the help of hand gestures, and he believed their ex-changes, which developed into a kind of acquaintanceship, saved him from being killed or sent to Pakistan.

The commander's son asked him why the Soviet Union had invaded. "Do you think there are Americans or Chinese fighting here?" he asked. "No, there are only Afghans. Like my own rela-tives, people from my little village. We're protecting our country, over which you came to take control."

"We never wanted to control your country," Olenin replied. "We came to help you."

"No, you're not here for our sake. You're here because of the communists, and they're our enemies."

The two young men discussed religion. Although Olenin was an atheist like most Soviets, he took an interest in the Koran—the only book available for him to read—and began learning the Pashto alphabet. After some time, he converted to Islam and took the name of Rakhmatullah.

Another captive joined him. Olenin had heard about a Ukrai-nian deserter named Nikolai and believed the new prisoner, a Ukrainian in an officer's uniform, was that man. Olenin came to despise his unbalanced-seeming and sometimes violent comrade. The two would spend years living side by side, during which the base twice came under Soviet attack. Surviving the shelling, Olenin went on to spend a dozen years in captivity and to remain in Af-ghanistan after the Soviet withdrawal, when he married an Afghan woman.

In 1994, after warlord Rashid Dostum negotiated a release of prisoners of war with the Russians, Olenin's parents traveled to Sheberghan to meet their son, whom they hadn't seen since he was little older than a boy. The father of another prisoner of war who also made the trip brought a bottle of vodka to celebrate the reunion with his son, but the former captives begged him to hide it, for fear of angering the Afghan Muslims. After seeing his parents for an hour, Olenin was asked, under the glare of Russian television cameras, whether he wanted to return home. He did, but didn't dare say so for fear of angering the Afghans on whom he'd come to depend.

That night, Olenin and the other prisoner were flown from Khairaton to Peshawar, where ISI officers handed them to the Russian embassy. When Olenin arrived home in Samara, its private shops and beggars amazed him, both new since the collapse of communism. But his new religion and rumors that he'd deserted made life back at home difficult, and it wasn't long before he returned to Afghanistan. He spent another ten years in Afghanistan, running a grocery store and selling fruit, before he returned to Russia once again to make another try of living at home.

VI

The mujahideen leadership largely sidelined the Durrani tribe during the Soviet War. That deeply rankled the group that had traditionally led Afghanistan since its leader Ahmed Shah Durrani had carved out the empire that formed the basis for modern Afghanistan two hundred years ago. But in late summer 1994, some Durrani members reasserted their claim to power by rallying behind a new group emerging in southern Afghanistan. Religious students called Taliban, or "students of Islam," had long been a part of local life. During the Soviet War, many thousands of young Afghan men had studied radical Islam in the border madrassas of northern Pakistan.

In the 1990s, they formed a militia backed by previously marginalized Durrani leaders who now sought to expand their power.

Stories of the Taliban's rapid rise are steeped in legend. But it's believed that when a local strongman in Kandahar raped several girls, locals appealed to the Taliban leader, a mullah named Mohammed Omar, for help. His religious students executed the rapist and threatened his followers. Soon other victims of violence appealed for help to the new group, whose members portrayed themselves as idealistic, pious fighters for justice.

The Pashtun-dominated Taliban grew out of Afghanistan's violent anarchy. Its young adherents were largely the product of an uprooted society who latched on to the messianic Islam preached by fundamentalist mullahs. The group was greatly aided by Saudi money and trained by Pakistan's ISI, which saw them as an alternative to the old Pakistani favorite Hekmatyar, who was helping destroy what was left of Kabul in his bitter feud with Massoud.

When a warlord named Mansur captured a Pakistani aid convoy, Pakistan's prime minister Bhutto turned to the Taliban to rescue it. Mansur was shot and his body was said to have been paraded hanging from the barrel of a tank. The Taliban then captured an arms cache from Hekmatyar and soon went on to take Kandahar. Locals welcomed the new movement out of a desperate desire for some kind of stability. Volunteers flocked to join.

In late August, Mullah Omar launched a fierce offensive and soon took Jalalabad, cutting off the transit route from Kabul to Pakistan. Over the next two years, the Taliban pushed steadily north, forcing Massoud to evacuate bombed-out Kabul in September 1996. The following day, the Taliban broke into the UN compound where Najibullah had taken refuge, castrated and killed him and his brother, and strung them up in public.

The Taliban forced women to wear head-to-toe burkas and barred them from working. Justice took the form of severed ears, hands, and heads. Adultery was punished by public stoning. The Taliban banned television, music, photographs, even whistling and kite flying, among the only forms of entertainment for poverty-stricken children. Women were beaten for showing even an arm. Kabul and other cities, lorded over by the Department for the Propagation of Virtue and Suppression of Vice, descended into a medieval hell.

Once again, Massoud began organizing resistance to Kabul—now in the hands of the Taliban—from his base in the Panjshir Valley. He called the rebel forces together to form the United Front for the Liberation of Afghanistan, known as the Northern Alliance. But its fighters fared badly against the Taliban, which took over 90 percent of the country. Pinned down next to Tajikistan, the Northern Alliance essentially controlled only the Panjshir Valley.

In May 1996, Osama bin Laden and his Al Qaeda group returned to the cave complexes he'd helped carve out south of Jalalabad, this time sheltered by the Taliban, which gladly accepted his money and jihadi-networking influence in return. In late summer 2001, Massoud agreed to be interviewed by two Algerian television journalists. During the interview, a bomb hidden inside a television camera exploded, fatally wounding Massoud. The Algerians were Al Qaeda members. The next day, other Al Qaeda members, most of them Saudis, hijacked four jetliners in the United States. Two smashed into the World Trade Center, one into the Pentagon, and one crashed in the Pennsylvania countryside after passengers fought the hijackers.

VII

When post-Soviet Russians bothered to remember the Afghanistan War at all, most thought of it as a conflict fought by the old regime. The new regime supplied its own military disaster. When Moscow launched an assault on the breakaway province of Chechnya in 1994 in order to suppress an independence movement—among other reasons, the Kremlin was afraid secession by the North Caucasus Mountains region would encourage other provinces to follow suit—the war went horribly. Lessons from the bitter experience of the Afghanistan War, which had ended a mere five years earlier, were brushed aside. Hardened local fighters who knew the terrain far better and had far more at stake mowed down thousands of poorly trained, badly equipped conscripts of the new, post-communist Russia.

The Chechen War was the latest in a long series of Russian military exercises in the Caucasus, a frontier territory not unlike Afghanistan's. Bloodied in battles against a new partisan force in the mountains, the Russians expressed their frustration on the local population, killing many thousands of civilians, leveling villages, and destroying Grozny, the capital.

After rebels under warlord Aslan Maskhadov recaptured Grozny in 1996, the two sides signed a peace agreement that left the shattered province essentially independent. Isolated and impoverished, the region became a hotbed of kidnappings, torture, and summary execution. In 1999, then–Prime Minister Vladimir Putin launched a second attack on Chechnya after Islamist Chechen warlords staged incursions into the neighboring Russian region of Dagestan. Moscow also blamed a series of apartment bombings in Russia on Chechens, despite a lack of evidence—and far greater indication the bombings may have been the work of the security forces as a pretext for war. Ruslan Aushev, the Afghan War hero and former commander of the 108th MRD—and one of Valery Vostrotin's closest friends—was then leader of the neighboring region of Ingushetia. Moscow rejected Aushev's many efforts to mediate in the conflict and eventually removed him in favor of a pro-Kremlin puppet on whose watch violence began spreading into Ingushetia from Chechnya.

The new Chechen War enabled Putin to rally political support among a Russian population fed up with a decade of humiliating post-Soviet decline. Nothing had struck harder at Russian pride than the dismal showing in the first Chechen conflict, but now the country's once-gloried military again became mired in a brutal stalemate, in which guerrilla attacks were answered with abduction, murder, torture, and rape of many thousands of civilian Chechens. Moscow's forces were able to bring some measure of stability to the region only by destroying most of what was left of the province.

By 2008, Chechnya was ruled by a former rebel named Ramzan Kadyrov, a thirty-one-year-old many believe has tortured and killed with his own hands. Kadyrov's swaggering authority rests on fear, tribute, and massive support from Moscow. The Kremlin's claim to victory in Chechnya is true only in the sense that the scorched-earth tactics learned in Afghanistan have been applied to a logical conclusion: a far smaller population has been literally bombed into submission, and its infrastructure rebuilt under an enthusiastically pro-Moscow administration. Where "Afghanization"—turning the conflict over to locals—failed, "Chechenization" has succeeded, at least temporarily.

But the regime that came out of Moscow's brutal suppression of Chechen independence is highly unstable. Kadyrov depends on a private militia, Kremlin backing, and the work of death squads. The Kremlin calls the rebels "bandits" and "terrorists"—echoing the same words the Soviet Union used to describe the Afghan mujahideen—and claims the conflict in Chechnya was part of the global war against terrorism. In fact, Moscow has done far more to create future terrorists from Chechnya's desperate and destitute population. Violence has spread from Chechnya to previously peaceful regions elsewhere in the North Caucasus, which threatens to become a hotbed of ethnic and sectarian conflict.

VIII

Putin's eight years as president were greatly aided by the skyrocketing of global oil prices. New wealth beyond the Kremlin's wildest dreams enabled him to marginalize Russia's opposition parties and all but silence the Kremlin's opponents. New parties sprang up that were either styled by the Kremlin or created with its sanction. The most prominent and influential figures in politics and business joined the main pro-Kremlin party, United Russia. Among them was Franz Klintsevich, the former reconnaissance chief of the 345th Paratroop Regiment.

Klintsevich had remained in the 345th after the war. In 1994, the regiment was sent to the former Soviet republic of Georgia to help secure a truce between the government and separatists in the breakaway Black Sea region of Abkhazia. Soon after, Klintsevich retired from the military to head the Russian Union of Afghanistan Veterans. He was later elected to parliament, where he became deputy head of United Russia's parliamentary faction.

Helicopter pilot Vladimir Kostiuchenko became Klintsevich's deputy in the veterans' union. In 2006, he too went into politics, forming the For Motherland party, which promised to champion veterans' interests in the burgeoning competition for Russia's growing nationalist vote.

Once thin and fit, Klintsevich is now corpulent. His massive, leather-upholstered office in the Stalin-era Duma building opposite Red Square looks out on the Kremlin. Far down the hall, another veteran of the 345th shares a cramped room with his assistant. The regiment's famed commander Valery Vostrotin is also a Duma deputy and a United Russia member. A large oil portrait of his nineteenth-century war hero Denis Davydov hangs on the wall behind his desk. On the windowsill, Vostrotin keeps a model of the loathed BMD infantry fighing vehicle in which he was twice wounded. After leaving Afghanistan, Vostrotin held several top military posts before serving as deputy emergency situations minister—in which capacity he returned to Afghanistan with cargoes of humanitarian aid—before winning election to parliament. One of his legislative aides is none other than former general Nikolai Serdyukov, who, as commander of the 345th Regiment in December 1979, had punished Vostrotin and the other men of Company 9 for looting the Taj-Bek palace they'd just helped storm.

To most Afghan War veterans, Vostrotin personifies heroism and even-handedness perhaps more than any other officer who fought in the war. Every February 11—the anniversary of the day in 1989 when the 345th Regiment officially pulled out of Afghanistan—veterans gather in central Moscow in front of the neoclassical Bolshoi Theater across the street from the Duma building. The weather is invariably cold, and usually overcast, making it bitterly raw. Veterans, family members, and friends stamp their freezing feet while waiting for their comrades to arrive. But Vostrotin's appearance produces shouts of greeting and murmurs of awe. In the crowd that surrounds him, congratulations are exchanged, war stories traded, and shots of vodka downed before the group breaks up for more serious reminiscing and drinking elsewhere. Still angry with the Soviet handling of the war and its aftermath, the veterans take solace in their deep comradeship and lingering grief over their dead comrades.

But attitudes to the war are changing. Oil-rich, twenty-first-century Russia has sought new confrontation with the West in a bid to reestablish its lost power on the world stage. And in Moscow, outward displays of patriotism and political loyalty again have become the going currency for getting ahead in business and politics. Veterans and students of the war are increasingly looking back at the conflict through a Cold War prism, speaking less about Moscow's mistakes in Afghanistan and more about the war's lessons for dealing with the United States. The huge flow of dollars Washington poured into the war in the hope of killing Soviet boys merely fulfilling their duty to help their comrade communists is increasingly taken as a warning about the danger of entertaining illusions about American friendship. U.S. support for the mujahideen is seen as an indication of Americans' real feelings about Russians—and proof of Washington's unwillingness to understand the Soviet Union really invaded Afghanistan only because it wanted to spread peace among its neighbors. When Russia invaded Georgia in 2008, partly in an attempt to split decisively with the West in addition to establishing its own sphere of influence, angry Kremlin propaganda sounded no different from the Soviet variety, and to great effect: many Russians believed American forces had fought alongside Georgians attacking Russian soldiers.

Still, feelings about the Afghanistan War remain deeply mixed and often confused. Many veterans are proud of their service, fiercely loyal to their comrades, and highly critical of how the conflict was fought. Much criticism of the authorities is directed at their decision—having made the mistake of invading Afghanistan—to pull out. Valery Kurilov, the Zenit *spetsnaz* officer who helped storm the Taj-Bek palace in 1979, isn't surprised that Al Qaeda found fertile ground in Afghanistan. "Why should Afghans share our values and respect us? What values are we even talking about? We invaded their country, robbed and killed them, then simply packed up and left. Why in the world *wouldn't* terrorism grow there?"

In 2005, Dmitri Lekarev, the private who fought with the Seventieth Brigade in Kandahar and returned to Moscow after his two years there, came across his battalion commander, Valery Dunayev, while walking in a park. The former colonel was sitting on a bench in civilian clothes. Lekarev, who respected Dunayev and felt lucky to have served under his command, somehow felt like a schoolchild in front of an old teacher.

Dunayev recognized Lekarev too. "Ah, sergeant, come here!" he beckoned warmly, then followed their exchange of greetings with a joke: "Maybe you've got a job for me?" It took the former private a moment to realize he was serious; the colonel who had four Orders of the Red Star and two Orders of Lenin was now unemployed. Lekarev didn't know whether the tears he managed to choke back were for him, for them both, or for the whole long venture whose seas of pain were still rising three decades after the mindless decision to launch it.

I

The sprawling mud walls of the Qala-i-Janghi fortress rise above the desert flats and pomegranate orchards surrounding Mazar-i-Sharif. The fantastical nineteenth-century castle contains a large compound with stables, a prison, and an armory. Two groups of television reporters drove there on November 25, 2001, planning to shoot a routine story, inasmuch as anything in war can be routine.

A month earlier, the United States had joined the series of great powers that invaded Afghanistan over the course of millennia. In October, American planes began bombing the frontline positions of Afghanistan's fervent Islamic Taliban regime to the north of Kabul: the opening salvos in Washington's war on terrorism. The provocation was September 11, when a group of mostly Saudi Arabian fundamentalist Islamists trained in Afghanistan by Osama bin Laden's Al Qaeda piloted two planes into the World Trade Center and a third into the Pentagon.

Soviet units had used the Qala-i-Janghi fortress during their war in Afghanistan, after which Taliban groups took it over. In early October, General Dostum, the feared Uzbek warlord and a leader of the Northern Alliance, drove out the Taliban and made the fortress his headquarters. Known for his ruthlessness, Dostum was said to impose discipline by killing even his own men—

including at least one accused of theft by lashing him to the tracks of a tank.

With the support of American B-52 bombers and special forces units, the alliance was fast crushing its enemy. Washington's plan was to minimize American casualties by relying on local forces and aerial bombardments. Ten days before the Russian reporters approached Qala-i-Janghi, Dostum had taken Kunduz, eighty-five miles due east. There the warlord negotiated the surrender of some five hundred fighters, mostly hard-line Arabs and other foreigners who had joined the Taliban. With little to lose, they had threatened to hold out to the end, until Dostum, offering terms that remain unclear, convinced them to submit. He then marched his prisoners to the fortress, where they were held by one of his top commanders, Aka Yasin.

Yasin had first met Dostum during the Soviet War in 1987, when he was in jail in the town of Sheberghan, in neighboring Jowzjan Province. He'd been sentenced for injuring two government soldiers with a pistol when they challenged him at a checkpoint. Dostum secured his release with a trade of prisoners. After the Soviet War, Yasin became severely critical of the mujahideen for having destroyed Afghanistan during their infighting. But he despised the Taliban even more for their medieval laws and cruelty. Having taken refuge in Pakistan during most of their severe rule, he returned to rejoin Dostum in the effort to help free Afghanistan soon after September 11.

Inside the Qala-i-Janghi fortress, Dostum's intelligence chief, Said Kamel, was directly responsible for the prisoners. Their interrogators included two CIA officers who had spent more than a month in the northern mountains, mostly with Yasin's men while they were fighting to oust the Taliban. The Americans were helping coordinate the Northern Alliance's movements according to American notions and designs.

The captives were held within the grimy, green-and-white-painted walls of the underground prison. On the day the television reporters arrived, the CIA's "Mike" and "Dave" were above the holding cells in a small brick building at ground level, questioning prisoners for intelligence that might help the U.S. invasion. Northern Alliance sentries searched the detainees for weapons and tied their arms behind their backs. The guards were wary—not least because the previous day, a Taliban fighter had exploded a grenade, killing himself and a guard.

For their part, the prisoners were growing increasingly worried about their fates. Although Dostum had been quoted saying he'd hand them to the UN, his brutal reputation suggested no one could be certain of his intentions. No doubt the presence of the Americans, with their brusque manner and threats of retribution if information was not supplied, inspired little confidence. Some of detainees would later say they feared execution.

When three guards went downstairs to bring up more prisoners, one inmate decided to act. He lobbed a rock at a guard's head and snatched his rifle. The small victory inspired other prisoners to fight. As some overpowered the guards, others began making their way to a narrow flight of stairs. When they reached the top, they threw themselves on the CIA officers, firing their weapons and detonating a grenade. Johnny "Mike" Spann, a thirty-two-year-old former marine, became the first known American casualty of the U.S. invasion. Other prisoners attacked his partner, "Dave." He grabbed his pistol, killed at least one, then shot his way forward until he could run from the building while the Taliban men continued fighting their guards and untying their fellow prisoners.

Minutes earlier, just after eleven a.m., a Reuters television producer named Nikolai Pavlov had been waiting impatiently with his cameraman at a tall gate outside the prison complex while a Northern Alliance commander went inside for permission to admit them. Two loud explosions followed by rifle fire thundered from within. The Russian reporter and his cameraman dove to the ground beneath some nearby trees.

A German ARD Television crew and a Red Cross delegation were also visiting the compound. As reporter Pavlov pressed himself to the ground outside, all hell—in the form of explosions and automatic weapons fire—broke loose around him. Northern Alliance guards shot from the prison roofs at the rebels, who returned fire. Deciding he needed better shelter, Pavlov dashed to a thick fortress wall, where he joined the German television crew, the Red Cross personnel, and flak-jacketed "Dave," who had also made his way there. Borrowing a satellite phone from the Germans, Dave screamed for air strikes.

By now, the prisoners had seized the prison building and broken into an arsenal of rifles, ammunition, and grenade launchers. Bullets whizzed past Pavlov's head when he raised it to try to see what was happening. Another attempt brought explosions of grenades in the nearby dust while guards fled for their lives to the fortress walls and began climbing over them. The reporters remained pinned down for hours, until early dusk, when Dave convinced the group it too must make a run for safety. He dashed to a wall, jumped over, and tumbled down the ramparts to the ground outside. (During several days of continuing mayhem at the fortress, international media would often replay Pavlov's footage of the CIA officer's successful flight.) Pavlov and the others followed. Outside the fort, they ran to a main road, hailed a passing car, and bounced over deep potholes toward Mazar-i-Sharif.

Spann's death seriously distressed Northern Alliance commander Aka Yasin. Tears came to his eyes when he described the event to me five years later. He'd come to respect the stern young man with the chiseled face and floppy hat whose work was helping achieve the impossible—ousting the Taliban—in a few short weeks. Yasin believed the mistake that made the uprising possible was permitting the guards to take weapons into the underground holding cells. He said the decision had been made by Said Kamel, Dostum's intelligence chief.

As the uprising dragged on, U.S., British, and Northern Alliance forces unleashed barrages on the fortress, including two-thousand-pound bombs dropped by American planes on the final night. Fearsome AC-130 helicopter gunships fired up to eighteen hundred rounds a minute at the Taliban fighters. When the rebellion finally subsided—after water had been pumped into the prison—the compound was littered with corpses, body parts, and bomb fragments. (Black Taliban turbans remained scattered there when I visited in 2006.) Only some 80 of the approximately 450 prisoners survived what was some of the fiercest fighting of the U.S. invasion.

Overall, however, the campaign went well, with minimal American casualties. Thousands of Taliban fighters surrendered or switched sides. Northern Alliance troops had marched into Kabul on November 13, just over a week before the Qala-i-Janghi uprising. As in many other cities, the enemy had simply abandoned it.

But although many of its members reverted to old allegiances, mostly of Pashtun tribal groups, the Taliban survived. Washington's most wanted man, Osama bin Laden, eluded American-backed Afghan troops in the caves and tunnels he'd helped carve out of the Tora Bora Mountains. American forces also missed several opportunities to capture or kill Taliban leader Mullah Omar, who had given bin Laden safe haven and close cooperation in return for funds from the Saudi construction business of bin Laden's family and connections to his global terrorist network.

II

The failure to net bin Laden and Omar after a gratifyingly successful invasion was less circumstantial than a reflection of a central aspect of warfare in Afghanistan: the difficulty of decoding the Afghan tradition of shifting allegiances. Soviet soldiers had marveled at the loyalty of Afghans who traded their vital supplies, even their food, for pilfered Red Army fuel and weapons—even as warlords who'd been cooperating with Red Army forces suddenly turned at opportune moments. Although the Taliban's melting away in the face of the U.S. invasion made the execution of Operation Enduring Freedom easier than expected, it also became the cause of one of the most intractable problems for the 21,000-strong U.S.-led coalition and 10,000-strong NATO-led peacekeeping force stationed in a country where warlords dominate and whose central government's authority barely extends beyond the capital.

The centuries-old struggle for domination of the country continues. But its new configuration as an international struggle with a fervent fundamentalist Islamic organization was a direct result of the Soviet War. Some of that conflict's all-but-forgotten lessons bear heavily on Iraq, which lies on the other side of Iran from Afghanistan. It took years following the U.S.-led invasion of 2003 for the American public to begin discerning the real nature of Iraq's bitter ethnic and sectarian conflicts between Sunnis and Shias, Arabs and Kurds. Former 345th Regiment commander Valery Vostrotin was astounded during a seminar with NATO officers he attended after the beginning of the war in Iraq. Sharing lessons learned fighting there, one NATO officer instructed the Russian participants about the importance of respecting Muslim customs during house searches. Don't hold your rifle in attack position, he advised, or go barging into women's quarters. Vostrotin stifled an anguished chuckle—he'd known that twenty years earlier.

No doubt many more years will pass before the interested public will grasp the complete truth about the motives for invading Iraq in 2003, the conduct of military operations there, and the change to international relations wrought by September 11. All that is very relevant to Afghanistan. To a startling degree, the Politburo's 1979 deliberations about how to deal with it mirror the Bush administration's close-minded and secretive decision-making that led to *its* invasion. The Bush White House might have modeled itself on the Soviet gerontocracy under Brezhnev that brushed aside warnings from military and regional experts who knew the situation in Afghanistan to be far more complicated than the Politburo stated.

Although genuinely happy to be freed from Taliban rule, many Afghans have since grown wary of American intentions, which they interpret partly from swaggering soldiers who seem to represent an "imperial" army. When NATO forces commanding streets and searching houses failed to respect local traditions and denigrated local officials by ignoring them, Afghan eyes easily saw them in the shoes of their Soviet predecessors. "Collateral damage"—an Orwellian euphemism for untold civilian pain—naturally generated even more resentment. When U.S. bombs shattered villages, anger at high-altitude bombing, seen as a tactic for lessening American casualties by reducing fighting on the ground to a minimum, pushed some as far as praise of the formerly hated Soviets. They were at least more willing to engage their enemy in the field.

III

After fleeing on the heels of the Soviet withdrawal, Aman Ashkrez, a former correspondent for Radio Kabul, lived in Russia for sixteen years. His new home was in a close-knit community of Afghans who run a teeming "business center" in a Moscow suburb, a concrete-slab structure that encompasses a mosque and a school.

Ashkrez has less than great hope for his native country. Sitting in his cramped office in Moscow, he pointed out that most of Afghanistan's recent rulers were killed or forced into exile. "Habibullah was hanged in 1929. His successor Nadir Khan was shot, *his* successor Zahir Shah fled, Daoud was killed, Taraki suffocated, Amin murdered, and Najibullah hanged; even Massoud was blown up. Deaths of heads of state in other countries are followed by periods of mourning and visits by heads of state from abroad. That never happens in Afghanistan."

Ashkrez's unhappy comparison helps suggest the great odds Afghanistan's shattered society must battle to build a normal way of life. The countless mines scattered throughout the countryside might be seen as symbolic as well as physical because they pose a serious threat to anyone who dares take a step off well-beaten paths.

Atta Mohammed Noor, the former rebel commander who was one of Massoud's closest lieutenants, is now governor of Balkh Province. In his natty, well-tailored suits, with his once-long beard fashionably close-cropped, he occupies several gleaming, mirror-windowed residential and office compounds in Mazar-i-Sharif, the provincial capital. Photographs of him in the field during the Soviet War, often with Massoud, line the walls of one of the buildings.

Noor believes the Afghan War of 2001 opened the best possibility of finally stabilizing his country. But he regrets the many opportunities already lost. Without promised international aid, he is convinced, the reconstruction needed to persuade the population to back the government as an alternative to warring will remain a fantasy. In his own Balkh Province, NATO's International Security Assistance Force, or ISAF, troops undermined the Afghan authorities by making arrests without informing the local officials who are legally responsible for such activity. Noor also believes the West must do much more to train and equip the Afghan National Army.

Of the mujahideen commanders who joined the Northern Alliance, among the first to hand in his weapons to Hamid Karzai's government after the Taliban ouster was Aka Yasin, the Tajik who had fought with General Dostum. He now lives in an opulent house on a teeming main thoroughfare leading to central Mazar-i-Sharif. Yasin wants to see Afghanistan become a liberal democracy. Unlike

Balkh Province governor and former mujahideen commander Atta Mohammed Noor in 2006 in one of his residences in Mazar-i-Sharif, next to a photograph of him with Massoud during the Soviet war. *(Gregory Feifer)*

many of his peers, he also believes women should enjoy equal rights. He says American troops who behave arrogantly and refuse to respect Afghan traditions, most seriously by violating women's privacy during house searches, are helping undercut American goals.

Former Education Minister Abdul Rakhman Jalili—the leading supporter of former President Hafizullah Amin poisoned by the Soviets—spent the war in jail. Freed in 1990 after more than ten years, he was reinstated teaching in Kabul University. The following year, he fled the mujahideen infighting for Pakistan, where he established the National Unity Party, of which he's now president. He later returned to Kabul and is now a representative in the Wolesi Jirga, the national parliament.

Satisfied that Afghanistan under Amin had been on its way to becoming truly modernized, Jalili blames the Soviet invasion for the country's myriad woes. He attributes the Kremlin's mistake to an inability to tolerate the prospect of an independent democratic state on its southern border and to a wish to demonstrate its strength to the West. The professor and political activist believes, together with almost all Afghans interviewed for this account, that Moscow was partly driven by its historic ambitions to acquire a warm-water port on the Indian Ocean.

After years in exile in Russia, Said Mohammed Guliabzoi returned to Afghanistan and was also elected a member of parliament. A member of the "gang of four" of Taraki supporters who served as communications minister under Amin and interior minister after the Soviet invasion, Guliabzoi still lives in Kabul's Soviet concrete-slab Microrayon. He says despite the similarity between the Red Army's situation in Afghanistan and NATO's current predicament, the cardinal difference is that the current force is backed by the United Nations, comprised of many nationalities, and was Afghanistan's only hope of throwing off the Taliban. Nevertheless, he too, like so many others, worries that rough tactics by NATO troops and their failure to observe Afghan social protocol is fast putting them in the same category as the Soviets in Afghan minds.

Mohammed Jan, the mujahideen commander in Logar Province

south of Kabul, survived the war and the Taliban occupation. His new, modest two-story house overlooks the road south to Kandahar, along which he'd led ambushes against Soviet convoys. Groves of trees and a growing collection of farms line the fertile valley, but their numbers are still paltry compared to before the war. Jan's rebel group has continued fighting the resurgent Taliban under Hamid Karzai's government. Several weeks before his interview for this book, he was shot in the head, next to his ear, when his headquarters came under attack. The bullet exited without causing permanent damage. Another bullet shattered bones in his hand. Miraculously, he was set to make a full recovery. Contemplative and soft-spoken, Jan says he first took up arms when there was no other way to protect his country, and that he'll continue fighting for the same purpose.

Massoud commander Abdul Nasir Ziyaee was named chief of political affairs in the military (mujahideen) Panjshir division under Rabbani's government in 1992. Later the tall man with a close-cropped gray beard became frontline chief commander against the Taliban and the Northern Alliance's head of ideology. Under Karzai, he was appointed military chief of political affairs in the Afghan National Army. Massoud named Ziyaee to that post twelve days before his assassination by the Taliban on September 9, 2001.

Ziyaee vividly remembers Massoud as fearless. During the Taliban's push north into the Salang Valley in the mid-1990s, the mujahideen leader climbed to the top of one of the tallest mountains of Panjshir's Shotol District to inspect the Northern Alliance's receding front line. Peering into the darkness through a pair of binoculars, Massoud asked Ziyaee, who hadn't slept for days, if he was tired. "No," he lied.

Massoud didn't believe him, and tried to raise Ziyaee's spirits. "If we flinch and run," Massoud said, "the future will be lost. We've no alternative but to fight. Even if we die in battle, history will remember us kindly."

Ziyaee believes the Taliban successfully copied Massoud's strategy during the Soviet War. Specifically, he sees the Taliban's spread of extremist Islamic ideology and their attempt to act as a surrogate government as coming straight from Massoud's book, although Massoud's ideology and government were of a different kind. But Ziyaee finds the Taliban fighters' certainty they will prevail the most threatening of their characteristics.

IV

Despite the mistakes and shortcomings of the American-led invasion in 2001, many in desperately poor Afghanistan continue to cling to the historic opportunity to turn their country into a viable state. But the subsequent invasion of Iraq—which diverted American resources—has provided one of the biggest obstacles to any measure of success in Afghanistan.

Twenty-four years after the Politburo's contemplation of a "quick" invasion of Afghanistan in 1979, the Bush administration believed it could withdraw within months of invading Iraq. The inherent contradictions of the American use of force to try to plant democracy in countries with no tradition of representative government differ little from the Soviet attempt to build communism in Afghanistan. Never mind the failure of Brezhnev's great gamble, and that the billions of Soviet rubles and American dollars poured into Afghanistan in the 1980s helped create a ruin of humanity and a homeland for today's worldwide fundamentalist terrorist network.

Needless to say, however, the circumstances of all wars differ. The United States went on to become more powerful than ever after its failure in Vietnam, while the Soviet Union crumbled shortly after it lost its counterinsurgency war in Afghanistan. Although the war can't be said to have ended the Soviet dictatorship, it hastened its demise by enlarging the drain on a crumbling economy and exposing the empire's corrupt ideology. As with France and England after the Suez crisis in 1956, the Soviet War in Afghanistan marked the end of empire. As with so many past wars, the consequences turned out vastly different from, even opposed to, the initial intentions.

ACKNOWLEDGMENTS

Censorship and propaganda were central to the Soviet War in Afghanistan, as they have been to almost every other military conflict. But the first casualty of the Afghanistan War wasn't truth. That had long before succumbed to the onslaught of Soviet lies about *all* aspects of life. The all-encompassing brainwashing makes the task of discerning what actually took place in Afghanistan especially difficult. The manufactured justifications that enabled many to close their eyes to the war's unspeakable abuses continue to influence perceptions—although the Soviets had no monopoly in that. Murderous hatreds among Afghans and Washington's belief that it won the Cold War in Afghanistan have also helped obscure our understanding of the conflict.

My first thanks go to those interviewed for this book: the veterans of the war living in Russia, and to their allies and adversaries in Afghanistan who believed it was important to their stories.

Zamir Gotta of Trident Media convinced *me* of their importance, then worked tirelessly to arrange interviews and give help in many other ways. Thanks also to Anna Zaitseva, who did a terrific job transcribing tapes.

I'm hugely indebted to my father, George, who spent countless days poring through rough drafts. His meticulous editing improved them immeasurably. My wife, Elizabeth, also provided invaluable editing. *The Great Gamble* couldn't have been completed without their help and encouragement.

Tim Duggan of HarperCollins did a terrific job editing the resulting product and dispensing sage advice. It was a real pleasure working with him and Allison Lorentzen.

Many thanks to historian and Afghanistan War veteran General Alexander Liakhovskii, who generously provided guidance and shared stories about some of the hundreds of veterans he knows. Most of the book's photographs come from his colossal archive.

Iqbal Sapand provided help in Afghanistan, arranging interviews, translating, and urging on his jeep when it was dangerously overheating in thin mountain air.

Thanks also to Robert Gottlieb and John Silbersack of Trident Media for undertaking the project.

Thanks finally to NPR's foreign desk for allowing me the time off needed to complete the book. I wrote much of it in the Moscow bureau, where Boris Ryzhak, Sergei Sotnikov, and Irina Mikhaleva went out of their way to give me help, for which I'm grateful.

GLOSSARY OF NAMES

Sergei Akhromeyev, Soviet Armed Forces General Staff chief, 1984–1988

Hafizullah Amin, prime minister of Afghanistan, March 1979–September 1979; president, September 1979–December 1979

Yuri Andropov, KGB chairman, 1967–1982; Soviet general secretary, November 1982–February 1983

Leonid Bogdanov, KGB Kabul station chief, August 1978–April 1980

Leonid Brezhnev, Soviet general secretary, 1964–1982

William Casey, director of U.S. Central Intelligence Agency, 1981–1987

Mikhail Gorbachev, Soviet general secretary, 1985–1991

Leonid Gorelov, chief Soviet military adviser to the Afghan government, 1975–1979

Boris Gromov, Fortieth Army commander, 1987–1989

Andrei Gromyko, Soviet foreign minister, 1957–1985

Said Mohammed Guliabzoi, Afghan communications minister, April 1978–September 1979; interior minister, 1979–1992

Gulbuddin Hekmatyar, fundamentalist mujahideen commander, Party of Islam leader

Mohammed Jan, mujahideen field commander, Logar Province

Nikolai Kalita, KGB Alpha Group special forces lieutenant, 1986

Babrak Karmal, Soviet-installed Afghan president, December 1979–November 1986; head of the Parcham, or Banner, wing of the Afghan communist party, the PDPA

Ismail Khan, Herat mujahideen commander, member of Rabbani's Society of Islam

Franz Klintsevich, 345th Paratroop Regiment special propaganda group leader, 1986–1989

Alexei Kosygin, Soviet prime minister, 1964–1980

Vladimir Kostiuchenko, helicopter pilot, Kandahar, 1981–1982; Jalalabad, 1985–1986; Bagram, 1988–1989

Valery Kurilov, KGB Zenit special forces officer, 1979

Dmitri Lekarev, private, Seventieth Separate Motorized Rifle Brigade, Kandahar, 1987–1989

Ahmed Shah Massoud, Panjshir Valley mujahideen commander; member of Rabbani's Society of Islam

Mohammed Najibullah, Afghan KhAD intelligence service director, 1980–1986; Afghan president, 1987–1992

Vladimir Polyakov, 108th Motorized Rifle Battalion reconnaissance lieutenant, Charikar, 1980

Alexander Puzanov, Soviet ambassador to Afghanistan, 1972–1979

Burhannudin Rabbani, mujahideen leader, Society of Islam founder

Alexander Rutskoi, Fortieth Army air force deputy chief, 1988

Vladimir Redkoborodyi, KGB's Ninth Directorate colonel, head of Afghan president Babrak Karmal's security, 1979–1984

Sergei Salabayev, Fifty-sixth Air Assault Brigade private, Gardez, 1984–1986

Asadullah Sarwari, Afghan security service chief, 1978–1979

Sergei Sokolov, Soviet ground forces commander, 1979; defense minister, 1984–1987

Yar Mohammed Stanizi, Afghan Army district commander, Ghazni Province, 1979

Mohammed Taraki, president of Afghanistan, May 1978–September 1979; head of the Khalq, or People, wing of the Afghan Communist Party, the PDPA

Dmitri Ustinov, Soviet defense minister, 1976–1984

Valentin Varennikov, Soviet General Staff deputy head; head of the Soviet Southern Theater of Military Operations, 1984–1989

Valery Vostrotin, Company 9 commander, 1979–1980; 345th Regiment commander, 1986–1989

Abdul Nasir Ziyaee, mujahideen field commander, Panjshir Valley; aide to Ahmed Shah Massoud

NOTES

Introduction

5   "Something the British were eager to prevent": Martin Ewans writes that the British spent two years putting down a Pashtun uprising that broke out after Afghanistan's southern border was demarcated. *Afghanistan: A Short History of Its People and Politics* (New York: HarperCollins, 2002), p. 78.

5   "The northern population consists chiefly of Turkic peoples": According to Louis Dupree, the widespread belief the Hazaras are descendants of Genghis Khan's hordes is incorrect. *Afghanistan* (Princeton, NJ: Princeton University Press, 1973), chart 6.

1. Invasion Considered: A Short, Victorious War

11   "Because he was ill": That possibility is according to Georgy Kornienko, in *Kholodnaia voina: Svidetel'stvo ee uchastnika* [*The Cold War: Testimony of a Participant*] (Moscow: Mezhdunarodnye otnosheniya, 1994), p. 194.

11   "I don't have one of those" is related by Leonid Zamyatin, head of the Central Committee's information office at the time, in Genrikh Borovik's film *Za deviat' let do kontsa voiny* [*Nine Years Before the End of the War*], part 1. Moscow: Telemir, 1993.

12   "An undesirable turn for us" is from Andropov's memorandum posted by the Woodrow Wilson International Center for Scholars Cold War International History Project (CWIHP) [http://wwics.si.edu/index.cfm?topic_id=1409&fuseaction=library.document&id=39], Daniel Rozas, trans. Text located in the Russian Federation Presidential Archive, from notes taken by Soviet ambassador to Washington Anatoly Dobrynin and provided to the Norwegian Nobel Institute; provided to CWIHP by Odd Arne Westad, director of research, Nobel Institute.

12   "His hawkish and secretive deputy": Hard-line Kryuchkov would later succeed Andropov as KGB chairman and become a leader of the attempted coup d'état against Mikhail Gorbachev in 1991.

12   "Gromyko spoke against invasion until October" is from Kornienko, p. 193. Kornienko cites his conversations with Gromyko.

16   "Eight Mi-8 transport helicopters, a squadron of An-12 turboprop cargo planes, a signal center, and a paratroop battalion" is from Lester Grau, "The Take-Down of Kabul: An Effective Coup de Main," in *Urban Operations: An Historical*

Casebook (Fort Leavenworth, Kansas: Combat Studies Institute, Command and General Staff College, October 2002) [http://www.globalsecurity.org/military/library/report/2002/MOUTGrau.htm].

17   "Yuri Andropov ordered Oleg Kalugin to draft a report" is according to Kalugin, interviewed in *Za deviat' let do kontsa voiny*, part 2.

17   "Kryuchkov ordered the four men to combine the channels of information" is from many accounts, including interviews with the KGB's chief representative in Kabul, Leonid Bogdanov, and according to Oleg Kalugin, in *Za deviat' let do kontsa voiny*, part 2.

21   "The Soviet leadership learned the news from a Reuters report" is according to Georgy Kornienko, first deputy foreign minister at the time, in an interview in *Za deviat' let do kontsa voiny*, part 1.

22   "The army . . . supported his action" is from Barnett Rubin, *The Fragmentation of Afghanistan* (New Haven, CT: Yale University Press, 1995), p. 102.

23   "Brezhnev was furious" is from Stephen Tanner, *Afghanistan: A Military History from Alexander the Great to the Fall of the Taliban* (New York: Da Capo Press, 2002), p. 230.

23   "A reconciliation that posed the president a serious threat" is from Ewans, p. 135.

23   "His funeral turned into an antigovernment demonstration" is from Tanner, p. 130.

23   "The communist coup d'état . . . caused some two thousand deaths" is from Ewans, p. 136.

23   "A clear pro-Soviet coup": The contents of the memorandum to Cyrus Vance are quoted in *Za deviat' let do kontsa voiny*, part 1.

23   "The KGB . . . was actually caught completely off-guard" is according to Kalugin in *Za deviat' let do kontsa voiny*, part 1.

24   "The principles of Islam, democracy, freedom and the inviolability of the person" is cited in Tanner, p. 231.

25   "Unrest all over the country": Larry Goodson writes the PDPA's reforms were probably aimed directly at undermining the power of family, tribal, or clan authority. *Afghanistan's Endless War: State Failure, Regional Politics, and the Rise of the Taliban* (Seattle: University of Washington Press, 2001), p. 56.

25   "Tens of thousands suffered": The Pul-i-Charkhi prison was built according to Michel Foucault's description of the "panopticon"; the wheel-shaped structure was still under construction in 1978 and provided miserable conditions for inmates. Many of them were tortured. Methods included beatings, pulling out of fingernails, sleep deprivation—but the favorite form of torture was the administration of electric shocks. ("Casting Shadows: War Crimes and Crimes Against Humanity: 1978–2001: Documentation and Analysis of Major Patterns of Abuse in the War in Afghanistan." The Afghanistan Justice Project, [http://afghanistanjusticeproject.org/warcrimesandcrimesagainsthumanity19782001.pdf], p. 29.)

29   "Pashtun tribesmen formed antigovernment strongholds" is from Tanner, p. 231.

29   "Washington could do little" is described in Milt Bearden and James Risen, *The Main Enemy: The Inside Story of the CIA's Final Showdown with the KGB* (New York: Random House, 2003), p. 221.

30 "Bodies of the publicly tortured and murdered were paraded on pikes" is from Ewans, p. 143.

31 "Which took the lives of some five thousand people": Some estimates put the number of casualties during the Herat uprising at over twenty thousand.

31 "Speaking to Soviet Premier Kosygin": Taraki's telephone conversation with Kosygin on March 17 or 18, 1979, is from a transcript posted by the Woodrow Wilson International Center for Scholars Cold War International History Project [http://wwics.si.edu/index.cfm?topic_id=1409&fuseaction=library.document &id=39]. Aired on the Russian Television Network *Special File* program, July 1992, as translated in FBIS-SOV–92–138 (July 17, 1992), pp. 30–31.

33 "The move would worsen the situation": Kosygin's conversation with Taraki is described in *Za deviat' let do kontsa voiny*, part 1.

33 "In August, the Fifth Brigade of the Ninth Infantry Division joined a revolt" is from Tanner, p. 232.

33 "Two hundred T-55 and a hundred T-62 tanks and twelve Mi-24 gunship helicopters" is from Tanner, p. 232.

33 "A historian noted": Larry Goodson writes the Kerala massacre was "a clear deviation from the stylized tribal violence." Goodson, p. 57.

34 "But most Afghans perceived the aging former journalist" is from Vasily Mitrokhin, "The KGB in Afghanistan," Woodrow Wilson International Center for Scholars Cold War International History Project working paper, February 2002, p. 17. (According to Oleg Kalugin, Taraki wasn't a KGB operative; rather, he retained friendly relations with Soviet intelligence, doing little more than exchange general information. *Za deviat' let do kontsa voiny*, part 1.)

34 "Disappearances, torture, and summary executions" are described in "Casting Shadows," The Afghanistan Justice Project, p. 10.

34 "That kind of crudeness": Guliabzoi himself was hardly blameless of committing violence. He'd go on to become interior minister during much of the Soviet War, when the ministry's Sarandoi national police would bear responsibility for a great number of killings, along with the KhAD secret service.

35 "Mojaddedi has many followers": Mojaddedi would become one of the seven main rebel leaders in exile during the war. After the overthrow of the Soviet-installed government, he would be named Afghanistan's president for two months. Later, following the American invasion of 2001, he would become speaker of parliament.

39 "But the prime minister outmaneuvered them" is from Alexander Liakhovskii, *Tragediia i doblest' Afghana* [*The Tragedy and Valor of Afghanistan*] (Moscow: Nord, 2004), p. 153.

43 "Hoping to save their jobs" is from Liakhovskii, p. 153.

43 "The prime minister ordered an antiaircraft battery": A number of different accounts, many of them contradictory, describe the events of that day and the following weeks. Amin supporters say it was Taraki who was surprised at the airport—because he'd ordered Amin to be assassinated on the way there.

45 "Despite the evidence about Amin's intentions" is according to Gorelov, interviewed in *Za deviat' let do kontsa voiny*, part 2.

46 "He'd finally decided to sack Sarwari": Other reports, including Mitrokhin's, say Taraki told Amin he'd also fire Guliabzoi, and transfer the other two ministers to other positions.

47   "He ordered Taraki's guards to stand aside": There are dozens of differing accounts of this central event. Amin supporters claim the guards opened fire from above without waiting for an explanation from the visitors. According to Guliabzoi and other Taraki loyalists, the guards made it clear only Amin, unarmed, was authorized to pass—after which Tarun fired first. Guliabzoi says Tarun was shot from behind by Amin's own men. He says proof lay in the unscarred walls behind the men: if Taraki's men were shooting, the walls would have borne bullet holes.

48   "Told the four Soviet representatives were inside" is from Liakhovskii, p. 164.

48   "He was quickly buried": According to Guliabzoi, Amin was undecided over Taraki's fate until his top supporters in government convinced him the president would pose a great risk as long as he remained alive.

48   " 'What a scum that Amin is' " is from Liakhovskii, p. 186.

49   "The Kremlin had provided more than $1 billion in military aid and $1.25 billion in economic aid" is from Tanner, p. 227.

49   "A top-secret cable": Cyrus Vance's cable is described in *Za deviat' let do kontsa voiny*, part 1.

49   "A cable to Washington": The U.S. embassy cable is cited in *Za deviat' let do kontsa voiny*, part 2.

51   "Amin accused them of helping Taraki" is from a number of sources, including Mitrokhin, p. 76.

2. Storm-333: The Invasion

56   "Guliabzoi's account of his fate": Bogdanov says Guliabzoi's refusal to acknowledge his flight from Afghanistan is a bid to improve his political reputation.

57   "He used his time there": Alexander Liakhovskii describes Paputin's report in "Inside the Soviet Invasion of Afghanistan and the Seizure of Kabul, December 1979," Gary Goldberg, Artemy Kalinovsky, trans., Woodrow Wilson International Center for Scholars Cold War International History Project working paper no. 51 (January 2007), p. 8.

57   "He committed suicide": Most Western accounts have it that Paputin was killed in fighting in Afghanistan, where he traveled to help launch the war.

57   "Zaplatin's testimony was less alarming" is according to Zaplatin, interviewed in *Za deviat' let do kontsa voiny*, part 3.

58   "The conflict's preeminent historian": During the war, Liakhovskii was assistant to Valentin Varennikov, commander of Soviet ground forces. One of the war's chief architects, Varennikov later became its military supremo. Liakhovskii's history is rich in detail, facsimiles of many source documents, and verbatim accounts. But Liakhovskii often fails to probe Soviet motives behind the war and sometimes engages in hagiography.

59   "Between December 10 and 30, various units were given some thirty various directives" is according to Colonel Vladimir Bogdanov, director of the general staff's main operative department in 1979, interviewed in *Za deviat' let do kontsa voiny*, part 4.

61 "Sarwari had been talking": While Guliabzoi claims never to have left Afghanistan, he admits to having taken refuge in Bagram along with other members of the "gang of four."

62 "An elite unit formed by KGB chief Andropov": Group A was set up in 1974 as a counterterrorist special force operating within the Soviet Union, as opposed to Zenit, which was created for duty abroad.

64 "That day, he signed a directive" is from *Za deviat' let do kontsa voiny*, part 4.

65 "The 860th Separate Motorized Rifle Regiment, 56th Separate Air Assault Brigade, 2nd Air Defense Brigade, and 34th Composite Aviation Corps" is from Grau, "The Take-Down of Kabul: An Effective Coup de Main."

65 "Drozdov didn't even have a floor plan" is from Yuri Drozdov, *Vymysel iskluchen [Fiction Is Out of the Question]* (Moscow: Vympel, 1997), p. 195.

68 "An Afghan tank unit was instructed to drain its vehicles of fuel" is from Tanner, p. 235.

69 "The Soviet forces would be leaving on December 28": According to Jalili, that part of the speech was inserted to put pressure on the Soviets to pull out their forces.

70 "Waziri immediately departed for the Soviet embassy" is according to Waziri, interviewed in *Za deviat' let do kontsa voiny*, part 4.

70 "The new Soviet ambassador . . . knew no more than anyone" is according to Kornienko in *Za deviat' let do kontsa voiny*, part 4.

70 "The doctors immediately understood they'd been poisoned" is according to Alexeev, who describes the experience in *Za deviat' let do kontsa voiny*, part 4.

70 "Alexeev administered liquids" is from Grau, "The Take-Down of Kabul: An Effective Coup de Main."

70 "Waziri now suspected" is according to Waziri, in *Za deviat' let do kontsa voiny*, part 4.

71 "Amin's guards manned positions within the palace" is from Grau, "The Take-Down of Kabul: An Effective Coup de Main."

71 "The regiment's twelve 100-mm antiaircraft guns and sixteen dual-barreled DShK heavy machine-guns" is from Grau, "The Take-Down of Kabul: An Effective Coup de Main."

77 "The doctor believed now they'd come for Amin" is according to Alexeev, in *Za deviat' let do kontsa voiny*, part 4.

78 "An officer of Group A shot Amin": There are many conflicting accounts of Amin's death. The general consensus in interviews for this book backs Liakhovskii's account that the Group A officer was responsible. Amin was alleged to have been shot again after the grenade detonated. *Spetsnaz* officers then wrapped his body in a carpet and carried it out of the palace.

80 "By the end of the month, there were eighty thousand Soviet troops stationed in Afghanistan" is from Tanner, p. 238.

82 "A telephone call interrupted their discussion" is according to Kalugin, in *Za deviat' let do kontsa voiny*, part 4. It was the last time Kalugin met Andropov. The counterintelligence chief who had been the KGB's fastest-rising star was soon banished to Leningrad.

83 "Withdrawing would be a serious mistake" is according to Vladimir Bogdanov in *Za deviat' let do kontsa voiny*, part 4.

83   "No discussion preceded the approval" is from *Za deviat' let do kontsa voiny*, part 4.

84   "Nineteenth-century muskets, World War II–era British Lee Enfield rifles, and AK-47s" is from Tanner, p. 243.

3. The Soviets Dig In

89   "MRCs also included a mortar battery" is detailed in a report by the Russian general staff, translated and edited by Lester Grau and Michael Gress in *The Soviet-Afghan War: How a Superpower Fought and Lost* (Lawrence, KS: The University Press of Kansas, 2002), p. 35.

93   "Karmal announced a broad-based unity government" is from Mark Urban, *War in Afghanistan* (New York: St. Martin's Press, 1988), p. 51.

93   "To court the country's Islamic clergy" is from Urban, p. 52.

95   "The Afghan Eleventh Division deserted" is from Tanner, p. 243.

95   "A riot in which three hundred people died" is from Tanner, p. 243.

96   "The Kremlin failed to understand its new mujahideen enemy" is from Grau and Gress, p. xix.

98   "A resistance movement took most control over Bamian, Ghowr, and Uruzgan provinces" is from Urban, p. 55.

99   "Mujahideen Lee Enfield rifles were ineffective against Soviet armor" is from Tanner, p. 246.

100   "Damaging bridges to bring long armored columns to a screeching halt" is from Tanner, p. 248.

100   "He faced difficulties convincing them": Mohammed Yousef describes training Afghan rebels in *The Bear Trap: Afghanistan's Untold Story*, with Mark Adkin (Lahore, Pakistan: Jang, 1992) [online excerpts cited: http://www.sovietsdefeatinafghanistan .com/beartrap/english/06.htm].

104   "'He was supposed to be hiding'": The oral testimony is from a paratrooper named Yuri Yurchenko, who contributed to a volume of soldiers' narratives. Anna Heinämaa, Maija Leppänen, and Yuri Yurchenko, *The Soldiers' Story: Soviet Veterans Remember the Afghan War* (Berkeley: University of California Berkeley International and Area Studies research series no. 90, 1994), pp. 25–26.

104   "'He split the boy's skull'" is from Heinämaa, et al., p. 26.

105   "Ethnic Slavs suspected their fellow soldiers" is from Alexander Alexiev, *Inside the Soviet Army in Afghanistan* (Santa Monica: The RAND Corporation, 1988), p. 42.

105   "The native army would shrink from ninety thousand" is from Tanner, p. 244.

106   "The Soviet 201st Motor Rifle Division sent armored columns up the Kunar Valley" is from Urban, p. 60.

106   "The enemy took cover" is from Tanner, p. 246.

106   "Mujahideen estimates put the number at eighteen hundred civilians" is from Ali Ahmad Jalali and Lester Grau, *Afghan Guerrilla Warfare: In the Words of the Mujahideen Fighters* (London: Compendium, 2001), p. 271.

106   "'They came looking for U.S. and Chinese mercenaries'" is from Jalali and Grau, p. 271.

106   "The mujahideen struck back the following month" is from Tanner, p. 246. The

mujahideen—reinforced with Arab and other foreign recruits—would later cut off the Gardez-Khost road for extended periods. Freeing it would be the objective of the war's biggest operation late in the conflict.

106 "Then the guerrillas overwhelmed them" is from Urban, p. 63.
117 "Some of the most dreaded mines" is from Robert Kaplan, *Soldiers of God: With Islamic Warriors in Afghanistan and Pakistan* (New York: Vintage Books, 2001), p. 4.
119 "The rest of the . . . world signed onto that prospect" is from Tanner, p. 240.
119 "Reservists drafted to top up the seven motorized rifle divisions" is from Urban, p. 64.

4. The Mujahideen Fight Back

121 "The Pashtuns are believed to have emerged as a distinct population" is from Ewans, p. 13.
122 "Afghanistan's first native ruler oversaw its greatest territorial expansion" is from Ewans, p. 23.
123 "The bombers flew sorties" is from Tanner, p. 248.
127 "The 108th MRD destroyed several of the mujahideen bases" is from Urban, p. 84.
127 "The division turned north toward Herat" is from Tanner, p. 249.
127 "Another tactic was to rig dummy explosives" is from Tanner, p. 249.
127 "Soviet and Afghan fighter jets bombed the area" is from Urban, p. 86.
131 "Massoud received almost no assistance": Massoud was much closer to the British—MI6 provided him some assistance—as well as the French.
131 "The Saudi General Intelligence Department . . . contributed hundreds of millions of oil-profit dollars" is from Steve Coll, *Ghost Wars: The Secret History of the CIA, Afghanistan and bin Laden, from the Soviet Invasion to September 10, 2001* (New York: The Penguin Press, 2004), p. 71.
132 "They were Shias" is from Tanner, p. 251.
132 "The CIA continued buying British Lee Enfield rifles" is from Coll, p. 58.
133 "He's believed to have received most of the $39 million Saudi supporters sent that month" is from Urban, p. 77.
133 "Engineer Esmatullah claimed to command five thousand men" is from Urban, p. 82.
135 "An attack that killed thousands" is reported in Urban, p. 96, citing Kabul Radio, TASS, and the *Guardian*. One would expect the Soviet commander to play up mujahideen losses. That he doesn't calls into question the accuracy of media reports at the time.
136 "But the Panjshir Valley" is from Edward Girardet, *Afghanistan: The Soviet War* (New York: St. Martin's Press, 1985), p. 79.
138 "While huge Mi-6 transports unloaded the soldiers" is from Tanner, p. 251.
138 "Massoud allowed the Afghan troops" is from Girardet, p. 84.
138 "Near the village of Ruha" is from Liakhovskii, pp. 633–634.
139 "But they failed to dislodge the mujahideen" is from Tanner, p. 252.
139 "Three to four hundred of their men had been killed" is from Urban, p. 104.

139 "Soviet destruction of villages, fields, and irrigation facilities was thorough" is from Tanner, p. 252.

139 "Panjshir's civilian population of around eighty thousand" is from Girardet, p. 86.

142 "Typhus, cholera, and malaria": Some veterans say more Soviets died in Afghanistan from illness than in combat.

147 "By 1982, the security service of an estimated eighteen hundred members" is from Urban, p. 112.

147 "The torture was conducted in houses around Kabul" is from "Casting Shadows," The Afghanistan Justice Project, p. 35.

147 "A new organization called the Democratic Youth Organization of Afghanistan" is from Urban, p. 76.

5. The Soviets Seek Victory

153 "Burnes reported to the Indian governor-general" is from Peter Hopkirk, *The Great Game: The Struggle for Empire in Central Asia* (New York: Kodansha America, 1994), p. 170.

153 "Burnes reported something else" is from Hopkirk, p. 171.

153 "Sixty of the animals were required" is from Tanner, p. 136.

154 "The Ghilzai tribe attacked a caravan" is from Ewans, p. 48.

155 "General Konstantin Kaufman sent a mission to Kabul" is from Hopkirk, p. 381.

155 "Abdur Rahman Khan . . . had lived twelve years in Russian-controlled Tashkent" is from Ewans, p. 69.

156 " 'It does not disappoint me' " is quoted from Charles Metcalfe MacGregor, *War in Afghanistan, 1879–80: The Personal Diary of Major General Sir Charles Metcalfe MacGregor* (Detroit: Wayne State University Press, 1985), p. 106.

157 "Nothing about Massoud" is from Tkachev's testimony, quoted in Liakhovskii, p. 640.

158 "Burgeoning new weapons arsenals" is from Tanner, p. 253.

158 "The prospect of profit" is from Coll, p. 66.

159 "The volumes were printed in Uzbek" is from Coll, p. 90.

160 "Some of them inside Afghanistan" is from George Crile, *Charlie Wilson's War: The Extraordinary Account of the Largest Covert Operation in History* (New York: Atlantic Monthly Press, 2003), p. 462. Wilson railed against ISI's attempts to stop him from entering Afghanistan because of security concerns.

164 "Standard Mi-8T models" is from John Everett-Heath, *Helicopters in Combat: The First Fifty Years* (London: Arms and Armour Press, 1992), p. 140.

168 "As low as twenty thousand" is from Rubin, p. 131.

168 "Ten to fifteen desertions a day" is from Girardet, p. 137.

168 " 'Contemporary photos of young women' " is quoted from Tanner, p. 255.

169 "Forcing people from their land" is from Tanner, p. 255.

169 "Up to 2 million people" is from Ewans, p. 158.

171 "The situation in Afghanistan is . . . difficult": Gromyko's comments are from

a Politburo transcript posted by the Woodrow Wilson International Center for Scholars Cold War International History Project [http://wwics.si.edu/index.cfm?topic_id=1409&fuseaction=library.document&id=39], Daniel Rozas, trans., provided by Mark Kramer.

171 "Andropov eventually realized Moscow couldn't win" is according to Sarah Mendelson in *Changing Course: Ideas, Politics, and the Soviet Withdrawal from Afghanistan* (Princeton, NJ: Princeton University Press, 1998), p. 74. Mendelson writes that the military's First Deputy Chief of Staff Sergei Akhromeyev, one of the main planners of the Soviet invasion, believed Andropov had become too sick to implement any change to the Kremlin's Afghanistan policy.

172 "Mines intended for children" are described in the *New York Times*, December 3, 1985. Afghan witnesses described pens, harmonicas, and radios used as booby traps aimed at children. The UN document was one of many such reports.

172 "In 1983, the Soviet 108th MRD" is from Urban, p. 119.

174 "Five thousand Afghan Army troops" is from Urban, p. 144.

174 "Abdul Wahed" is from Urban, p. 148.

174 "They were stopped by snow" is from Tanner, p. 260.

174 "Mi-24s accompanied the battalions" is from Tanner, p. 260.

175 "Kabul Radio announced" is from Urban, p. 147.

176 "Failing to crush us by force": Girardet quotes Massoud in Girardet, p. 77.

177 "His death undermined what little unity there had been" is from Rubin, p. 238.

186 "Cluster bombs with sixty highly lethal bomblets" is from Urban, p. 121.

187 "Drought on top of the destruction" is from Rubin, p. 231.

187 "A battalion of some five hundred men" is from Urban, p. 172.

187 "The rebels killed an Afghan general" is from Urban, p. 173.

187 "Helicopter-borne troops found the Soviets' corpses" is from Tanner, p. 264.

188 "An important mujahideen logistics base": The Zhawar base later would be used by the Taliban—and become the focus of heavy American bombing during the post–September 11 offensive.

188 "After intense fighting in the hills" is from Urban, p. 194.

189 "He also set up a 'national reconciliation commission'" is from Ewans, p. 165.

189 "His successful undermining" is from Urban, p. 182.

190 "He was sent to Moscow" is from Kaplan, p. 175.

190 "Najibullah boosted his authority" is from Urban, p. 184.

191 "American intelligence claimed" is from Tanner, p. 266.

6. The Tide Turns

193 "Although their destination was secret": Like other special forces officers' families, Kalita's found out about his assignments through the grapevine.

194 "Ordinarily forbidden to Red Army soldiers": Still, equipment such as combat boots was so inferior and uncomfortable, those regular troops who could get their hands on sneakers—usually Soviet- or Chinese-made, and fourth-rate—

wore them as often as possible. (Some soldiers preferred the heavier, Communist-made knockoffs to Nike or Adidas models.)

197   "Whether or not Pahlawan's mujahideen group": Pahlawan would be assassinated in the 1990s by his rival and sometime ally General Rashid Dostum, another Uzbek warlord who fought for the Afghan Army during the Soviet War before joining the mujahideen and later the Northern Alliance against the Taliban.

205   "A mujahideen rocket attack lit up the night" is from Bearden and Risen, p. 227.

209   "Only one of the choppers turned to fire" is from Bearden and Risen, p. 248.

209   " 'Go out there and win' " is from Bearden and Risen, p. 214.

210   "Almost $500 million in 1986" is from Coll, p. 151.

210   "Moscow's underhanded participation in the Vietnam War": In a January 1998 interview with *Le Nouvel Observateur*, President Carter's national security adviser Zbigniew Brzezinski said Washington had first provided the mujahideen aid in July 1979, six months before the war had begun. When the Soviets invaded, he told Carter, "We now have the opportunity of giving the USSR its Vietnam War."

210   "Washington was wary" is from Tanner, p. 267.

210   "His relenting in January 1986" is from Bearden and Risen, p. 212.

212   "The CIA's estimation" is from Tanner, p. 267.

214   " 'Those who don't intend to adjust' " is quoted in *Time* magazine, March 3, 1986.

214   "Addressing members of the Politburo": Gorbachev's comments and those of the other Politburo members on November 3, 1986, are from a Politburo transcript posted by the Woodrow Wilson International Center for Scholars Cold War International History Project [http://wwics.si.edu/index.cfm?topic_id=1409&fuseaction=library.document&id=39], Daniel Rozas, trans., provided by Mark Kramer.

7. Endgame

218   "The Fortieth Army was to fight solely to defend itself" is described by the Russian general staff in Grau and Gress, p. 28. Among the many exceptions to the Kremlin's order would be the biggest offensive operation of the entire war. The brutal Operation Magistral, or Highway, began in November, described by the general staff report as an "operation to safeguard convoys."

218   "Washington would spend some $630 million" is from Coll, p. 151.

220   "Massoud had formed a new political group": The Supreme Council of the North would later become the Northern Alliance that fought the Taliban.

220   "In July, he staged a number of attacks" is from Urban, p. 228.

221   "Suicide or being shipped home": *Dedovshchina* also drove some soldiers to kill *dedy* in revenge. Alexiev, p. 38.

227   "The Afghan form of Farsi": The Soviets taught a simplified version of Afghanistan's many dialects. Meeting Najibullah on several occasions—one dur-

ing which his unit helped provide security for the president's visit to a village school—Klintsevich found the relatively erudite Afghan leader to be one of the few Dari speakers he could understand because initially he often discovered the dialects too complicated to comprehend.

229 "Vostrotin's friend Colonel Ruslan Aushev": Vostrotin had met the war hero during his first tour in Afghanistan. The friends later studied together at the Frunze academy. After the collapse of the Soviet Union, Aushev would become the popular head of the Russian region of Ingushetia. Many Ingush revere him, partly for his efforts to aid hundreds of thousands of refugees who spilled out of neighboring war-torn Chechnya.

230 "He estimated his forces killed six hundred resistance fighters" is from Liakhovskii, p. 554.

231 "Khost's forty thousand residents" is from Urban, p. 229.

231 "Haqqani had attracted considerable support" is from Coll, p. 157.

234 "A popular television correspondent": Leshchinskii's reputation was big enough for him usually to get what he wanted, and he often claimed to be working on the Central Committee's direct orders. Some officers and soldiers despised him for that, the inevitable propaganda his reports generated, and for endangering soldiers' lives by asking them to fire rounds for the camera during operations such as Magistral.

235 "Parachutes thrown out of helicopters" are described in a Red Army field report, translated and edited by Lester Grau in *The Bear Went Over the Mountain: Soviet Combat Tactics in Afghanistan* (London: Frank Cass Publishers, 1998), p. 62.

235 "Klintsevich and others had seen them": Klintsevich also believes the rebels were drugged, probably from smoking marijuana, judging by their bravado.

237 "The cost of Company 9's valiant holding": The battle was the centerpiece of a 2005 feature film called *Deviataia rota [Company 9]*. The film—one of newly wealthy Russia's first Hollywood-style, special effects–heavy movies—proved wildly successful. Its Soviet nostalgia, depiction of soldiers' heroism, and glorification of violence also heralded an emerging new popular attitude toward the war. One of the film's main themes was the battle's futility. But apart from simply distorting facts, the film did far more to whip up pride in the Soviet effort than to draw attention to its mistakes.

239 "The incident was apparently an eerie coincidence" is from Tanner, p. 268.

240 "The Soviets would videotape their handover procedures" is from Lester Grau, "Breaking Contact Without Leaving Chaos: The Soviet Withdrawal From Afghanistan," *Journal of Slavic Military Studies*, April–June 2007, vol. 20, no. 2.

242 "One of his pilots was a spy": Twenty years after the operation, a white-haired, booming Rutskoi told me the pilot eventually defected to Canada, where he has since died.

247 "He could not have been prepared": Bearden describes his telephone conversation in Bearden and Risen, p. 341.

247 "Some ten Toyota pickup trucks": Bearden denies the CIA exchanged Rutskoi for a U.S. intelligence officer. He told me Rutskoi was brought down by a lucky shot from a 14.5-mm machine gun around Parachinar, that he was treated well by a militia group that "knew it had something of value—his plane—and that

it might get something for him as well. I got his plane and him in a deal that involved Toyota Hilux pickups and 107-mm multibarrel rocket launchers. There was no torture and no trade."

247 "Rutskoi would turn against Boris Yeltsin": In October 1993, Rutskoi led nationalist members of parliament in an uprising against the government after the legislature declared him "acting president." It was a key moment in post-Soviet history. The standoff turned violent after anti-Yeltsin protesters broke through police cordons around the government building and Rutskoi called on his supporters to storm Moscow's main television studio complex. The Kremlin ended the standoff by shelling the parliament building. Almost two hundred people died during the standoff. Yeltsin enacted a new constitution giving him vast new powers. A decade later, Vladimir Putin would use them to help bring authoritarianism back to Russia. After the 1993 revolt, Rutskoi was jailed for several months until the new parliament pardoned him. He was elected governor of the southern Kursk Region in 1996. His campaign for reelection ended in 2000—now under Putin's presidency—when his name was struck off the ballot the night before the election. Rutskoi is now a businessman.

248 "It was attacked by rebel rocket fire" is from Liakhovskii, p. 617.

248 "Hoping to minimize casualties": Klintsevich says he also saved the lives of many Afghan civilians by refusing artillery units permission to shell populated areas.

250 "General Varennikov flew to the city" is from Liakhovskii, p. 594.

250 "The Soviets also introduced SCUD surface-to-surface missiles" is from Ewans, p. 168.

250 "Assassinating rival mujahideen commanders" is from Coll, p. 181.

254 "Officially, 13,833 died": The figures of dead and wounded are from Grau, *The Bear Went Over the Mountain*, p. xix.

254 "Among the equipment lost": The amount of matériel and equipment lost is from Grau, *The Bear Went Over the Mountain*, p. xix.

8. Aftermath

255 "A third of the prewar population" is from Grau, *The Bear Went Over the Mountain*, p. xviii.

256 "The Arab millionaire was said to have promised": Gareev claims to have met bin Laden during the siege.

257 "Thirty-six men were killed" is from Tanner, p. 272.

257 "Varennikov would be in a Moscow jail": Varennikov was the only participant in the 1991 coup attempt who didn't accept a pardon. Instead he was tried three times before his eventual acquittal by the Russian Supreme Court in 1994. The following year, he was elected to the Duma lower house of parliament, where he remains a legislator.

261 "Najibullah fled on April 15" is from Ewans, p. 178.

262 "Their ascendance struck a devastating psychological blow" is from Tanner, p. 276.

262   "An estimated eighteen hundred civilians" is from Rubin, p. 272.

268   "When a shell hit the base's arsenal" is from TASS, June 5, 1985 (from BBC *Monitoring Report*, June 12, 1985).

272   "Durrani members reasserted their claim" is from Goodson, p. 99.

276   " 'Chechenization' has succeeded, at least temporarily": Some even believe Moscow succeeded only in giving complete independence in all but name to Kadyrov, who has realized the centuries-old dream of Chechen emancipation.

277   "A truce between the government and separatists": The truce ended a violent civil conflict, but Georgia would soon accuse Russia of using its peacekeepers to back Abkhazia and other separatist regions in a bid to cripple—and influence—its former Soviet subject-state. Later, Tbilisi accused Moscow of aming to annex the Georgian provinces.

Epilogue

281   "A Taliban fighter had exploded a grenade" is from a report in the *Sunday Times*, December 2, 2001.

282   "The presence of the Americans": It wouldn't have been the first time American swagger created enmity in Afghanistan. In the 1950s and 1960s, when U.S. engineers helped build roads, the Kandahar airport, and other infrastructure in the south of the country, at least one case of insensitivity to local conditions threatened the success of a dam and irrigation project along the Helmand River (Tanner, p. 226). Soviet engineers in the north had greater success.

282   "They threw themselves on the CIA officers" is from the *Sunday Times*, December 2, 2001.

283   "Gunships fired . . . at the Taliban fighters": Among them was twenty-year-old John Walker Lindh, the so-called American Taliban, now serving a twenty-year prison sentence in the United States.

This book is based chiefly on interviews with veterans of the Soviet War, many of whom appear in the narrative. I also interviewed former mujahideen fighters and commanders in Afghanistan, and other participants, such as former CIA officers.

Of the documents on which I've relied, some have been collected and posted online by the Woodrow Wilson International Center for Scholars Cold War International History Project. Others have been compiled by historian Alexander Liakhovskii, whose book—*Tragediia i doblest' Afghana* [*The Tragedy and Valor of Afghanistan*] (Moscow: Nord, 2004)—is the most comprehensive account of the war.

Military historian Lester Grau has translated and edited invaluable Soviet military documents. Among them, Grau and Michael Gress's *The Soviet-Afghan War: How a Superpower Fought and Lost* (Lawrence, Kansas: The University Press of Kansas, 2002) is a translation of the Russian general staff's report about the war. *The Bear Went Over the Mountain: Soviet Combat Tactics in Afghanistan* (London: Frank Cass Publishers, 1998) is a translation of the Frunze Military Academy's compilation of officers' reports about combat incidents. Grau's commentary in the abovementioned volumes was indispensable.

Of secondary sources on which I've relied, also crucial have been Stephen Tanner's *Afghanistan: A Military History from Alexander the*

Great to the Fall of the Taliban (New York: Da Capo Press, 2002); Mark Urban's *War in Afghanistan* (New York: St. Martin's Press, 1988); Steve Coll's tour de force *Ghost Wars: The Secret History of the CIA, Afghanistan and bin Laden, from the Soviet Invasion to September 10, 2001* (New York: The Penguin Press, 2004), and Barnett Rubin's important scholarly work *The Fragmentation of Afghanistan* (New Haven, CT: Yale University Press, 1995).

A selected bibliography of other works on which I've relied follows.

Books

Bearden, Milt, and James Risen, *The Main Enemy: The Inside Story of the CIA's Final Showdown with the KGB* (New York: Random House, 2003)

Borovik, Artyom, *The Hidden War: A Russian Journalist's Account of the Soviet War in Afghanistan* (New York: Grove Press, 1990)

Crile, George, *Charlie Wilson's War: The Extraordinary Account of the Largest Covert Operation in History* (New York: Atlantic Monthly Press, 2003)

Drozdov, Yuri, *Vymysel iskluchen* [*Fiction Is Out of the Question*] (Moscow: Vympel, 1997)

Dupree, Louis, *Afghanistan* (Princeton, NJ: Princeton University Press, 1973)

Elphinstone, Mountstuart, *An Account of the Kingdom of Caubul* (London: Oxford University Press, 1972)

Everett-Heath, John, *Helicopters in Combat: The First Fifty Years* (London: Arms and Armour Press, 1992)

Ewans, Martin, *Afghanistan: A Short History of Its People and Politics* (New York: HarperCollins, 2002)

Girardet, Edward, *Afghanistan: The Soviet War* (New York: St. Martin's Press, 1985)

Goodson, Larry, *Afghanistan's Endless War: State Failure, Regional Politics, and the Rise of the Taliban* (Seattle: University of Washington Press, 2001)

Heinämaa, Anna, Maija Leppänen, and Yuri Yurchenko, *The Soldiers' Story: Soviet Veterans Remember the Afghan War* (Berkeley: University of California Berkeley International and Area Studies research series no. 90, 1994)

Hopkirk, Peter, *The Great Game: The Struggle for Empire in Central Asia* (New York: Kodansha America, 1994)

Jalali, Ali Ahmad, and Lester Grau, *Afghan Guerrilla Warfare: In the Words of the Mujahideen Fighters* (London: Compendium, 2001)

Kaplan, Robert, *Soldiers of God: With Islamic Warriors in Afghanistan and Pakistan* (New York: Vintage Books, 2001)

Kornienko, Georgy, *Kholodnaia voina: Svidetel'stvo ee uchastnika* [*The Cold War: Testimony of a Participant*] (Moscow: Mezhdunarodnye otnosheniya, 1994)

Mendelson, Sarah, *Changing Course: Ideas, Politics, and the Soviet Withdrawal from Afghanistan* (Princeton, NJ: Princeton University Press, 1998)

Metcalfe MacGregor, Charles, *War in Afghanistan, 1879–80: The Personal Diary of Major General Sir Charles Metcalfe MacGregor* (Detroit: Wayne State University Press, 1985)

Shiverskikh, Anatoly, *Razrushenie Velikoi Strany: Zapiski Generala KGB* [*The Ruin of a Great Country: A KGB General's Notes*] (Smolensk: Smolensk Publishers, 2005)

Yousef, Mohammed, and Mark Adkin, *The Bear Trap: Afghanistan's Untold Story* (Lahore, Pakistan: Jang, 1992) [online excerpts cited: http://www.sovietsdefeatinafghanistan.com/beartrap/english/06.htm]

Reports and Papers

The Afghanistan Justice Project, "Casting Shadows: War Crimes and Crimes Against Humanity: 1978–2001: Documentation and Analysis of Major Patterns of Abuse in the War in Afghanistan" (2005)

Alexiev, Alexander, *Inside the Soviet Army in Afghanistan* (Santa Monica: The RAND Corporation, 1988)

Grau, Lester, "The Take-Down of Kabul: An Effective Coup de Main," in *Urban Operations: An Historical Casebook* (Fort Leavenworth, Kansas: Combat Studies Institute, Command and General Staff College, October 2002)

Mitrokhin, Vasily, "The KGB in Afghanistan," Woodrow Wilson International Center for Scholars Cold War International History Project working paper (February 2002)

Liakhovskii, Alexander, "Inside the Soviet Invasion of Afghanistan and the Seizure of Kabul, December 1979," Gary Goldberg, Artemy Kalinovsky, trans., Woodrow Wilson International Center for Scholars Cold War International History Project working paper no. 51 (January 2007)

Articles

Grau, Lester, "Breaking Contact Without Leaving Chaos: The Soviet Withdrawal From Afghanistan," *Journal of Slavic Military Studies*, April–June 2007, vol. 20, no. 2

Grau, Lester, and Ali Ahmad Jalili, "The Campaign for the Caves: The Battle for Zhawar in the Soviet-Afghan War," *Journal of Slavic Military Studies*, vol. 14, no. 3, September 2001

New York Times, December 3, 1985

Sunday Times, December 2, 2001

TASS, June 5, 1985 (from BBC Monitoring report, June 12, 1985)

Time, March 3, 1986

Documentary Films

Borovik, Genrikh, *Za deviat' let do kontsa voiny* [*Nine Years Before the End of the War*]. Moscow: Telemir, 1993

Ren-TV, *Kabulskaya Zhara* [*Kabul Heat*]. Moscow, 2005

INDEX

Page numbers in *italics* refer to maps and photographs.